1. Paul Warburg 6

2. ... refuses to co-operate in Public Senate hearing 7

3. ... handled large sums of money furnished by Germany for Lenin & Trotsky 7

4 Colonel House 8

5 Owen [?] Glass Bill 6, 9

6 William Jennings Bryan

AF863841

9

*The Great American Ripoff*

# *The Great American Ripoff*

## *An Indictment of the Federal Reserve Board*

**F.W. Maisel**

CONDIDO PRESS
*A Private Publishing House*

Design and Production:
George Djordjevic Design Studio

Typography:
Cheryl Gilman, Hillcrest Graphics

Charts:
Simpson Graphic Design

**FIRST EDITION**

To order additional copies of this book, send $9.95 to:

Condido Press
P.O. Box 27551
Rancho Bernardo
San Diego, CA 92128



ISBN: 0-911863-00-1

Library of Congress Catalog Card Number: 82-84739

Printed in the United States of America

# Table Of Contents

# PREFACE

For the record, the first draft of this book contained nothing about David Rockefeller or the Trilateral Commission. The book began as a criticism of Federal Reserve policy by a concerned American. As I wrote, the absurdities of our national economic policy were so evident that I thought I was mistaken. The Board's policy was an enigma—I could not understand Volcker's commitment to high interest rates. The record showed that the Fed had increased interest rates to control inflation on five previous occasions without success. I became curious. What was motivating Volcker? Then I discovered the relationship between the Chairman of the Federal Reserve Board, David Rockefeller and the Trilateral Commission. Then I understood the high interest rates.

The American people have been duped in a very artful way. I was reminded of the story of the Emperor and his Clothes. With brazen audacity, the Emperor's ministers and tailors convinced the Emperor and his subjects that the Emperor's new clothes were of the finest and rarest material. And the subjects agreed. Some even touched the make-believe fabric and commented on how soft and luxurious it was.

The American public has been conned with the same audacity, and many of us, like the Emperor's subjects, believe the hype and praise Volcker for a job well done.

It was a child's honesty that revealed the hoax against the emperor and his subjects. Perhaps we need to approach our national problems with that same basic honesty. By seeking the truth and ignoring the shadows cast by ingeneous, manipulative men, we can redirect our economy and country towards permanant growth and prosperity.

# *Dedication*

This book is dedicated to the farmer whose way of life is threatened by high interest rates, to the middle-class family who must bear the brunt of the financial burden, to the businessman who faces bankruptcy, to the carpenter who is unemployed, to the family that lost its home by foreclosure, to the black whose chance of achievement with dignity is threatened, to the single mother who sacrifices beyond endurance to hold her family together—in short, to all Americans who have suffered the financial and emotional trauma of the Federal Reserve Board's corrupt monetary policies.

# FOREWORD

## *A Declaration Of Economic Independence*

***"Practical men, who believe themselves exempt from intellectual influences, are usually the slave of some defunct economist."***

***Lord John Maynard Keyenes***

This book is written in anger. I am angry that the American public has been the victim of the biggest sting in history, perpetrated by one of its most venerable institutions—the Federal Reserve Board. I feel somewhat like the patient who submits himself in complete trust to a doctor, and then finds while on the operating table that the doctor is on the undertaker's payroll.

After reviewing the policies of the Board I asked how any prudent government body charged with the public's trust could have possibly followed their disastrous policies for twelve years? How persons qualified in the field of economics and statistics could be so blind to the results of their policies? I felt that there had to be an explanation for their dismal performance. And there was: my research showed that David Rockefeller's "Financial Junta" ran the Board. Only then did the Board's policy make sense—it was not public policy, but Rockefeller policy designed to implement the profit strategy of the Rockefeller Syndicate. I did not look for conspiracies, nor did I need to, since the facts are there for anyone to see and understand. The Board was corrupted by an elite clique of money lenders led by David Rockefeller and his Trilateral Commission. They executed a coup d'etat and installed a "financial junta." Paul Volcker is the head honcho. President Carter was their man in the White House and paid for his presidency with billions of our dollars.

Though written in anger, this book is written with an objective viewpoint. I hope that it presents a strong argument for public vigilance that will free our economy from the corruption of the "money changers." Every American should have the right to pursue his economic goals without the burden of paying tribute to economic pirates who create power for themselves by restricting the life blood of free enterprise—the supply of money and credit.

This book is not anti-bank or anti-finance. On the contrary, it is an argument for a healthy, honest, non-monopolistic banking system.

This book is not anti-bigness if it operates within the dictates of the law. It is not anti-Rockefeller or anti-Chase Manhattan Bank. I believe that they should earn their money the "old-fashioned way:" they should work for it.

This book is not isolationist. Some of the aims of the Trilateralists in promoting international commerce are desirable, but I believe that national economic policy ought to be a decision made by our Congress and by the people. It should not be made for us by "Big Brother."

This book is not slanted to the "right" or to the "left." Rather, it is written about a common problem that concerns all Americans. I found that "aware" conservatives and liberals agree that the Federal Reserve Board has failed us and is under the control of David Rockefeller and his Syndicate.

Although I consider myself a liberal, I have always admired Barry Goldwater because he is honest and an honest conservative is a national treasure. I was especially pleased to find that he saw the Rockefeller Trilateral threat to the nation and spoke out candidly in his excellent book, *With No Apologies*.

I look forward to the day when debate between conservatives and liberals can democratically chart the destiny of our country, instead of it being done for us by a "financial junta." We do not have that privilege today because double-digit interest rates, double-digit unemployment, double-digit inflation, and tripple-digit deficits obliterate the consideration of all other problems.

My final reason for writing this book is that America today stands at the threshold of economic cornucopia that boggles the mind. The technology to implement the twenty-first century is here and it is improving at an accelerated gallop. There is a millenium that invites our enjoyment and participation. Like a seductive partner, it waits to caress us and provide us with new comforts, new intrigue, and new pleasures. And the beautiful part of the scenario is that these delights come to us in a new dimension. Until now, we have sought pleasures in our 4000-pound V-8 sex symbols. Now we can be seduced by a ten-pound set of controls that will make our lives more luxurious. They will give us intense visual and audio experiences and extend the perimeters of our minds. The genesis of the new lifestyle is here, and the greatest thing about it is that it can be ours at imperceptible inconvenience to our environment. It does not require a scarred earth and smoke-belching mills; it comes from pretty little plants with lawns located in Silicon Valley.

The technology is willing and waiting, and waiting, and waiting. But, the Federal Reserve Board has retarded our evolution into this new lifestyle. We have become the victim of economic instability because of "tight-money, high-interest" policies of the Federal Reserve Board, and it is impossible to program for our nation's future. Because of a restrictive Federal Reserve Board, we are becoming just another nation that looks back at its glorious golden age.

Before we completely lose our competitive edge and join the ranks of second-rate nations, we must find the courage to force a change in our monetary system. Economic progress is a tenuous opportunity. We must not allow a corrupt Board to sabotage our future.

I am an economic pragmatist from Texas and believe that if gum doesn't work, use bailing wire. I have no illusions that this book will please the conventional theoretical economist. Indeed, I would be disappointed if it did. I do not believe that the Federal Reserve Board was sanctified in heaven or that Volcker is an economic Messiah, nor do I believe that our economic system was designed by God. Instead, I believe that the economy works because we act when necessary to make it work; and to make it work better, we must be willing to correct abuses. Now is the time to make necessary changes to heal our sick economy. This book is a call to action, it is an attack on the power structure of the Rockefeller Syndicate and threatens the source of their enormous windfall profits.

This book is chauvinistic in the sense that an affluent America is the most powerful and benign force for democracy and a better quality of life throughout the world. Without an economically strong America, the drive toward worldwide democracy and better economic conditions for all people would be blunted. Despite all of our failures, we still remain "the guys in the white hats."

# *Acknowledgments*

I want to thank Steve Wozniak of Palomar College, who reviewed my first draft and provided editorial help. I want to thank William Gladstone of Waterside Productions, who ruthlessly edited the final version with a critical eye. Glayds Collins and Dan Arnsan of the library at Palomar College were very helpful in providing research guidance. Barbara Brill did magic with her fingers to complete the manuscript in record time. Thanks also to Laurie Buchanan and Virginia Bezoenik for their patience and stenographic skills. I also want to thank Joseph Craiger for blocking out the world and running interference while I completed the toughest assignment I have ever had.

# PART I

## *Introduction*

The American public is the victim of the biggest rip-off in history. Our most trusted institution, the Federal Reserve Board, has been instrumental in a swindle that has cost the public and our government over a trillion dollars in the last decade.

The evidence will show that in 1970, the Federal Reserve Board became a money machine for David Rockefeller and his Syndicate. When Arthur Burns was appointed chairman (1970), the Federal Reserve Bank became the feifdom of David Rockefeller. His control of the Board was solidified and strengthened when Jimmy Carter, the "Capon" President, appointed Rockefeller's personal aide, Paul Volcker, to the chairmanship. For the last twelve years, the policy of the Board has been determined by the profit strategy of the Rockefeller Syndicate. The Federal Reserve Board had no "public policy." The facts will show that the high interest policy of the Board was never intended to fight inflation. It was simply a subterfuge to create high interest rates. (During the last decade, 1972-1982, the prime rate increased from 4 to 22%, nearly a 500% increase while inflation spiraled at a record rate averaging 10% per year.)

The Rockefeller Syndicate is a $500 billion combine that derives much of its income from interest. The Syndicate, like all massive conglomerates, has a carefully designed plan to maximize profits and expand its dominion of power. The paramount objective of the Syndicate's profit strategy is high interest.

The first part of this book tells the story of how the rip-off happened. It begins with the origin of the Federal Reserve Bank. Chapters 2 and 3 explain David Rockefeller's role and the formation of the Trilateral Commission, followed by the saga of how he created a surrogate President, *(The Capon Presidency),* to guarantee that the "right" people were appointed to the Federal Reserve Board. Chapter 5 *(The Board of Governors),* analyzes the unknown, unelected dictators of the American economy, the members of the Federal Reserve Board. Chapters 6 and 7 are an analysis of the Board's fraudulent no-win policy. Chapter 8 answers the question of how faithfully Chairman Volcker represented the public interest. Chapter 9 explains why a balanced budget is so elusive.

Subsequent chapters detail the horrendous cost to the public, the consequences of the Board's policies on the American economy, and the subversion of our democracy. The concluding chapters offer an alternative program to correct the mis-management of our economy and a series of reforms to prevent their recurrence.

A word of encouragement to the reader. This book is written in simple, easy to understand copy. It is not difficult to understand economic concepts. However, most people fear books in economics because they think the text is beyond them. That is how you are expected to react and forfeit your right to participate in economic decisions. Do not be intimidated. National economic decisions are vital to your welfare. All its takes is common sense, and you probably have more of that than many of the economists that are making the decision for you.

# CHAPTER 1

# *The Origin Of The Federal Reserve Bank*

> ***This Act establishes the most gigantic trust on earth. When the President signs this bill, the invisible government by the Monetary Power will be legalized. The people may not know it immediately, but the day of reckoning is only a few years removed . . . The people must make a declaration of independence to relieve themselves from the Monetary Power . . . Wall Streeters could not cheat us if you Senators and Representatives did not make a humbug of Congress . . . The greatest crime of Congress is its currency system. The worst legislative crime of the ages is perpetrated by this banking and currency bill.***
>
> ***Congressman Charles Lindberg, Sr. 1913***

According to most history books, the Federal Reserve Bank was created by the Federal Reserve Act of 1913 in response to a growing need for an organized central banking system to provide national banking service. Congress approved it because the American public needed a flexible money supply and low, stable interest rates for a growing exuberant economy. This is the usual explanation for the establishment of the Federal Reserve Bank.

This chapter offers a viewpoint different from the sanitized version found in most texts. It will show that the Federal Reserve Bank was misrepresented to Congress and to the public by a group of American and international bankers. They never intended to create a bank for the benefit of the people. It was a well-conceived plan that gave the banking aristocracy a vehicle to dominate and control our money supply. For years, European bankers manipulated interest rates through central banks profitably. The international banking families of Rothschild and Warburg sent a brilliant young banker, Paul Warburg, to design an American version of a central bank.

The origin of the Federal Reserve Bank is a tale of deceit and international intrigue with a Paul Erdman plot. It is a story of powerful American and international financiers who established a central bank in the United States. It depicts how the Congress of the United States forfeited its constitutional powers to control the nation's money supply to a private, secretive, independent organization: the Federal Reserve Bank.

From the beginning the Federal Reserve Bank was tainted by intrigue, secrecy, and the ulterior motives of the men who formulated the plan. To study the operations of European central banks, the National Advisory Commission, which was composed of sixteen Congressmen, traveled to Europe in 1908 to research a report that was to contain their recommendations. Senator Aldrich, a strong proponent of a central bank, was chairman of the commission. Upon completing the trip, the Committee issued a report, but the document that was issued over their signatures was not their report. The report was written at a secret meeting at Jekyll Island, the result of a deception that would significantly change the course of the economic history of the United States.

In November 1910, a group of bankers and financiers led by Senator Aldrich went to the Jekyll Island Hunt Club, which was owned by J.P. Morgan and other New York bankers. The group of money lenders represented the most powerful economic force in America at that time:

- Frank Vanderlip – National City Bank of New York (Rockefeller); (a partner of the Rockefeller's investment syndicate known as the Standard Oil Gang)
- H.P. Davidson – J.P. Morgan Company
- Paul Warburg – Kuhn, Loeb Company (a financial firm that controlled much of America's railroads)

According to the Pujo Committee report, this consortium, whose holdings at that time exceeded $24 billion, represented a trust that controlled a large part of American finance, transportation, and heavy industry. The central member of the group that met at Jekyll Island was Paul Warburg, a central bank expert who, in fact, formulated the plan that was to eventually become our Federal Reserve System.

Secret meetings by a group of the most powerful financiers in America led by an alien international banker who ghostwrote a congressional report does not constitute an auspicious beginning for America's most important economic institution – the Federal Reserve Bank.

The private car that left Hoboken Station was supplied by Senator Aldrich, John D. Rockefeller's son-in-law, David Rockefeller's grandfather. The shades were drawn, and during the trip to Jekyll Island, the participants referred to each other by their first names only to ensure that even the railroad personnel could not identify them. After returning to New York, they referred to themselves as the "first name club," in acknowledgment of their self-importance in an historic intrigue. This attitude of being an "insider" with the right to be secretive has continued in the Federal Reserve System. The Board members consider the Federal Reserve System a private organization.

The public was ambivalent towards a centralized banking system. Traditionally, Americans were wary of central banks because they feared that the concentration of economic powers represented a loss of economic freedom. Thomas Jefferson warned that "a private central bank was a greater menace to the liberties of the people than a standing army." Andrew Jackson, fearing the concentration of immense monetary power in private hands, fought the United

States Bank successfully. President Garfield, prior to his assassination, warned about the danger of a central bank: "Whoever controls the supply of currency would control the business and activities of all the people."

In 1910, Congress and the people were suspicious of a central bank. The rhetoric of William Jennings Bryan for bimetalism, the superficial trust-busting of Teddy Roosevelt, and the publicity resulting from the Pujo Committee, created a political atmosphere that opposed the formation of a central bank. Such was the political climate when the Aldrich Plan was submitted to Congress on January 16, 1911. Warburg, who formulated the plan, was politically astute enough to know that if the bill were sponsored by Aldrich (depicted as a bloated capitalist in contemporary political cartoons) it was doomed to defeat. Although Warburg argued against Aldrich's sponsorship of the bill, the venerable New Englander prevailed.

*Harper's Weekly,* May 7, 1910, editorialized: "Mr. Aldrich sums up in his personality the greatest and most sinister menace to the popular welfare of the United States." Senator Aldrich married into the Rockefeller Family and was a multi-millionaire with strong ties to the large financial trusts. He was portrayed as a pompous, dictatorial capitalist who would deliver America into the clutches of the greedy banking trust. Wilbur L. Stone wrote in the *North American Review,* September 1911:

> Senator Aldrich would take from the people and give to the bankers the absolute control of the people's money. It is apparent that in such a body of bankers there would be no opportunity for the people or their representatives to make their wishes known effectively, if their wishes conflicted with those of the banking interests.

Understandably, Congress defeated the Aldrich Plan.

But the mood of America was changing as a result of the intense lobbying of the proponents of the central bank. Despite the fear of financial concentration, the public and Congress were made aware of the need for a more resilient banking system that could provide a flexible money supply for a developing economy. The fantastic growth of transportation systems (railroads), the development of American heavy industry (steel), and the growing demand for fuel (coal and kerosene) required a more sophisticated banking system. This need was accentuated by our expanding economic frontier that was moving west and relied on local banks to finance the progress. Western industry depended upon Wall Street for capital. Even though the need for banking reform was evident, the people remained suspicious of a central bank.

The financial aristocracy, however, had too much to gain from a central bank to let it fail. After Senator Aldrich's trip to Europe, they realized that making money from a central bank was much easier and more lucrative than profits from industry and transportation. A central bank was the way to go.

Since the turn of the century, there had been serious attacks against industrial and transportation monopolies. In 1911 the Supreme Court ordered the break-up of the Standard Oil monopoly. This fortified the "Standard Oil Gang's" (Rockefeller, Aldrich, and Stillman group) resolve to pass a bill that would create a central bank. They experienced firsthand the tremendous financial rewards of monopolistic practices in the Petroleum Industry. They understood full well that the Federal Reserve Act would create a legal monopoly of the nation's money supply, and because of the way the bill was written, they would be in control if the proper people were appointed to the Board.

Ironically, the Supreme Court ruling that broke up the Standard Oil monopoly reinforced the resolve of the financial aristocracy to force through Congress a central bank that monopolized the money supply for the entire nation.

It cannot be stated too strongly that the clamor for the bank was not from the people but from the leaders of the banking industry whose aim was to monopolize the American money market and eliminate competition.

Warburg and his colleagues re-introduced the central bank disguised as a regional banking system. The new legislation that was drawn up became known as the Owens-Glass Act, or the Federal Reserve Act, named after Representative Carter Glass, Chairman of the House Banking and Currency Committee; and Senator Robert L. Owen, Chairman of the Senate Banking and Currency Committee. Ostensibly, the bill was written by Dr. Henry Parker Willis, who was retained by the House Banking and Currency Committee as an "expert" consultant during the writing of the Federal Reserve Bill from 1912 to 1913. With some important amendments, the Federal Reserve Act was passed by Congress in 1913 and signed immediately by President Woodrow Wilson.

There is no doubt that the Federal Reserve Act of 1913 was a modified version of the Aldrich Plan ghostwritten by Paul Warburg in complicity with the largest banking interests in America at Jekyll Island. (Warburg's concept of a "united" Reserve Bank of the United States had been published in *The New York Times* as early as March 24, 1910.)

Frank Vanderlip, who represented the National City Bank of New York and the Rockefeller's "Standard Oil Gang" at Jekyll Island, acknowledges this in his autobiography, *From Farm Boy to Financier:*

> Our secret expedition to Jekyll Island was the occasion of the actual conception of what eventually became the Federal Reserve System. The essential points of the Aldrich Plan were all contained in the Federal Reserve Act as it was passed.

Further evidence comes from Professor E.R.A. Seligman, head of the Department of Economics at Columbia University, who observes: "The Federal Reserve Act is the work of Mr. Warburg, more than any other man in the country."

Who was Paul Warburg?

Paul Warburg arrived in America around 1902. He was a member of the Hamburg banking family of M.M. Warburg, who was a member of the Reichsanleihe-Konsortium – the inner sanctum of German bankers. When he came to the United States, he was financed by the Rothschilds and became a partner in the banking house of Kuhn, Loeb Company of New York. Although he seemed to have spent little time with the firm, he was paid a salary of $500,000 a year (an exceptionally large salary for that period). From the time of his arrival, he spent most of his time promoting a central bank for the United States.

Paul Emden assessed Paul Warburg's contribution to international banking in *The Money Power of Europe*.

> The Warburgs reached their outstanding eminence during the last twenty years of the past century, simultaneously with the growth of Kuhn, Loeb Co. in New York, with whom they stood in a personal union and family relationship. Paul Warburg, with magnificent success, carried through in 1913 the reorganization of the American banking system at which he had, with Senator Aldrich, been working since 1911, and thus most thoroughly consolidated the currency and finances of the United States.

In his recent book, Senator Barry Goldwater noted that "Warburg was the Architect of our Federal Reserve System, creating a privately owned mechanism to control the currency and the credit of the United States." (Goldwater, p. 238)

Warburg did not become an American citizen until 1911, a year after the Jekyll Island conclave. In 1912, a year after he became a citizen, he was decorated by Germany's Kaiser. After the Federal Reserve Bank was approved by Congress, according to plan, Warburg was appointed to the Board by Woodrow Wilson in 1914. Warburg refused to cooperate in the Senate's Public Confirmation Hearings. He was afforded special treatment by the Senate, which granted him a secret, informal conference. On July 23, 1914, *The Nation* reported:

> Mr. Warburg finally had a conference with Senator O'Gorman and agreed to meet the members of the Senate Subcommittee informally, with a view to coming to an understanding, and to giving them any reasonable information that they might desire. The opinion in Washington is that Mr. Warburg's confirmation is assured.

Although the minutes of that meeting were never published, Warburg was confirmed by the Senate and served as the vice-chairman of the Federal Reserve Board until his resignation in May 1918, when a United States Navy report exposed him as having a brother who was the leader of German espionage. The official Federal Reserve records merely indicate that his term expired. The report went as follows:

> Warburg, Paul, New York City. German, naturalized American citizen 1911, was decorated by the Kaiser in 1912, vice-chairman of the Federal Reserve Board, handled large sums furnished by Germany for Lenin and Trotsky. Has a brother who is leader of the espionage system of Germany. (Mullins, p. 58)

To demonstrate that international bankers are good sports, his family's banking house, M.M. Warburg, financed the Kaiser's World War I effort, while their son, Paul Warburg, vice-chairman of the Federal Reserve Board, was responsible for financing the American and allied war effort. During his tenure on the Board, Warburg was the dominant personality and was referred to as the financial dictator of the Federal Reserve Bank until his resignation in 1918. While he was vice-chairman, there was speculation that he was the personal agent of the Rothschilds and other European bankers who wanted to influence the American economy and the international gold market through our central bank.

* * * * *

If the story of the origin of the Federal Reserve System seems a bit exotic, the story of the politics and politicians behind its passage borders on the bizarre: a particularly naive President (Woodrow Wilson), an unknowing plagiarist (Congressman Glass), a Senator (Owen) who sponsored the bill and later admitted that he did not understand it, the congressional consultant (Dr. Willis) who became the act's severest critic, and a foe of central banking (William Jennings Bryan) who successfully promoted the act through Congress.

Woodrow Wilson, the President of Princeton University during the panic of 1907, observed that, "All this trouble could be averted if we appointed a committee of six or seven public-spirited men like J.P. Morgan to handle the affairs of our country." Wilson, who was in awe of the wealthy and frequently paid them homage, was naively advocating a government of the super-rich—a financial dictatorship. Wilson endeared himself to J. Pierpont Morgan and the Rockefeller clique by being the first major educator to endorse the Aldrich Plan. Wilson's public endorsement resulted in substantial financial aid that enabled him to become Governor of New Jersey. After a visit with James Stillman, president of the Rockefeller-influenced National City Bank, and a promise to support the Federal Reserve Act, presidential candidate Wilson received strong financial backing from the powerful financial clique that was promoting the national bank. Shortly after taking office, according to Willis in his book *The Federal Reserve System,* Wilson personally directed that Colonel House, his aide, be given a copy of the draft of the Federal Reserve Act. Willis had prepared a digest of the bill which he then delivered to President Wilson and Congressman Glass. The New York bankers backed Wilson for president to ensure that the act would be signed promptly and that the "right" members would be appointed to the Board of Governors of the Federal Reserve System.

Wilson fulfilled his part of the agreement superbly, although he did not fully understand the bill or its implications.

> The new President admitted "he knew nothing" about banking theory or practice. Glass made the same confession to Colonel House in November, and this vacuum is of the utmost significance. The entire banking reform movement at all crucial stages was centralized in the hands of a few men who for years were linked financially, ideologically, and personally, with one another. (Kolko, p. 222)

Colonel House was personal advisor and confidant to President Wilson. He was dubbed "the unseen guardian angel of the Federal Reserve Act." He was the liaison between Wilson and the banking proponents of the act. His papers documented his role and the influence of the banking elite. Colonel House recorded on December 19, 1912:

> I talked with Paul Warburg over the telephone, regarding currency reform. I told of my trip to Washington and what I had done there to get it in working order. I told him that the Senate and the Congressmen seemed anxious to do what he desired, and that President-elect Wilson thought straight concerning the issue.

House reported another meeting on March 17, 1913:

> Mr. J.P. Morgan, Jr., and Mr. Denny of his firm came promptly at five. McAdoo [Secretary of Treasury] came about ten minutes afterward. Morgan had a currency plan already printed. I suggested that he have it typewritten, so it would not seem too prearranged, and send it to Wilson and myself today.

On October 1913:

> Paul Warburg was my first caller today. He came to discuss the currency measure. There are many features of the Owen-Glass Bill that he does not approve. I promised to put him in touch with McAdoo and Senator Owen so that he might discuss it with them. *(The Intimate Papers of Colonel House)*

Congressman Carter Glass, a man with very little understanding of money or banking, was the conduit through which the Federal Reserve Act was manifested. As chairman of the House Banking and Currency Committee, he was made to think that he co-authored the bill.

Co-author Senator Owen, who owned the First National Bank of Muskogee, Oklahoma, was a relatively unsophisticated country banker who was confused by the bill. Owen's political orientation is paradoxical: although he was the nation's chief advocate of popular government, he nonetheless co-authored a bill that created a board of governors insulated from the public. He was president of the National Popular Government League, which advocated a government directly responsible to the people through recall, referendum, and initiative, yet none of these instruments of public recourse can be used against the Federal Reserve Board because of his bill. Senator Owen tried to insert only one major modification into the bill that required the Federal Reserve Board "to assure the stabilization of the price level," but it was stricken out. For a period of time he was a strong apologist for the Federal Reserve Act, but he ultimately became an outspoken critic of the bank and its Board. In later years, he regretfully admitted that he had not understood all of the provisions of the bill.

When Congressman Glass realized that neither he nor Senator Owen could deliver the votes to pass the bill, the silver-tongued William Jennings Bryan was seduced into supporting the Federal Reserve Act. Without Bryan's support, according to Willis, "It was clear that no progress could be made and that the Glass Bill might as well be abandoned."

(X) - SP's LIBRARY

Bryan was a populist who realized that money must be made available throughout the economy, but he fought against a central bank. He had attacked the big money trust and monetary politics in his "Cross of Gold" speech. Instead, he advocated bimetalism, a currency backed by both gold and silver.

Although Bryan, the "Great Commoner," had applied the coup de grace to the Aldrich Plan, the power of the proponents of the Federal Reserve Act proved too strong, and Bryan succumbed. Although he was enticed into banking the act, Bryan insisted on three important modifications:

(1) The notes would be Treasury currency, issued, payable, and guaranteed by the government;

(2) The section setting up the Federal Reserve Board would be revised to ensure a geographically and economically diversified public board and that its members would be appointed by the President and confirmed by the Senate to assure public control of the bank.

(3) The sections dealing with public deposits would be modified to ensure government control of government funds.

When these provisions were accepted and written into the act, his seduction was complete. On December 23, 1913, the Federal Reserve Act was passed by both houses and signed into law by the President.

Many of the key people responsible for the enactment of the Federal Reserve Act of 1913, including William Jennings Bryan, later regretted their support and condemned the Federal Reserve System and especially its Board. After watching the operation of the Federal Reserve and the public-be-damned policies of its Board, Bryan wrote, "In my long political career, the one thing I genuinely regret is my part in getting the banking and currency legislation enacted into law." Commenting on the Federal Reserve Board's role in causing the Agricultural Depression of 1920-1921, Bryan stated that the action of the bank double-crossed the farmer and caused a deflation of the agricultural industry that cost the farmer billions of dollars. He accused the Board of a deliberate criminal act.

Bryan was not the only disillusioned sponsor of the bill. Senator Robert Owen, who co-sponsored the bill because he believed that the act would stabilize the purchasing power of the dollar and provide a stable price level, was outraged because the big banks gained control of the Fed. He believed that the Federal Reserve System should have been the people's bank. Like everyone else, he had been fooled and then disenchanted. He became a severe critic of the Federal Reserve System and made this very astute observation:

> The people did not know the Federal Reserve Banks were organized for profit-making. They were intended to stabilize the credit and currency supply of the country. That end has not been accomplished. Indeed, there has been the most remarkable variation in the purchasing power of money since the System went into effect. The Federal Reserve men are chosen by the big banks, through discreet little campaigns, and they naturally follow the ideals which are portrayed to them as the soundest from a financial point of view.

Although the personnel of the Fed has changed over the years, its allegiance to the big banks has not wavered. Owen's comment is still true today: "The Federal Reserve men are chosen by the big banks . . . and they naturally follow the ideals which are portrayed to them." These comments by the Senate sponsor of the Federal Reserve Act seem timeless, for they aptly describe the Federal Reserve Board of today.

Dr. Henry Parker Willis also worked to pass the act but became disappointed in the operation of the bank. He was hired by Congressman Glass and the House Banking and Currency Committee as an expert consultant to draft the various versions of the bill. (He was secretary of the Federal Reserve System from 1914 to 1918.) In *The North American Review,* May 1929 ten years after his resignation from the Board, Willis attributed the agricultural depression of 1920-1923 directly to the Federal Reserve Board:

> Since the inauguration of the Federal Reserve Act, we have suffered one of the most serious financial depressions and revolutions ever known in our history, that of 1920-1921 . . . One million farmers left their farms, due to difficulties with the price of land and the odd status of credit.

Until 1931, Willis, editor of *The Journal of Commerce,* attacked all aspects of the Federal Reserve System. He condemned the Board, its personnel, its policies, the operation of the System, and even the structure of the System. He bitterly accused the Federal Reserve Board of complicity in a bankers' conspiracy that caused the stock inflation of 1926 and resulted in the Crash of 1929. Willis charged that the purposes and objectives of Congress in passing the act were ignored by the Board. The first and foremost was that the Federal Reserve Bank would guarantee an "elastic credit supply."

Willis was disillusioned and disappointed because he felt that he had been used, that the American public had been used, that the Congress of the United States had been used. Only the Federal Reserve Bank and the large banks were pleased. Willis observed that, "it was well-known during the spring of 1913 that they [bankers] were already parcelling out the directorships and executive positions which would be at their disposal as soon as the Glass Bill became the law."

There was strong opposition to the Federal Reserve Act from a Cleveland, Ohio, attorney named Alfred Crozier, who was an outspoken critic of what he referred to as the "Wall Street Banking Fraternity." He commented to a Senate committee:

> . . . the so-called administration currency bill grants just what Wall Street and the big banks for twenty-five years have been striving for, that is, *PRIVATE INSTEAD OF* public control of currency . . . The measures rob the government and the people of all effective control over the public's money, and vest in the banks exclusively the dangerous power to make money *among* the people scarce or plenty.

The origin of the Federal Reserve Bank was the result of a plot that deceived the American public. In the final analysis, it was a successful attempt by American and international bankers to monopolize the currency of the United States and place total control in private hands.

To paraphrase Congressman Lindberg: this act establishes the most gigantic monopoly on earth; the invisible government by bankers will be legalized. The greatest crime of Congress is the Federal Reserve Act. . . . The people must make a declaration of independence to relieve themselves from the control of the banking monopoly.

The course of events has proven Congressman Lindberg right. The history of the Federal Reserve is a woeful tale of corrupt, ineffectual policy, consistently contrary to the welfare of the American public. The unfortunate and devastating truth is that the Federal Reserve Board was corrupt to begin with and has worsened with age.

# CHAPTER 2

## *The Corrupters*

> *The United States has always been a corrupt society. Periodically, good citizens band together and elect to office political opportunists who are presented to the public as non-politicians. Briefly, things appear to be clean. But of course bribes are still given; taken. Nothing ever changes nor is there ever going to be any change until we summon up the courage to ask ourselves a simple if potentially dangerous question: Is the man who gives a bribe as guilty as the man who takes a bribe?*
>
> *— Gore Vidal*

". . . the general public, even usually informed persons, are as much in the dark about what is going on in the U.S. as in the center of Tibet." (Lundberg, *The Rockefeller Syndrome)*[1]

It is difficult for the man in Sweetwater, Texas, or Atlanta, Georgia, or Escondido, California, to comprehend how political and financial power brokers are dominating our government. Theoretically, we elect a President and a Congress to run our country. But do we in fact? In 1980 the supposed democratic election of a President actually involved no more than choosing between preselected candidates. With such an arrangement, the public could not win, and the power brokers could not lose. Unfortunately, it is not unique for political machines or unseen forces to control our government, as will be shown here.

It is only normal that David Rockefeller thinks of the Federal Reserve Bank as a family heirloom since his grandfather, Senator Aldrich, organized the secret meeting at Jekyll Island. David probably became interested in the banking business because he subscribed to his grandfather's philosophy that controlling a central bank was a quicker and easier way to make money than being in the oil business. For more than a decade, the "People's Bank"—the Federal Reserve—has been the fiefdom of David Rockefeller, run by his vassals who have set a policy that has benefited the Rockefeller Syndicate first, and the national interest second, if at all. To assure his control of the Fed, power broker David Rockefeller corrupted the Presidency of the United States so totally that Jimmy Carter turned the reins of government and the Federal Reserve Bank over to Rockefeller's "Financial Junta," which now exercises

*All footnotes are placed at the end of each chapter.

considerable control over our national government and absolute control over our national bank.

The average American may ask why David Rockefeller would bother. He has more economic wealth than one man would possibly use—mansions, ranches, jet aircraft, and yachts that could satisfy any ambitious man. Obviously all this is not enough. In *With No Apologies,* Barry Goldwater observes that it is not comfort but the quest for power that motivates men like David Rockefeller:

> History is more than a record of man's struggle for physical survival. Food and shelter are elementary needs, but in the minds of many, the acquisition of power is more important.
>
> In the world of nature, the predator stalks his prey, killing to satisfy hunger. In the society of man, the predators pursue sovereignty, not sustenance. (Goldwater, p. 282)

There is no doubt that David Rockefeller pursues sovereignty and, as will be pointed out in this book, has elevated himself to the status of "king-maker." Congressman Lawrence McDonald described the greed for power of the Rockefellers this way:

> Money alone is not enough to quench the thirst and lusts of the super-rich. Instead, many of them use their vast wealth, and the influence such riches give them, to achieve even more power. Power of a magnitude never dreamed of by the tyrants and despots of earlier ages. Power on a worldwide scale. Power over people, not just products. (Gary Allen: *Introduction: The Rockefeller File)*

To understand David Rockefeller, it is necessary to understand the mental attitude of most bankers. The higher their position, the more they are devoid of empathy or sympathy. They are concerned with their "bottom line"—not with the moral or human consequences of their goals.

Most of us have vaguely heard of David Rockefeller. He is described by Ferdinand Lundberg, an authority on American power and wealth, as "the Chairman of the Board of the ultrapowerful Chase Bank, as close to God as anyone can get." (Lundberg, p. 203) Lundberg further observed that, "What Leonid Brezhnev is to the Politburo and Central Committee of the Communist Party, USSR, David Rockefeller is to the Rockefeller family and the Rockefeller Syndicate. . . ." (Lundberg, p. 287) Bill Moyers, Press Secretary to Lyndon B. Johnson and Trustee of the Rockefeller Foundation, offers this view:

> David Rockefeller is the most conspicuous representative today of the ruling class, a multi-national fraternity of men who shape the global economy and manage the flow of its capital. Rockefeller was born to it, and he has made the most of it. (Bill Moyers, *The World of David Rockefeller).*

David Rockefeller is the grandson of John Rockefeller. In 1901, David's father, John D. Rockefeller II, married Abby, the daughter of Senator Aldrich (the senator who went to Europe to study the central bank and then promoted the idea in America). Even Rockefeller's critics acknowledged that Abby was the best thing that ever happened to Junior. She ran a happy, spirited household and enhanced the personality of her children with the quality of her lifestyle. Perhaps her style was the reason for the good humor and leadership qualities of some of her sons. She gave birth to five Rockefeller boys and one daughter: John D. III, Laurence, Nelson, Winthrop, David, and Abby. Within the status quo, the sons are moderate, enlightened, and, in certain ways, progressive. Winthrop was sometimes referred to as a radical, but only by some of his southern antagonists, while Nelson was considered too moderate for the Republican Party. Had he switched parties, perhaps he would have become president.

David, the family leader, is a brilliant innovator, an internationalist, and probably the most powerful international banker in history. He has a Ph.D. in economics and has written two books. David is reserved, not as outgoing as Nelson, and prefers to rule by status. There is a rumor that if the President of the United States cannot reach someone by phone, David Rockefeller can. He is a benevolent aristocrat, believing that his personal prescription for world development should be followed since it is unwise to leave such important matters to public whim. David seems to be at his best with the human equation. He knows how to use his position and status to exact subservience from a coterie of very able, intelligent, and influential people.

The Rockefeller brothers, despite their differences, generally operate together in matters of finance. By careful planning, they have kept most of the family's wealth intact. It is difficult to separate their power from their finances since most of their wealth is held in trusts, such as the Rockefeller Foundation and the Rockefeller Brothers' Fund. When Nelson Rockefeller was nominated for Vice President in 1974, he modestly indicated his worth at something over $218 million. Surely this was too low, for in 1964 an expert on America's wealthy families, Ferdinand Lundberg, estimated the family's wealth at $5 billion!

But this is only a small fraction of the financial resources controlled by the Rockefeller family.

The financial power base of David Rockefeller is extremely broad. According to Professor James C. Knowles (author of *The Rockefeller Financial Group)* of the University of Southern California, in 1969 the Rockefeller Syndicate controlled assets in excess of $113 billion. Among these assets were 25% of the assets of the fifty largest commercial banks in the country and 30% of the assets of the fifty largest life insurance companies. The financial backbone of the Rockefeller Syndicate includes the Chase Manhattan Bank, First National Bank of New York, and the First National Bank of Chicago, which ranked, respectively, second, third, sixth, and tenth nationally in 1969.

The Syndicate also includes three mammoth mutual life insurance companies—Metropolitan, Equitable, and New York Life—which are run by "friendly" trustees. In addition, the Rockefellers have significant influence in the major oil companies: Exxon, Mobil, Standard Oil of California, and others. But the personal base for David's prodigious financial power is the

Chase Manhattan Bank. Lundberg estimated that Chase and the Rockefeller Syndicate controlled assets of over $200 billion in 1974, and current evaluation (1982) would exceed $500 billion.

Over this vast economic empire, David Rockefeller reigns as "his eminent grace," the leader of the Syndicate. But it would be indelicate to suggest that he is the godfather, even though his family comes down hard on its competition and critics.

The Rockefeller clan is not above publicly defiling the reputations of its political foes. When Nelson was running against Justice Arthur J. Goldberg for Governor of New York, the family paid Victor Lasky to write a derogatory biography, entitled *Arthur J. Goldberg, the Old and the New,* which was distributed free to the New York State Republican organization. Brother Laurence paid $65,000 to have the book written and distributed by Literary Properties, Inc. While being considered for Vice President and subjected to intense questioning, Nelson confessed to his indiscretion: "In regard to the financing of the book on Mr. Justice Goldberg, let's face it—I made a mistake."

Others felt the Rockefeller wrath included Senators Birch Bayh and Gaylord Nelson because they opposed Nelson's nomination for Vice President, and Senator Frank Church because he wanted an accounting of David's international banking practices.

In 1976, Senator Ted Kennedy was methodically smeared in his bid for the Democratic presidential nomination by the Rockefeller group's orchestrated propaganda blitz on Chappaquiddick, slandering him to assure Jimmy Carter's nomination. In most cases, the Rockefellers do not personally wield the axe, preferring to have the hatchet job performed by a hireling who is paid through a Rockefeller Foundation or committee.

Sometimes the Rockefellers use their propaganda machinery to build up their public image. When Nelson was seeking congressional approval of his nomination as Vice President, the family contributed $89,952 to the Academy of Political Science, that, according to a *Time* magazine story by Martin Tolchin, published a laudatory book, *Governing New York State: The Rockefeller Years,* which was circulated through Congress and appropriate committees.

Nor is the Rockefeller family against buying favors. Just before Henry Kissinger joined the Nixon Administration, Nelson made him a gift of $50,000, and when Nelson ran for Governor of New York, he made a gift of $86,000 to Judson Morehouse, the Chairman of the New York State Republican Party. Nelson said that he made the gift to Morehouse to keep him "independent of temptation." A New York *Post* headline read: "MOREHOUSE RAN ROCK $$ UP TO $600G." Later, Nelson granted Morehouse an additional loan of $49,000 to finance an investment in a company that brother Laurence was funding. Ultimately, Nelson commuted Morehouse's felony bribery conviction. In all, Nelson gave gifts amounting to $1,778,878 to important members of the political community, including eighteen current and former state officials and a number of his staff members. Beneficiaries of the Rockefeller largess included:

- William Ronan, Chairman of the Metropolitan Transportation Authority, then Chairman of the Port Authority, and a Trustee of the New York State Power Authority, received $600,000 in gifts (loans that were forgiven).
- Other recipients were Henry Diamond, State Environmental Conservation Commissioner; James Gaynor, Commissioner of Housing and Community Renewal; G. Russel Clark, State Superintendent of Banks.
- One noteworthy case of obtaining political influence by a well-placed mega-buck involved William Miller. When Congressman Miller was the Republican National Committeeman, Nelson requested that brother Laurence loan Miller $30,000 to invest in two of Laurence's companies. Laurence made the loan.

Philanthropy to the right officials is the essential element in the making of Rockefeller power, an act which, if practiced by lesser men on a smaller scale, would be called bribery.

In his opening statement to a congressional committee, Nelson asked, "Am I the kind of man who would use his wealth improperly in public office. . . . I think the answer is no." You, the reader, be the judge.

The fact is that the Rockefellers have flagrantly used their wealth for political advantage and control.

It is rumored that David Rockefeller has been offered the post of Secretary of the Treasury by three presidents, who must have naively thought that he would do for our Treasury what he did for his Chase Bank.

In David's role as head of the most powerful financial group in America, he has influenced our national government for many years. Between him and brother Nelson, every administration since Eisenhower was subjected to Rockefeller pressure. John Kennedy felt the influence but did not succumb to it. Johnson also resisted and his clamor for low interest rates was a source of irritation to the Rockefellers.

But, when Nixon became President, the Rockefeller influence grew to impressive proportions. Nelson and Dick were fellow travelers of sorts. Their relationship of political intrigue went back to the Eisenhower Administration, when they were appointed by the president to serve on a covert committee to secretly enlist the services of certain Nazis and Nazi collaborators for espionage against the Russians. (It is probable that the recent collaborator, Barbie, the butcher of Lyons, was such an agent.) A brief résumé of the Nixon-Rockefeller relationship is enlightening.

An unusual meeting between Nixon and Nelson occurred during the 1960 Republican convention in Chicago. When Nixon was sure he had his party's nomination sewed-up, he flew to New York to meet with Nelson. Nelson made some extraordinary prerequisites for the meeting:

> In *The Making of the President, 1960,* Theodore White noted that Nixon accepted all the Rockefeller terms for this meeting, including provisions 'that Nixon telephone Rockefeller personally with his request for a meeting; that they meet at the Rockefeller apartment

> . . that their meeting be secret and later be announced in a press release from the Governor, not Nixon; that the meeting be clearly announced as taking place at the Vice President's request; that the statement of policy issuing from it be long, detailed, inclusive, not a summary communique.' (Allen)

The press dubbed this meeting the "compact of Fifth Avenue" and Barry Goldwater described it as the Munich of the Republican Party. Nelson had replaced the Republican platform with his own, and Nixon accepted it. The *Wall Street Journal,* July 25, 1960, commented that the fourteen points "are a far cry from the thing that conservative men think the Republican Party ought to stand for. . . ."

Nixon lost the Presidency to Kennedy and then lost the California governorship to Brown. Although he had little money when he left California, he moved into a $100,000 a year apartment in New York in a building owned by the Rockefellers, and went to work with John Mitchell, Rockefeller's personal attorney. (*Wall Street Journal,* January 17, 1969). Mitchell became Nixon's campaign manager and a strong voice in Nixon's cabinet. Nixon's miraculous political rebound was financed by the Rockefellers. Gary Allen noted that the rapid growth in Nixon's financial statement "may have been part of Nixon's deal with Rockefeller and the insiders that Mr. Nixon's personal property problems should be solved." (Allen, *None Dare Call It Conspiracy,* p. 108)

He went on to comment ". . . Rocky arranged the '68 election so that if he could not be President, someone whom he controlled would be."

There is no doubt that the Rockefellers got what they wanted from Nixon:

(1) Nixon appointed Arthur Burns as Chairman of the Federal Reserve Board.

(2) Nixon appointed David Rockefeller's personal aide and V.P. of Chase's forward planning committee, Paul Volcker, Under-Secretary of the Treasury, who became the chief architect of Nixon's international monetary policy.

(3) Nixon appointed the Rockefeller's international advisor, Henry Kissinger, Secretary of State.

(4) Nixon appointed John Mitchell, Rockefeller's personal attorney, Attorney General, the chief law enforcement officer of the nation.

(5) Nixon's "ping-pong" diplomacy opened relations with Red China. (Nixon had previously said that he would have nothing to do with "those Commies.")

Then something happened to the Dick and Nelson relationship, and it deteriorated. Rockefeller expert Gary Allen posed an interesting question: "Was Nixon Watergated?" (Allen, *The Rockefeller File*) Allen's thesis is credible enough to warrant serious consideration. The scenario went something like this:

Although they had a political alliance, Nelson and Nixon detested each other, according to Allen. But they needed each other — a combination of Nelson bucks and power at the top and Nixon's grass roots appeal. Allen speculated that, "Nixon grew too accustomed to the prerogatives of power, and believed that he had become an equal partner in the deal." (p. 174) Allen suggests that it was Kissinger and Haig, as Rockefeller agents, who masterminded

Nixon's early retirement. ". . . and as we unravel the twisting threads of this strange saga, we find that each tug that ultimately toppled Nixon from the throne can be traced to Rockefeller." (p. 175)

Kissinger insisted that White House leaks be stopped and he set up a special White House Investigating Unit, known as the Plumbers. Kissinger named a member of his staff, David Young, a Wall Street attorney who had worked for the Rockefellers, to head the unit. The Plumbers were used for more than security leaks. As we know, they broke into the Democratic Headquarters at Watergate.

According to Allen, the Watergate burglary was intentionally bungled.

This theory was supported recently on the television show *Lie Detector* by one of the men convicted of the break-in. Frank Sturgis claimed that he was recruited by the CIA to get data on subversive Donors to the Democratic Party. He also claimed that they were set up to be caught on the last burglary to destroy the office of the Presidency. He said that the Plumbers were the creation of David Rockefeller, Kissinger, and CIA Director Helms. He speculated that Rockefeller told Kissinger to do what he could to destroy Nixon.

But Watergate would not have been a problem for Nixon had it not been for the tapes. It was the tape cover-up that did Nixon in. He would have survived Watergate if Alexander Butterfield, his liaison with the Secret Service, had not offered the information to the congressional committee. Butterfield had been a CIA informant and is suspected of working with the CIA while he was in charge of the taping of the White House. Did Butterfield drop his bomb intentionally on orders from Rockefeller, Kissinger, or the CIA?

But why didn't Nixon destroy the tapes when Butterfield divulged their existence? Even Watergate prosecutor Leon Jaworski admitted that "if Mr. Nixon had destroyed the tapes at the time their existence was disclosed in July 1973, he would still be President."

Allen theorizes that he could not, that he was not in control of the tapes. It has also been suggested that there were duplicate tapes, and even if he had been able to destroy the White House copies, duplicates would have found their way to the proper people. Allen presents a good argument that someone had access to those tapes who was hostile to Nixon. There was the mysterious "deep throat" who supplied the press with damaging information. The details of Judge Sirica's orders proves that someone with access to the tapes was supplying the judge with specific information: "The entire segment of tape on the reel identified as 'White House telephone start 5/25/72 (2:00 P.M.) (skipping 8 lines) 6/23/72 (2:50 P.M.). . . ." Obviously someone told Judge Sirica what to look for. The Nixon tapes were under the control of the Secret Service, according to the report in *Newsweek* on September 23, 1974.

> While former White House chief of staff H.R. Haldeman awaits trial for his part in Watergate, the Secret Service chief he ousted from the White House last year has landed a plum job. Robert H. Taylor, 49, who tangled with Haldeman over Nixon security procedures, is now head of the private security forces for all the far-flung Rockefeller family enterprises.

Allen comments:

> Hmmm. Once Nixon is deposed, the head of the Secret Service—the man in charge of the agency which was in charge of the tapes—gets 'a plum job' with the Rockefeller Empire. And what of the Rockefeller's number one man in the White House?
>
> We know that Henry Kissinger was deeply involved in wiretapping his own staff and several journalists. But the one member of the White House staff who apparently never had his remarks taped in the Oval Office was Herr Kissinger—who also, as it happens, was chief of all U.S. intelligence gathering operations. And who also, we now know, was responsible for establishing the Plumbers in the first place!
>
> But through all of this, Kissinger's loyalty was not with his President, it was with the Rockefellers!*

Allen writes that: "While it was Henry Kissinger who set Nixon's head on the chopping block, it was another Rockefeller agent, General Alexander Haig, who applied the ax. Haig was appointed—at Kissinger's suggestion—as an interim replacement for the hastily deposed Bob Haldeman." (Allen, p. 181) Kissinger met Col. Haig when he was a member of the Council on Foreign Relations while David Rockefeller was president of the association. In 1969, Colonel Haig became an assistant to Kissinger. By 1973, he had jumped 240 generals to a four-star rank.

Haig, it was reported, took the evidence against Nixon to Republican Senators and Congressmen and Barry Goldwater was provided the damaging tape of June 23. After a congressional group made up of Senators Goldwater and Scott and House Minority Leader John Rhodes called on Nixon, "that night," Lloyd Shearer of *Parade* magazine reported, "after again talking to Kissinger and Haig, Richard Nixon decided to resign."

Ford's administration was unique because after he appointed Nelson Vice President, he spent the rest of his Presidency dodging Nelson's persistent clamor to elevate himself to domestic *charge d'affairs* parallel to Kissinger's international status. To Ford's credit, he refused and found himself faced with a vindictive Rockefeller clan. Nelson took himself off Ford's re-election ticket, (some say at the request of Ford) and threatened not to help Ford against Carter. As we know, Ford lost to Carter.

Brother David had Carter groomed and ready to run as the Democratic candidate in 1976. Carter was elected and the Rockefellers had a tenacious hold on the White House.

David Rockefeller's intimidation of Congress can be demonstrated by his successful efforts to squelch an inquiry into the effect on American banks of the Arab oil billions flowing into the country. At the beginning of 1975, there was a massive flow of Arab funds into American banks, particularly into large international banks such as Rockefeller's Chase Manhattan. From 1974 to 1977, $108 billion of OPEC money migrated to the United States, including

$38 billion as deposits or purchase of U.S. Treasury notes. Fearing that the Arabs' billions could be used to influence American foreign policy, a Senate subcommittee attempted to determine the facts. However, the most powerful lobbyiest in America, David Rockefeller, put an end to the inquiry. Although Senator Frank Church, Chairman of the Multi-National Subcommittee of the Senate Foreign Relations Committee, insisted that the international banks disclose the amount of their OPEC funds, the larger banks (including Chase) refused to divulge any information. Paul Volcker, who had just been appointed President and Chief Executive Officer of the Federal Reserve Bank of New York (later to be appointed chairman of the Federal Reserve), dutifully interceded on behalf of David Rockefeller, his ex-boss and benefactor. Volcker argued for confidentiality, calling disclosure an extremely dangerous precedent. Then Senator Charles Percy, whose daughter had married John D. Rockefeller IV, vigorously opposed the disclosures, arguing, "I think we are dealing with dynamite right now and I think it is a cause for concern for Arthur Burns [then Chairman of the Federal Reserve Board], David Rockefeller, for a lot of them." David Rockefeller flew to Washington, had breakfast with Senator Chase, and happened to have a chance meeting and lunch with Senator Church, who was forced to accept an agreement that the banks would supply confidential figures to the Fed and not to Congress. David obviously has a way with words.

David's influence is not limited to the American government; he is very strong on the international circuit. He has the ability to make his presence felt even in far-off Iran, as demonstrated by his relationship with the Shah. In the late 1960s, as the Shah's oil revenues grew, so did David's affections for the Shah. Anthony Simpson describes the romance this way:

> David Rockefeller flew in and out of Tehran, staying at the Hilton with his large entourage and impressing the Shah with his influence and his benign concern: on one visit he presented the Shah with a hunting rifle; on another he bought a whole collection of paintings by Iranian artists. It was a friendship of mutual interest. Rockefeller enjoyed the reassurance of a fellow-prince, as well as the prospect of business; and the Shah saw Rockefeller as a key to American support—with all the mystique of his name, his foundations and international connections, personifying the traditional links between the Chase Bank and the oil industry. (Anthony Simpson, *The Money Lenders*)

Using sophisticated, highly respected intellectual committees, commissions, and think tanks, David Rockefeller has learned to marshal public opinion where and when it counts. He is so adroit in manipulating the public that he displays a true genious for propaganda. Perhaps it is because he is somewhat shy and unassertive in public that he has learned to speak so effectively through the mouths of others. When David wants to make a statement of policy, he can call upon the most prestigious leaders in the world to make the statement and top academicians and economists to defend it. (Think how helpless a Congressman or an ordinary citizen would be against people like Arthur Burns, Henry Kissinger, Zbigniew Brzezinski, and the Rockefeller think tanks.) David's grandfather, John D. Rockefeller, said, "The ability to deal with people is as purchasable a commodity as sugar or coffee, and I pay more for that ability than for any other under the sun." Having learned that lesson well, David has brought under his wing the talents of many of the most important men in government, academics, economics, and finance throughout the world. And, once under the Rockefeller wing, the individuals become ever more powerful and more indebted to their sponsor.

Ferdinand Lundberg astutely assesses the Rockefellers' dedicated proclivity to bring the "right" people into their sphere of influence: "The secret relates to people. For in addition to collecting money, properties, works of art and the general run of investments, the Rockefellers also carefully collect people — key people — some of them brilliant. And it is the people they collect that is one of the major sources of their pervading power." (Lundberg, p. 115) "If one listed all of the people the Rockefellers are connected with through the magic power of money, all the investments of their various philanthropic and personal funds, and all the agencies in receipt of supplementary revenues from them, one would get a book equivalent in size to a big city telephone directory — nothing but lists, lists, lists." Then he comments, "But more interesting to me among the spin-offs from the Rockefeller phenomenon and more significant culturally and socially, are the large number of Syndicate professors and Syndicate commentators who look upon the Rockefellers much as devout Muslims look upon direct descendants of Mohammed." (Lundberg, pp. 366-369)

Like the Medici, who used their wealth to bestow favors on promising people, David grants patronage generously, expecting and getting total allegiance in return. He creates projects and then funds them, sometimes using study and research groups like the Brookings Institute, the American Enterprise Institute (AEI), the Hoover Institute, and a variety of other think tanks. His patronage has served him well, for being chosen to serve on a Rockefeller commission is a mark of achievement, an indication of being accepted by the inner circle. Being chosen elicits the "K.A. Factor,"* even among men who should know better. To create a feeling of obligation, the Rockefellers sometimes resort to direct payment to obtain loyalty (as in the case of Kissinger).

Arthur Burns, Chairman of the Federal Reserve Board from 1970 to 1978, is an example of how the Rockefellers use patronage to develop a relationship that will enhance their power structure. In 1958, when the Rockefeller Brothers' Fund created a panel called "International Security: The Military Aspect," headed by Nelson Rockefeller, Arthur F. Burns (a Columbia University professor and president of the National Bureau of Economic Research), was chosen as a director of the panel. Though Professor Burns was a distinguished economist who had established himself as an expert on business cycles, he knew nothing about international security. After being offered this position, Burns became part of the Rockefellers' inner circle and was later chosen as a member of the Trilateral Commission. On February 1, 1970, Nixon appointed Burns Chairman of the Federal Reserve Board, and for eight years he served

Rockefeller's interest so well that David could not have fared better if he had held that post himself. After Burns left the Federal Reserve Board, the Committee to Fight Inflation was formed in June 1980, with Burns as its director. The Commission is supported by AEI, a Trilateralist-connected think tank where Burns was rewarded with a distinguished scholar-in-residence appointment. (Sklar, p. 575)

To appreciate the scope of David Rockefeller's ability to collect people, you need only to look at the influence and importance of the other members of the panel on International Security:

- Nelson Rockefeller, Chairman.
- Adolf A. Berle, Jr., Author.
- Chester Bowles, former Ambassador to India and former Governor of Connecticut.
- Arthur F. Burns, Columbia University Professor, Ex-President of the National Bureau of Economic Research and Ex-Chairman of the Federal Reserve Board.
- General Lucius D. Clay, Chairman of the Continental Can Company and former Commander-in-Chief of U.S. Forces in Europe, as well as Military Governor of the U.S. Zone, Germany.
- John Cowles, President of the Minneapolis *Star* and *Tribune,* and Chairman of the Des Moines *Register* and *Tribune.*
- Justin W. Dart, President of Rexall Drug Company and member of the Reagan Kitchen Cabinet.
- Gordon E. Dean, former Chairman of the Atomic Energy Commission and Senior Vice President for Nuclear Energy of General Dynamics Corporation.
- John S. Dickey, President of Dartmouth College.
- John W. Gardner, President of the Carnegie Corporation of New York and creator of Common Cause.
- Lester B. Granger, Executive Director of the National Urban League.
- Caryl P. Haskins, President of the Carnegie Institution.
- Theodore M. Hesburgh, President of the University of Notre Dame.
- Margaret A. Hickey, Public Affairs Editor of *Ladies Home Journal.*
- Oveta Culp Hobby, President and Editor of the Houston *Post,* former Secretary of Health, Education and Welfare, and Director of WACS.
- Devereau C. Josephs, Chairman of the New York Life Insurance Company.
- Milton Katz, Director of International Legal Studies, Harvard University Law School, former Ambassador, and Chief of the Marshall Plan in Europe.

- The late Henry R. Luce, Publisher of *Time, Life,* and *Fortune.*
- Thomas B. McCabe, President of the Scott Paper Company.
- General James McCormack, Vice President of M.I.T. and former Director of Research and Development, United States Air Force.
- Professor Richard P. McKeon, Department of Philosophy, University of Chicago.
- Lee W. Minton, President of the Glass Bottle Blowers Association.
- Charles H. Percy, Ex-President of Bell & Howell, United States Senator, and Rockefeller in-law.
- Jacob S. Potofsky, President of Amalgamated Clothing Workers of America.
- Anna Rosenberg, Industrial Relations Consultant and former Assistant Secretary of Defense.
- Dean Rusk, former Secretary of State, President of the Rockefeller Foundation.
- David Sarnoff, Chairman of the Radio Corporation of America.
- Charles M. Spofford, Wall Street Corporation Lawyer and former Deputy Representative to NATO.
- Edward Teller, Professor of Physics, University of California, Associate Director, University of California Radiation Laboratories, and the "father" of the hydrogen bomb.
- Frazar B. Wilde, President of Connecticut General Life Insurance Company.
- Robert B. Anderson, Ex-Secretary of the U.S. Treasury.
- James R. Killian, Jr., President of M.I.T., former Special Assistant to the President.
- Henry A. Kissinger, Director of the panel, Associate Director of the Center for International Affairs, Harvard University, former Secretary of State.

(Source: Lundberg)

A second panel had an equal number of well-known personalities. And this is only one committee of many created and financed by the Rockefellers. According to Lundberg, "The prime objective of these 'studies' was to project an image of Nelson Rockefeller as a formidable public figure of possible presidential stature. Everything else about them was purely incidental. None of the 'studies,' for all the hullabaloo accompanynig them, was anything but routine." (Lundberg) Other Rockefeller study panels include:

- The Challenge to America – Its Economic and Social Aspects.
- The Pursuit of Excellence – Education and the Future of America.
- The Power of the Democratic Idea.
- The Performing Arts – Problems and Prospects.

Each committee member was an important figure in his respective field and a person of the same caliber as those listed above.

Although a legitimate study of problems in an attempt to reach objective, socially useful conclusions is laudable, it is apparent that the underlying purpose of the panels was to provide sophisticated support for the Rockefeller philosophy. More pointedly, there is the lingering suspicion that each panel was primarily an excuse to anoint the panel's members and to induct them into the Rockefeller power system.

*When Kissinger left public office, he joined the Chase Manhattan Bank as Chairman of the International Committee at the invitation of David Rockefeller and was appointed director of the Rockefeller Brothers' Fund.

*K.A. is a term that describes a subservient "yes-man."

# CHAPTER 3

# *The Financial Junta*

***Our non-elected rulers.***

***— Senator Barry Goldwater***

To use his position of great wealth, David Rockefeller uses organizations to speak for him and implement his strategy. These organizations have significantly influenced the policies of our government, particularly our foreign and monetary policies. In 1973, David Rockefeller, in one of the most adroit power plays in financial history, solidified his influence over the federal government and the nation's economy by creating the Trilateral Commission.

The Trilateral Commission is an outgrowth of and closely aligned with a number of influential Rockefeller organizations, some of which preceded the Trilateral Commission. Indeed, a large part of the power of the Trilateral Commission resulted from choosing the strongest, most effective members from these groups.

An important predecessor was the Council on Foreign Relations, which was founded at the end of World War I. Since its organization, the Council on Foreign Relations has been the architect of United States foreign policy. As Barry Goldwater points out, since 1944 every secretary of state except James F. Byrnes has been a member of the Council on Foreign Relations. On September 1, 1961, the *Christian Science Monitor* assessed the council in these terms: "The Council on Foreign Relations is composed of 1400 of the most elite names in the world of government, labor, business, finance, communications, foundations and academies. It has staffed almost every key position of every administration since that of FDR." Paul Warburg was one of the incorporators. The Rockefellers and their foundations contributed heavily to the council; and David Rockefeller became its chairman in the same year that he became chairman of the Chase Manhattan Bank. It is generally acknowledged that David Rockefeller still exercises a strong influence on the Council on Foreign Relations, so much so that he was able to replace a recent chairman of the council. Understandably, many powerful council members became members of the Trilateral Commission.

The Atlantic Council, an organization formed to promote international trade for the United States, is closely tied to the Trilateral group in that eleven Atlantic Council directors are Trilateral Commissioners: David Packard, Vice Chairman; David M. Abshire; Anne Armstrong; Sol C. Chaikin; George Franklin, Jr., Coordinator of the Trilateral Commission; Thomas L. Hughes; Henry A. Kissinger, member of the Executive Board of the Trilateral Commission; Winston Lord, Chairman of the Council on Foreign Relations; Charles W. Robinson; Robert V. Roosa; Phillip H. Trezise; Marina N. Whitman; George Ball, Honorary Director of the Atlantic Council.

Another Rockefeller organization, the Commission on Critical Choices for Americans (CCCA), describes itself as "a nationally representative, bipartisan group of forty-two prominent Americans brought together under the Chairmanship of Nelson A. Rockefeller." It is generally acknowledged that the commission, five of whose members are Trilateralists, is funded by the Rockefeller organization to perpetuate the philosophies that are basic to the Trilateral Commission. Interestingly, a number of important CCCA members, including Nancy Hanks, who later married Henry A. Kissinger, have reportedly received cash gifts from the Rockefellers.

An international group known as the Bilderbergers was a forerunner of the Trilateral Commission. Promoting "Atlanticism," trade and international banking between Europe and America, it was started in 1954 by Holland's Prince Bernhard. David Rockefeller was a participant, along with the most important political leaders, bankers, and intellectuals in the Western world. However, the Japanese were excluded from membership. Becoming aware of growing economic power of Japan and its potential in international banking and trade, David Rockefeller formed the Trilateral Commission to include the Japanese.

The Trilateralists are closely aligned with the Bilderbergers, whose international executive committee is made up of twenty-six members, almost half of whom are Trilateralists, including David Rockefeller and Henry Kissinger.

The term "Trilateral Commission" is a bit confusing because it sounds as if some "authority" appointed the commission to serve. In a sense this is true since David Rockefeller appointed the Commission to serve on his behalf. He and Zbigniew Brzezinski conceived the Trilateral Commission as an international organization made up of three branches—United States, Western European, and Japanese—hence, the name *Tri*lateral. Accordingly, the purpose of the organization is to promote internationalism among these three spheres of economic power.

David Rockefeller views the Commission benignly. In the Prospectus of the Trilateral Commission, he said that he intended to bring the best brains of the world together to bear on the problems of the future. In answer to criticism of the Commission, he responded, "My point is that far from being a coterie of international conspirators with designs on covertly ruling the world, the Trilateral Commission in reality is a group of concerned citizens interested in fostering greater understanding and cooperation among international allies." (Sklar, p. xi).

Another way to describe the Trilateral Commission is to compare it to a super international fraternity made up of all the big men on campus. It is composed of the most important international bankers, political leaders of the free world, multinational corporations, ambassadors, international economists, and, surprisingly, union labor leaders. One Trilateralist described the Commission very candidly:

> We do not like to call ourselves neo-federalists—that irritates too many sensitive souls. We call ourselves neo-functionalists who attain control over domestic policies by coordinating functional areas. But yet, there is an aspect of neo-federal supranationalism to our program. (Karl Kaiser, Trilateral Commissioner)

In reality, the Trilateral Commission is a politically powerful organization of the most influential world leaders in finance, politics, communications, and academics. It is the "shadow government" of the United States, an elitist underground that intends to control government policy domestically and internationally.

Guided by the strategy of David Rockefeller, the Commission is a clique of powerful people who manipulate governments to serve their own financial objectives. Barry Goldwater comments on the Trilateralists' motives: "What the Trilateralists truly intended was the creation of a world-wide economic power superior to the political governments of the nation states involved. As managers and creaters of the system they will rule the future." (Goldwater, p. 285). He further comments, "In my view, the Trilateralists represent a skillful, coordinated effort to seize control and consolidate the four centers of power—political, monetary, intellectual, and ecclesiastical." (Goldwater, p. 284).

Goldwater's viewpoint was substantiated by Jeremiah Novak, a knowledgeable observer of the Trilateral Commission.

> Far faster than people realize, the domestic and foreign policy of the United States is being influenced by a supra-national directory, operating on a governmental and private basis under the aegis of the Trilateral Commission. Inherent in the idea of Trilateralism is the neo-federalist supra-national unit to which individual nation-states are subordinated. (Sklar, *Trilaterialism*)

In the Commission's second report, *The Crisis of International Cooperation*, it called for the formation of an advisory commission of three heads-of-state to set policy for the Trilateral nations. "The international system which depended for its leadership in the past on the United States alone now requires a truly common management." Sklar outlined the Commission's purposes:

> The Commission's purpose is to engineer an enduring partnership among the ruling classes of North America, Western Europe and Japan—hence the term "Trilateral"—in order to safeguard the interests of Western capitalism in an explosive world. The private Trilateral Commission is attempting to mold public policy and construct a framework for international stability in the coming decades. (Sklar, p. 2)

Then she explains the Trilateralists' philosophy:

> To put it simply, Trilateralists are saying: the people, governments and economies of all nations must serve the needs of multinational banks and corporations . . . In short, Trilateralism is the current

> attempt by ruling elites to manage both dependence and democracy—at home and abroad. (Sklar, p. 4)

In the final analysis, as Senator Goldwater observes, the Trilateral Commission is David Rockefeller's alter-ego:

> The Trilateral Organization created by David Rockefeller was a surrogate—the members selected by Rockefeller, its purposes defined by Rockefeller, its funding supplied by Rockefeller. David Rockefeller and Zbigniew Brzezinski screened and selected every individual who was invited to participate. (Goldwater, p. 280)

The authors of *Trilaterals Over Washington* further comment that without "being accused of hastiness or bias one can reasonably conclude that David Rockefeller is the power behind the Trilateral Commission and presumably stands to gain the most from its activities." Sutton and Wood offer this assessment:

> Trilaterals represent an elite, kept afloat by sheer audacity and by the traditionally slow reaction of citizenry . . . unfortunately, reaction to elitism is usually stimulated only by overt oppression. The basic game plan of the Trilaterals is to blur the separation between "private wealth" and "public service" for Trilateral advantage; public wealth is to be oriented to private Trilateral ends. The essential point to hold in mind, however, is that a global multinational corporation (Chase Manhattan Bank) is in control of a power vehicle that controls the U.S. Government.

The Trilateral Commission is not yet a supra-government dictatorship nor is it a casual get-together. It is a forum conceived and formed by David Rockefeller to influence the course of international banking and commerce and to dominate the American government and its economy by controlling the Federal Reserve Bank. It is not a democratic commission with members chosen to represent diverse viewpoints, but David Rockefeller's carefully selected mercinaries: a "financial junta."

After a preliminary meeting of seventeen people, including Rockefeller and Brzezinski at the Pocantico, the Rockefeller estate in Tarrytown, New York, in July 1972, the Commission was formed in 1973 by David Rockefeller, with Zbigniew Brzezinski as director. As the "proper" members were chosen by Rockefeller and Brzezinski, the Commission grew until it reached approximately 300 members—one hundred members each in the United States, Western Europe, and Japan. The roster reads like a "Who's Who" of international financiers, corporate officers, and government officials: the political and banking elite of the world. Even knowing the nature of the membership, it is difficult to conceive of the enormous economic and political power of the Commission. But look at this line-up. At one time, its membership included the President of the United States, the Prime Minister of England, the Prime Minister of France, the Chairman of the World Bank, the Chairman of the largest bank in the world, two of our recent chairmen of the Federal Reserve

Bank, and the heads of many of the most important banks in the world.

It is imperative that the American public comprehends the political and financial power of the Trilateral Commission and the tremendous influence and control it exerts over our government. Keep in mind that the Commission is David Rockefeller's alter-ego and we are talking about Rockefeller power.

How powerful and how *extensive* is the Commission? In the world of finance, present or former Trilateral members have served in the following capacities to national central banks or world banks:

- Arthur Burns, past Chairman of the Federal Reserve Board; Paul Volckner, the present Chairman; and the man being groomed for future Chairman of the Federal Reserve, Anthony Solomon (now President of New York Federal Reserve Bank, having replaced Paul Volcker).
- Michael Belanger, President and Chief Executive Officer of the National Bank of Canada.
- T. Kenneth Whitaker, Governor of the Central Bank of Ireland.
- Guido Carli, Governor of the Bank of Italy.
- Alden Clausen (former Chairman of the Bank of America), Chairman of the World Bank.
- Many of the largest banks in the United States, Europe, and Japan are represented on the Trilateral Commission.

The following is a sample list of European and Japanese banks represented on the Trilateral Commission:

- Sir Anthony Tuke, Chairman of Barclay Bank, Ltd.
- Baron Edmond de Rothschild, President of Campaign Financier Holding.
- Lord Roll of Ipsden, Chairman of S. G. Warburg and Company, Ltd.
- Claudio Villalongs, Chairman of Banco de Madrid.
- Etc., etc., etc. . . .

In Japan, the banks are represented by:

- Yusuke Kashiwagi, President of the Bank of Tokyo.
- Toshio Nakamura, Chairman of Mitsubishi Bank.
- Takeshi Watanabe, former President of the Asian Development Bank.
- Yukio Shibayama, Chairman of Sumitomo Corporation (Bank).
- Etc., etc., etc. . . .

The following table (Sklar, pp. 14-16) shows that twenty-four out of the top fifty banks in the world are represented on the Trilateral Commission by an officer and/or director.

| Rank 1976 | Bank (Holding Company) | Home Country | Assets (Billion $ US) '76 |
|---|---|---|---|
| 1 | •BankAmerica Corp. | United States | 72.2 |
| 2 | Citicorp | United States | 63.1 |
| 3 | •Caisse Nationale de Credit Agricole | France | 52.7 |
| 4 | •Chase Manhattan Corp. | United States | 45.0 |
| 5 | Deutsche Bank | Fed. Rep. of Germany | 44.4 |
| 6 | Credit Lyonnais | France | 40.6 |
| 7 | Groupe BNP | France | 40.6 |
| 8 | Banco do Brasil | Brazil | 38.8 |
| 9 | •Dai-Ichi Kangyo Bank | Japan | 36.9 |
| 10 | Societe Generale | France | 36.5 |
| 11 | •Dresdner Bank | Fed. Rep. of Germany | 35.9 |
| 12 | •Barclays Bank | United Kingdom | 33.0 |
| 13 | Banca Nazionale del Lavoro | Italy | 32.7 |
| 14 | •Fuji Bank | Japan | 32.4 |
| 15 | •Sumitomo Bank | Japan | 32.4 |
| 16 | Westdeutsche Landesbank Girozentrale | Fed. Rep. of Germany | 30.9 |
| 17 | •Mitsubishi Bank | Japan | 30.7 |
| 18 | •Manufacturers Hanover Corp. | United States | 30.4 |
| 19 | •Sanwa Bank | Japan | 30.1 |
| 20 | National Westminister Bank | United Kingdom | 29.1 |
| 21 | Royal Bank of Canada | Canada | 28.6 |
| 22 | •J.P. Morgan and Co. | United States | 27.9 |
| 23 | Commerzbank | Fed. Rep. of Germany | 26.8 |
| 24 | Chemical New York Corp. | United States | 26.6 |
| 25 | Canadian Imperial Bank of Commerce | Canada | 26.0 |
| 26 | •Bank of Tokyo | Japan | 25.2b |
| 27 | Bayerische Vereins Bank | Fed. Rep. of Germany | 24.1 |
| 28 | •Industrial Bank of Japan | Japan | 23.7b |
| 29 | Tokai Bank | Japan | 23.2 |
| 30 | Algemene Bank Nederland | Netherlands | 22.8 |
| 31 | •Mitsui Bank | Japan | 22.7 |
| 32 | •Continental Illinois Corp. | United States | 21.8 |
| 33 | Swiss Bank Corp. | Switzerland | 21.6 |
| 34 | Union Bank of Switzerland | Switzerland | 21.6 |
| 35 | Taiyo Kobe Bank | Japan | 21.4 |
| 36 | Bankers Trust New York Corp. | United States | 21.1 |
| 37 | Co-operative Central Raiffeissen-Boerenleenbank | Netherlands | 20.8 |
| 38 | •Long-Term Credit Bank of Japan | Japan | 20.6 |
| 39 | Amsterdam-Rotterdam Bank | Netherlands | 20.5 |
| 40 | •Midland Bank Limited | United Kingdom | 20.2 |

| Rank 1976 | Bank (Holding Company) | Home Country | Assets (Billion $ US) '76 |
|---|---|---|---|
| 41 | •Bank of Montreal | Canada | 20.1 |
| 42 | •Lloyds Bank | United Kingdom | 20.1 |
| 43 | Banca Commerciale Italiana | Italy | 19.9 |
| 44 | •First Chicago Corp. | United States | 19.7 |
| 45 | •Western Bancorp. | United States | 19.7 |
| 46 | Bayerische Hypotheken und Wechsel Bank | Fed. Rep. of Germany | 19.6 |
| 47 | •Bayerische Landesbank und Girozentrale | Fed. Rep. of Germany | 19.2 |
| 48 | Daiwa Bank | Japan | 18.9 |
| 49 | Bank of Nova Scotia | Canada | 18.7 |
| 50 | •Bank fur Gemeinwirtschaft | Fed. Rep. of Germany | 17.1 |

• Represented on the Trilateral Commission through an officer and/or director.

The fact that there is a group to promote international banking is not unusual. What is unusual, however, is the close integration of the bankers with the most powerful government officials in the world, including President Carter; Prime Minister Edward Heath of England; Prime Minister Raymond Barre of France; Kiichi Miyazawa, Japanese Minister of State; Chief Cabinet Secretary; Jean Rey, the Belgium Minister of State; Manuel de Prado, Vice President of Spain and Oliver Giscard d'Estaing, brother of the former Prime Minister of France.

Trilateral Commission members dominate the State Department, and hence, the foreign policy of the United States. Kissinger, a Republican, and Cyrus Vance, a Democrat, both former Secretaries of State, were members. President Reagan's Vice President, George Bush, is a member. Trilateralist Casper Weinberger, Secretary of Defense, is the strongest member of the Reagan Cabinet. His close associate from Bechtel, George Schultz, was recently appointed Secretary of State when the Weinberger faction "pushed" Haig out. In addition, a substantial number of Trilateral members have served and are serving in key State Department posts.

In England, British Foreign Secretaries David Owen and Lord Carrington were members, as was Mitchell Sharp of the Canadian Ministry of External Affairs.

The number of ambassadors who are members of the Commission is alarming. Trilateralists have been ambassadors between the United States and Japan, between England and Japan, between the United States and England, between the United States and Italy, and even between the United States and China.

As we will see in the next chapter, "The Capon Presidency," Commission members ran the Carter Administration. When the commission had approximately seventy members, more than twenty-five of them were appointed to key posts in the Carter Administration. Additional members served in Congress, and others were directing our Federal Reserve Bank. And those members who were not running our government or central bank were helping David Rockefeller run his Syndicate.

This is frightening, especially since so many members of a small Commission were chosen to run our Government while other qualified potential candidates were passed over. If a man wasn't chosen by David Rockefeller for the Trilateral Commission, he was effectively excluded from top level service in the Carter Administration. It is as if the Sacramento Poker Club staffed the Governor's office, the legislature, and the judiciary for the State of California.

The power of the Commission is due largely to the "people manipulation" of David Rockefeller and his close aides, who planned their intrusion into government. Carter's Presidency was planned, just as Paul Volcker was systematically programmed and promoted for the position of Chairman of the Federal Reserve Board.

Rockefeller's effectiveness is testimony to the power of wealth and well-reasoned strategy.

It is embarrassing, but many Americans, regardless of their socio-economic status, are completely subservient to wealth. Some make fools of themselves trying to please the wealthy, while others are ambitious status-seekers who expect the touch of the wealthy to enhance their position in life. Carter, Kissinger, Brzezinski, and Volcker sought the acknowledgment and the backing of the wealthy. Besides being highly developed in both politics and business, the "K.A." system even dominates the prestigious field of academics. Despite stature and position in the intellectual and academic world, academicians grovel to please the grantors of patronage. Because the competition is intense, the "K.A." who pays his dues stands the best chance of receiving important appointments and grants. David Rockefeller, a master of the "light touch," knows how to organize and exploit this seemingly inexhaustible obsequiousness.

The Rockefeller group also contributes generously to religious causes, particularly if they are of the right political orientation. There is a strong indication that the Trilateral Commission is intimidating the political community by using the moral majority and other religous fundamentalists as hatchet propagandists to smear any troublesome adversaries. If the Rockefeller forces cannot meet the economic or political challenge of an adversary, they cast doubt on his morality by having the moral majority and other religious and "ethical" organizations attack him, thus using religion to slander political opponents. Goldwater himself was targeted for such an attack and had the guts to take them head-on. However, some liberal Senators and Congressmen such as Birch Bayh and Gaylord Nelson, who had the effrontery to lead the fight against the confirmation of Nelson Rockefeller as Vice President, were not successful. The moral majority mounted a vengeful campaign against them, and they were defeated, as was Rockefeller nemesis Senator Church. In the 1980 Democratic primary Senator Edward Kennedy lost to "pious" Carter due largely to the moralist attacks against him orchestrated by the Rockefeller Trilateralists.

It is not commonly known that the Rockefeller family created a foundation, the Isealantic Fund, to influence religious thinking. By 1970, the family had contributed $31.2 million to the fund so that it could make contributions to churches and theological schools that agreed with the Rockefeller philosophy. David Rockefeller served as president of the fund, and Laurence was the vice president. With such a large fund to buy religious favors, the Rockefellers had little difficulty enlisting hypocritical men-of-God into their corps of "moral assassins."

Most important to David, the Trilateral Commission has had the most fantastically successful financial promotional scheme in economic history. While the public image of the Trilateral Commission is to promote international cooperation, its real purpose is to implement the Rockefeller Syndicate's profit strategy. It does this by controlling the Federal Reserve Bank, enabling the Rockefellers' international banking operations to expand astronomically. Chase Manhattan Bank's profits from its international operation have increased from 22% in 1970 to 78% in 1978. David Rockefeller has become the most powerful international banker in history.

As an international bank, Chase deals in dollars or United States government securities. In effect, they sell dollars and government securities (actually, they loan dollars for a fee, but dollars, not pesos, are the commodity). As in any business, the quality of the commodity is extremely important. In the international money market, quality is measured by the value of the dollar in relation to other currencies. Consequently, Chase wants the dollar to be the most valuable currency in the world. Today, the dollar is the most demanded currency in the world, a condition that was skillfully achieved by Rockefeller's Trilateral colleague, Paul Volcker, Chairman of the Federal Reserve Bank, by forcing interest rates to record highs.

Understandably, then, Trilateralists Arthur Burns' and Paul Volcker's chairmanship of the Federal Reserve Board was of critical importance to the international expansion of David Rockefeller's Syndicate.

On August 17, 1979, Ann Crittenden of *The New York Times* commented on Volcker's initial increases in the discount rate.

> The Federal Reserve's aggressive moves in the last few days to raise short-term interest rates makes it clear that international considerations and specifically, the defense of the dollar, are now influencing American economic policy to a degree unparalleled in the post-war period.

The international value of the dollar was the prime concern of Volcker when he became chairman of the Fed's Board, superseding domestic economic problems. Volcker was chosen as chairman because he had effectively manipulated the international value of the dollar on two previous occasions as Undersecretary of the Treasury and was an unabashed proponent of high interest rates. He knew that high interest rates would strengthen the dollar. His first important act as chairman was to increase interest rates.

The domination of the Fed by the Trilateralists served two purposes for American international banks. First, it increased interest rates on U.S. securities in order to attract money from all over the world, especially OPEC dollars. Secondly, it increased the value of the dollar in relation to foreign currencies.

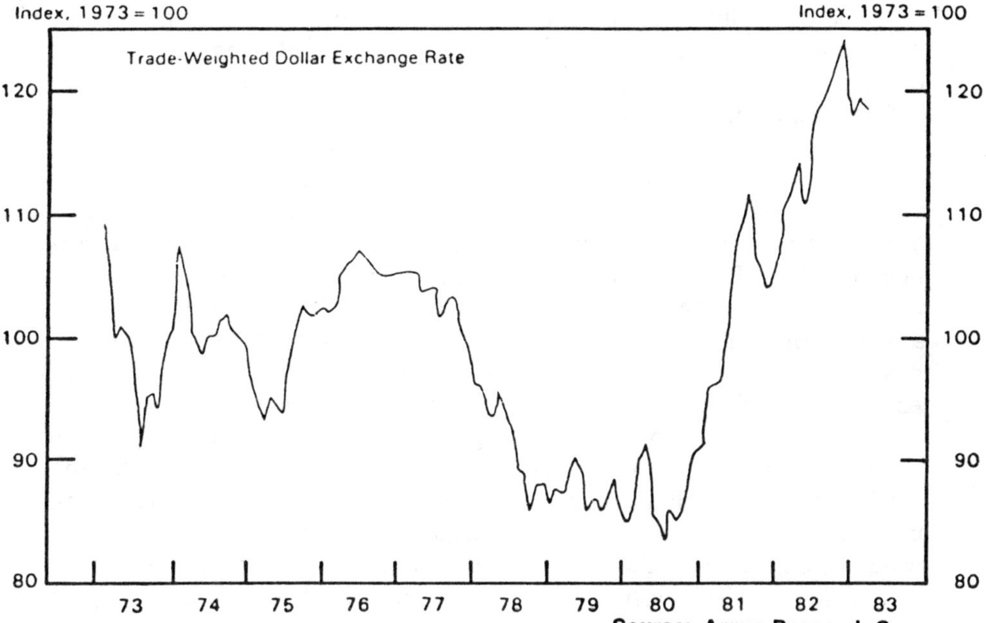


**Source: Argus Research Corp.**

**This chart documents Chairman Volcker's commitment to a strong international dollar. He increased the international value of the dollar 40% by doubling domestic interest rates from mid-1980 to the end of 1982.**

The formation of the Trilateral Commission in 1973 coincided with massive intrusion into America of Japanese products by Japanese Trilateral corporations, such as Nissan Motor Company, Mitsubishi Corporation, Sony Corporation, Toyota Motor Company, Sumitomo Corporation, and Hitachi, Ltd. Although Japanese products undoubtedly captured the fancy of the quality-conscious American consumer, the creation of an overseas market so quickly and so extensively is unusual and requires some clout. Japan now supplies the American market with one out of every five autos, nine out of every ten motorcycles, and a large share of electronic commodities.

The Japanese must have received powerful marketing know-how and financing for such a spectacular invasion. A plausible explanation is that Japan's success is due to the influence of the American branch of the Trilateral Commission. To facilitate the Japanese move into the American market, many government officials involved in Japanese-American relations were chosen to be members of the Trilateral Commission, both in Japan and in the United States. In addition, key posts in the Departments of State, Treasury, and Banking in both countries were held by Trilateral Commission members. Robert S. Ingersol, former U.S. Ambassador to Japan, was a member of the Trilateral Executive Committee. The founding session of the Trilateral Commission was held in Tokyo on October 20-23, 1973. On May 30 and 31, 1975, the first plenary meeting of the Commission was held in Kyoto, Japan. Although he was busy running for the presidency, Jimmy Carter found time to attend that meeting in Kyoto.

The difficulty in explaining American-Japanese trade is the fact that American businessmen have been virtually excluded from the Japanese market. The relation is so one-sided as to beg for explanation. The trade deficit against the United States in 1982 will amount to $18 billion, yet American entrepreneurs are not allowed fair access to the Japanese market.

Was the American market offered to the Japanese members of the Trilateral Commission of Japan in exchange for other favors? The head of almost every Japanese corporation that does massive business in the United States is a member of the Japanese Trilateral Commission. Doesn't it seem peculiar that Congress has not interceded on behalf of American businessmen to encourage a balance of trade with Japan, and isn't it strange that Carter would attend a meeting to promote trade with Japan when it was so one-sided against American firms? Why should we offer Japan such a one-sided advantage to the detriment of our economy and businessmen? We are not talking about free trade in this case since there is no free trade for Americans in the Japanese market. Not since colonial days have we tolerated such an unfair trade agreement. Japan eagerly imports raw materials from us and exports the finished product back to us in the same manner that England did when we were its colony. Meanwhile, finished American products are effectively kept out of the Japanese market or are allowed into Japan with such penalty as to make their prices prohibitive.

Yet another oriental Trilateral caper revolves around the "opening of China" and the appointment of labor leader Leonard Woodcock to the post of Ambassador to China in 1979. Though lacking foreign or diplomatic credentials, Leonard Woodcock was a Trilateral member. That was the only credential he needed. Chase Manhattan opened the first American bank in China and loaned $50 million for a trade center in Peking. J. Paul Austin, Chairman of Coca Cola and a Trilateralist friend of Rockefeller and Carter, established the first business relations with China by introducing Coca Cola to China. Exxon, a part of the Rockefeller Syndicate, sought an agreement with the Chinese to explore and develop Chinese oil deposits. Trilateralist Leonard Woodcock was not the American Ambassador to China; he was David Rockefeller's ambassador and personal trade emissary.

Another international development that occurred with the creation of the Trilateral Commission was OPEC's tremendous increase in income from petroleum. Because the billions of dollars waiting to be invested by unsophisticated national leaders was a mouth-watering morsel for David Rockefeller, he vigorously pursued the OPEC leaders, particularly those from the Near East, as we have seen in his romance with the Shah of Iran. The tremendous increase in petroleum prices was essentially the result of a Rockefeller/Kissinger financial plan to arm Iran.

When the Shah was encouraged to develop a military bastion to dominate the Persian Gulf, he had the problem of financing the armaments. Recall that David Rockefeller was the Shah's banker and financial advisor. As Secretary of State, Kissinger urged the Shah to raise the price of oil so that Iran could pay for its arms. The Saudi government strongly opposed the idea, claiming that it would cause worldwide inflation. Despite pleas to forestall the increase made by the American ambassador to Saudi Arabia at the insistence of the Saudi government, Kissinger encouraged the Shah to increase the price of oil.

Think about this: Rockefeller's paid agent Henry Kissinger was instrumental in promoting the rapid escalation of world oil prices over the objections of the Arabs. David Rockefeller wanted the increase in oil prices because it would enhance the value of the reserves held by Exxon, Mobil, Standard, and other oil companies that are part of the Rockefeller Syndicate. Kissinger made it happen.

As a result of the Rockefeller/Kissinger plan to encourage the Shah to increase oil prices, the American public has paid hundreds of billions of additional dollars to the OPEC nations. We can understand the oil-producing nations increasing the price of oil, but it is difficult to trust a Secretary of State who forced the price increase on them. In dealing with the Shah of Iran, Kissinger demonstrated his loyalty to his benefactor, David Rockefeller, while conveniently ignoring his obligation to the American people as their Secretary of State. Kissinger was aware that the Rockefeller Syndicate would benefit tremendously from the increase in oil prices, and, as we all know, the price increases were reflected in a tremendous rise in profits for Exxon, Standard, Union, and other oil companies.

Henry Kissinger may go down in history as America's most expensive Secretary of State. Kissinger tried to justify his part in increasing oil prices at a United Nations General Assembly meeting in September, 1974, stating, "Oil producers sought a better life for their people and a just return for their diminishing resources." (Stoessinger: *Henry Kissinger, The Anguish of Power.*)

The 1970s was a very good decade for the Syndicate. If Rockefeller had personally been the boss of the Fed, this is exactly what he would have done. But he didn't need to take the time since he had financial hit men like Burns and Volcker to do it his way.

We are not concerned with how much money the Rockefellers legitimately earn by pursuing their ethical business interests. But we must be alarmed when a large part of their income results from subverting the Federal Reserve Bank. David Rockefeller corrupted the fiduciary relationship between the chairman of the Federal Reserve Board and the American public. We are extremely naive—no, just plain stupid—if we fail to see that David Rockefeller's Trilateralists used their financial and political power to exploit the American public. They have caused the loss of jobs, jeopardized our investments, and threatened our way of life.

In 1976, the Trilateralists executed a coup d'état to gain control of the American presidency, and almost no one noticed. The next chapter is the tragic story of how they corrupted the presidency of the United States.

# CHAPTER 4

# *The Capon Presidency*

> ***Once the people rule again, we can reorganize our government and make it work with competence and compassion. Because we owe the special interest nothing. Because we owe the people everything. I see an American government that has turned away from scandals and corruption and official cynicism and finally become as decent as our people.***
>
> ***Jimmy Carter***
> ***Before the Election***

To most of us, in 1976 Jimmy Carter was an unknown populist from Georgia who was challenging the Washington establishment.

We all wondered where Jimmy Carter came from. In a recent book, Senator Barry Goldwater has a chapter entitled "Jimmy Who?" To an America that was tired of corruption in government, Jimmy Carter looked too good to be true, and his winning the presidency was a beautiful American saga that proved that democracy worked in America. Where else but in America could an obscure Georgia peanut farmer take on and defeat the political establishment to become President of the United States?

If it were only true.

Trusting American voters who accepted Jimmy Carter as an honest, smiling country boy did not realize that he was the confidant of the richest, most successful, and most politically sophisticated men in America.

The story of how Jimmy Carter sold his political soul to the Rockefeller Syndicate is the tragic story of the creation of an American presidential puppet. His participation in David Rockefeller's Trilateral Commission, the most powerful economic-political association in the free world, was the key to Carter's election.

In 1973, Zbigniew Brzezinski detailed the Trilateralists' qualifications for the ideal 1976 presidential candidate: "he would have to 'emphasize work, family, religion, and patriotism . . . and rely on a great deal of co-determination *between state and the corporations.*' " *(Trilaterals Over Washington*, pp. 3, 4.) The philosophy underlying Brzezinski's qualification is "neo-fascism," and his list of qualifications required a presidential puppet—a role Carter was willing to play.

The Trilateralists wanted to be sure that they won the presidency. Even at the time that Jimmy Carter was being groomed for the office, they hedged their bet with other potential candidates who were also members of the Commission: Senator Walter Mondale, a Democrat; and Elliot Richardson, at that time a highly visible Republican. The Trilateralists discouraged press coverage of candidates who were free of their influence, while flexing their muscles with friendly candidates to demonstrate that no one could win without Trilateral support.

"It was Brzezinski, in fact, who first identified Carter as Presidential timber and subsequently educated him in economics, foreign policy, and the ins and outs of world politics." (Suttan and Wood, p. 2.) Senator Goldwater confirms the Trilateralists' choice of Carter as their candidate.

> David Rockefeller and Zbigniew Brzezinski found Jimmy Carter to be their ideal candidate. They helped him win the nomination and the Presidency. To accomplish this purpose they mobilized the money-power of the Wall Street bankers, the intellectual influence of the academic community — which is subservient to the wealth of the great tax-free foundation — and the media controllers represented in the membership of the CFR and the Trilateralists. (Goldwater, p. 286)

A little-publicized fact was Carter's long-standing association with David Rockefeller. In 1971, Carter was on a Jet Star, courtesy of Lookheed, to meet David Rockefeller for lunch in the director's dining room of the Chase Manhattan Bank *(Jimmy Carter, The Man and The Myth*; 1979, Victor Lasky.)* It was rumored that Hedley Donovan, Editor-in-Chief of *Time* magazine, was at that meeting. Then, in 1973, three years before Carter was elected President, he was invited by Brzezinski and David Rockefeller to join the Trilateral Commission.

There is no doubt that the Trilateral group selected Carter and groomed him for the Presidency. The founding director of the Trilateral Commission, Brzezinski, told Peter Pringle of the London Sunday *Times*, "It was a close call between Carter and Reuben Askew of Florida, but we were impressed that Carter had opened trade offices for the State of Georgia in Brussels and Tokyo. That seemed to fit perfectly into the concept of the Trilateral." Brzezinski's statement indicates that the Trilateralists were considering a number of candidates and decided that Carter fit their specifications better than anyone else.

Nor can Jimmy Carter deny that he actively enlisted the support of the Trilateralists and attempted to attract their attention by showing his enthusiasm for the organization. As previously stated, Carter, while he was campaigning in 1975, attended the Trilateral meeting in Kyoto, Japan. Another Carter ploy that pleased the Trilateral Commission was cited in the Commission's First Annual Progress Report. "His distributing some 400 task-force reports to Democratic candidates for office in the 1974 United States elections." The Commission was obviously pleased with his proselytizing candidates and disseminating Commission philosophy.

All the ingredients for the corruption of the presidency of the United States were there. The basic ingredient was an ambitious, willing, pliable, cooperative, undistinguished candidate who understood that he had to play ball with the big boys. To mix the brew was the catalyst, Zbigniew Brzezinski, a super-ambitious academician and immigrant who could not become president himself, but who found himself in a position to select the president of the United States. The epicenter of the "move" on the presidency was David Rockefeller, who wanted to control our Federal Reserve Bank, assure a strong dollar abroad, and deregulate oil prices.

Carter's campaign workers realized the importance of his Trilateral connection. Gerald Rafshoon, the campaign's media expert, said, "One of the most fortunate accidents in the early campaign, and critical to his building support where it counted, was Jimmy Carter's membership in the Trilateral Commission." (Goldwater, p. 287.) Carter himself has acknowledged the importance of the Trilateralists to his presidency: "Membership on this Commission has provided me with a splendid learning opportunity, and many of the other members have helped me in my study of foreign affairs."

The Trilateral influence and domination of Jimmy Carter did not go unnoticed by some of his more perceptive aides. His personal confidant and campaign manager, Hamilton Jordan, voiced his dismay about the massive intrusion of Trilateral input during the campaign: "If after the inauguration you find Cyrus Vance as Secretary of State, and Zbigniew Brzezinski as head of National Security, then I would say that we failed. And, I'd quit." Predictably, Cyrus Vance was appointed Secretary of State, and Zbigniew Brzezinski did become the head of the National Security Commission; however, Jordan did not quit. Instead, he became Carter's White House Chief-of-Staff.

Jimmy Carter would have remained an unknown without the help of the Trilateral Commission. He "owed" them for his presidency, and he spent four years making payments.

Brzezinski headed the Jimmy Carter for president task force. Besides coaching Carter in matters of foreign policy, Brzezinski provided him with access to other influential men such as Hedley Donovan of *Time* magazine; Cyrus Vance; Harold Brown, President of the California Institute of Technology; and Michael Blumenthal, chairman of Bendix Corporation; all of whom were members of the Trilateral Commission. Some observers considered Trilateralist Richard Gardner, who was a member of David Rockefeller's inner circle and a trustee of the Rockefeller Brothers' Fund (assets of $238 million in 1971), to be one of Jimmy Carter's most important coaches.

Carter rewarded his benefactors well. Brzezinski was appointed Advisor to the President for National Security matters; Cyrus Vance was appointed Secretary of State; Harold Brown was appointed Secretary of Defense; Michael Blumenthal was appointed Secretary of the Treasury; Hedley Donovan was appointed Senior Consultant to the President; and Richard Gardner was appointed Ambassador to Italy. These appointments were significant political payoffs, but Carter's most flagrant payoff went to David Rockefeller. Carter allowed twenty-five of Rockefeller's personally chosen Trilateralists to run the administration and bestowed the Federal Reserve chairmanship on Rockefeller's protégé and fellow Trilateralist, Paul Volcker. As a final installment, he promoted the deregulation of oil and gas prices.

Brzezinski was the mastermind behind the political development of Jimmy Carter. In May 1976, Leslie H. Gelb wrote in *The New York Times*: "[Brzezinski] was the first guy in the community to pay attention to Carter, to take him seriously. He spent time with Carter, talked to him, sent him books and articles, educated him." (Sutton and Wood, p. 4.) Brzezinski was the guiding light in Carter's development, particularly in the development of his foreign policy. In the Carter campaign, the rule was to clear any matter with Brzezinski, especially if it dealt with foreign affairs. Before acting on anything that had to do with foreign policies, Carter would reportedly say, "Has Brzezinski seen this?"

Aware that media exposure was necessary to create a president, the Trilateralist secured the best. Carter's publicity was orchestrated adroitly by fellow Commission member Hedley Donovan, the Editor-in-Chief of Time, Inc.

> Donovan played a central role in the "faking of the President, 1976." Under his Trilateral direction, *Time* functioned as a black propaganda vehicle throughout the campaign and post-election period, painting Carter as an "outsider" with no connection with the corrupt politics of Washington, D.C. and Wall Street. This image-building provided the crucial cover for the planned fraud, and *Time* played a crucial cover up role. . . . (U.S. Labor Party, Campaign Publications, Inc., 1977, p. 13.)

In December 1975, Carter trailed Kennedy, Humphrey, Wallace, McGovern, Jackson, Muskie, and Bayh, the most popular and well-known Democratic presidential hopefuls. In January 1976, he was the first choice of only 4% of Democratic voters; however, by March 1976, he had jumped to 26% and even led incumbent President Ford by a few points. Because Senators Humphrey, Kennedy, Jackson, and Muskie, President Ford, and Governor Wallace had spent a lifetime in politics and already had long-standing national recognition, it was almost a Cinderella story for an unknown like Carter to be vaulted into the number one spot in the presidential race. But if you look as the impressive power of the pro-Carter Trilateral press, you will understand how this came to be. (Sklar, pp. 206, 207.)

As early as January 1975, Rex Gramun, a Georgia political commentator who later joined Carter's White House staff, noted Carter's favorable press coverage, pointing out the *The New York Times, The Washington Post*, and the *Wall Street Journal* had front-page stories on Carter's announcement for the presidency. Altogether, over 100 newspapers and magazines around the world ran stories on Carter. In January 1976, national news columnist Joseph Kraft, a Trilateralist, pointed out that Carter was "the media candidate for the Democratic Presidential nomination." Tom Wicker, another news columnist, wrote that Carter had received "good press" and was being promoted by the media as the "surprise" of the campaign. Morris Udall referred to Carter's coverage as "an incredible flow of press." What is noteworthy is that with all this coverage, the major media never mentioned Carter's Trilateral connection.

The power of the Carter press can only be explained by the connection between the media and the Trilateral Commission, which included the following media men as members: Hedley Donovan; Arthur R. Taylor, former head of CBS Network; Emmett Dedmon, Editorial Director of the Chicago *Sunday Times* (the sixth largest newspaper in the United States); Henry B. Schacht, a director of CBS; Sol Winowitz, a director of *Time*; J. Paul Austin, a director of Dow Jones *(Wall Street Journal)*; Harold Brown, Director of Times-Mirror Corporation *(Los Angeles Times)*; Archibald K. David, a director of Media General, Inc.; Peter G. Peterson, a director of Great Books Foundation and National Educational TV; William M. Roth, Director of Atheneum Publishers; and Cyrus Vance, a director of *The New York Times*. (Sutton and Wood, pp. 25, 26.)

Another Trilateralist who was almost as important as the news media in the election of Jimmy Carter was Andrew Young, the token black on the Trilateral Commission. In 1976, the year of the campaign, Andrew Young was invited to join the Commission to deliver the black vote. He was extremely effective since over 90% of the black vote went to Jimmy Carter, ensuring his election.

All in all, Jimmy Carter's election was a magnificent victory for the Trilateral Commission. Selecting, indoctrinating, and selling an unknown to the public was power politics par excellence.

When there is a coup d'etat in South America, the generals use guns to usurp political power and install a military Junta. But in the United States, David Rockefeller and his Trilateralists used their control of the money supply to usurp political power and install a Financial Junta. The coercion of money can be as effective as that of loaded guns.

After promoting and financing the Carter candidacy, the Trilateralists moved in and took control of the government. Carter simply turned the government over to David Rockefeller's "financial junta"—the Trilateral Commission-and became the Capon President. Like a neutered rooster, he scratched and strutted, but could do nothing. The Capon Presidency was so obsequious to the desires of David Rockefeller and his Trilateralists it was a national embarrassment. Evaluating Carter's performance as president, Goldwater writes, "The record is so incredibly bad, I'm compelled to suggest it appears to have been planned." It was planned. The major beneficiaries of the Carter Administration were David Rockefeller, The Trilateralists, and the money lenders. Carter ignored his promises to the American people on economic reforms that he advocated in his campaign. In most cases, he did not even attempt to live up to them, but simply made an about-face to accommodate the suggestions of those aorund him. When Carter moved into the White House, the Trilateral Commission moved in with him. One reporter caustically commented, "It would be unfair to say the Trilateral Commission dominates the Carter Administration. The Trilateral Commission IS the Carter Administration."

Carter publicists attempted a grass-roots diversion by stating that people from all walks of life would be considered for the new administration. But the record proves that this was a hoax. Twenty-five Trilateralists were appointed by Jimmy Carter to top administration posts, including Secretaries of State, Defense, and Treasury, three of the most important cabinet offices. The National Security Council members – Jimmy Carter, Zbigniew Brzezinski, Walter F. Mondale, Cyrus R. Vance, and Harold Brown-were all Trilateralists.

It is difficult to understand why a nation so rich in first-rate candidates for government positions had so many key officials from such a small group. The following list of Trilateralists shows how they dominated the Carter Administration, particularly in matters of national finance and international affairs:

CARTER'S PERSONAL STAFF

- Jimmy Carter, President.
- Walter Mondale, Vice President.
- Zbigniew Brzezinski, Assistant to the President for National Security Affairs.
- Lloyd N. Cutler, White House Counsel.
- Hedley Donovan, Senior Advisor for Domestic and Foreign Policy and Media Relations.
- Samuel P. Huntington, Coordinator of National Security, National Security Council.
- Sol Linowitz, Special Mid-East Negotiator; Director, President's Commission on World Hunger; Co-Negotiator of Panama Canal Treaties.
- Henry Owen, U.S. Ambassador-at-Large, Special Representative of President for Economic Summits.
- Elliot L. Richardson, U.S. Ambassador-at-Large with responsibility with U.N. Law of the Sea Conference.
- Gerald C. Smith, U.S. Ambassador-at-Large for Non-Proliferation Matters.
- Paul C. Warnke, Director, U.S. Arms Control and Disarmament Agency;
- Chief Disarmament Negotiator.
- Andrew Young, Ambassador to the United Nations.

CABINET MEMBERS

- Cyrus Vance, Secretary of State.
- W. Michael Blumenthal, Secretary of the Treasury.
- Harold Brown, Secretary of Defense.

STATE DEPARTMENT

- Cyrus R. Vance, Secretary of State.
- Leonard Woodcock, Ambassador to Peking.
- Richard Holbrooke, Assistant Secretary of State for East Asian and Pacific Affairs.
- Lucy Wilson Benson, Undersecretary of State for Security Assistance.
- Warren Christopher, Deputy Secretary of State.
- Richard N. Cooper, Undersecretary of State for Economic Affairs.
- Richard N. Gardner, Ambassador to Italy.

TREASURY
- W. Michael Blumenthal, Secretary of the Treasury.
- C. Fred Bergsten, Assistant Secretary of the Treasury for International Affairs.
- Anthony M. Solomon, Undersecretary of the Treasury for Monetary Affairs.

CIA
- Robert R. Bowie, Deputy to the Director of Central Intelligence for National Intelligence.

FEDERAL RESERVE BANK
- Arthur Burns, Chairman of the Federal Reserve Board.
- Paul A. Volcker, Chairman of the Federal Reserve Board.
- Anthony Solomon, President, New York Reserve Bank.

Those members of the Trilateral Commission who were not running Chase Manhattan or other Rockefeller projects were running our government for him!

It is incomprehensible that so many important members of an administration could have been chosen strictly by merit from such a small group. Because most of the appointees were not qualified for their positions, their collective inabilities constituted a very impotent administration – a whole barnyard of capons. Senator Goldwater's assessment of the Carter appointees hit the mark: "His administration has been severely damaged by the scandalous failure of the men to whom he has given authority." (Goldwater, p. 276.) But they had the necessary credential: David Rockefeller's stamp of approval as members of the Trilateral Commission.

There was a design, a plan to infiltrate Trilateral members into governmental positions of power, it was admitted in the Trilateral Commission's Fourth Annual Report. "An increase in the Trilateral Commission's impact, resulting in a large part from the number of Commissioners entering various governments was perhaps the special feature of the year 1976-77." The impact on our government was dramatic. In effect, the United States government was annexed by the Commission, as one group of conservative authors observed: "In 1976, the American voter thought he had elected Jimmy Carter; in fact, he had elected Chase Manhattan." (Sutton and Wood, p. 44.) Carter's mass appointment of Trilateralists to key administration posts and subsequent delivery of our government to David Rockefeller was not the end of the story. For good measure, he also threw in the Federal Reserve Bank.

In 1979, Jimmy Carter appointed Paul Volcker, a fellow Trilateralist and personal aide of David Rockefeller, to run our national banks.

We cannot help but ask, Why did Carter appoint Volcker? Volcker differed with Carter on monetary policy. It is interesting to review Carter's campaign promises with regard to employment, inflation, and interest rates. He pointed out in his *Position Paper* (April 22, 1976) that, "The major economic problem, however, is unacceptably high unemployment with double-digit inflation." (p. 43.) He said that full employment would require an expansionary fiscal and monetary policy. "Such an expansionary policy can reduce unemployment without re-igniting inflation because our economy is presently performing so far under capacity." (p. 143.) He promised a "steady flow of jobs and output." (p. 144.) "The number one domestic commitment of the next administration will be to create jobs and reduce unemployment." He set a goal of 3% adult unemployment and 4 to 4.5% for the general labor force. (p. 199.)

What was Carter's pre-election viewpoint on inflation, interest rates, and monetary policy? In commenting on GOP errors, he said, "Under the Nixon/Ford Administration, interest rates have reached their highest level since the Civil War." (p. 757.) In an interview he acknowledged that inflation was caused by "external circumstances" like grain sales, devaluation of the dollar, and oil price increases. Then he said, "I thought that the Federal Reserve was much too restrictive when the growth and the supply of money was reduced almost to zero." (p. 786.) He criticized the Republicans for using restrictive money policies to slow down the economy: "The Republicans have tried to halt inflation by slowing down the economy—by putting people out of work—and that policy has been a dismal failure." (p. 760.) Then he advocated that to curb inflation, we must "adopt a monetary policy which encourages lower interest rates and the availability of investment capital at reasonable costs," and he urged that we "increase the productive capabilities of our economy." (p. 145.)

In a comment printed in *U.S. News and World Report* in May 1976, Carter indicated that he planned to take a different approach. When asked how he was going to reduce unemployment to the range of 4% among adults, he responded, "We have to pursue an expansionary fiscal and monetary policy in the near future—with some budget deficits if necessary." On a number of occasions, Carter criticized the policy of the Federal Reserve Board, pointing out that the policy of restricting the economy through tight-money high-interest was an ineffective way to control inflation.

Carter said that Volcker's policies were diametrically opposed to his own, yet he appointed him. As a result, Carter's administration was characterized by the tightest money policy and the fastest escalating interest rates of any American presidency. The prime rate went from less than 5% in 1977 to 22% in 1980, a fantastic increase of 340% in four years—an average 85% increase per year! Despite his promises, unemployment increased until it reached the present double-digit level. Inflation also reached the double-digit mark, passing 13.5% in 1980.

Why wasn't Carter a more effective president? There are many possible explanations. He may have misled the people with his rhetoric to get elected, or he may have been overwhelmed and perplexed by the job and did not know what to do. Although both of the above factors probably played a part, the major reason for the ineptitude of the Carter Administration was the powerful role that Volcker played. Volcker dominated his presidency with massive and constant increases in interest rates. When interest rates rose to 22%, all other economic programs became inconsequential. The chairman of the Fed was defacto directing national economic policy.

The tight-money, high-interest policy of the Federal Reserve Board reduced the nation's level of economic activity and caused a rapid increase in unemployment during the Carter Administration. Historically, as interest rates rise, so does unemployment. Carter's promises to decrease unemployment and to expand the money supply were not compatible with the Board's commitment to high-interest rates. Carter was a sacrificial lamb, whose pre-election economic policy never had a chance.

The key to understanding the Carter presidency is to understand his relationship with the Federal Reserve Board. Either he was so in awe of the Board that he was afraid to act, or he was honoring his commitment to his benefactor David Rockefeller and the Trilateral Commission.

When Carter became president in 1977, he inherited the Federal Reserve chairman, Arthur Burns (1970-1978), an ultra-conservative who had been appointed by Nixon in 1970. Burns was an advocate of monetary intervention to control the economy. An acknowledged expert on business cycles and a master at manipulating business and economic activity, Burns perfected the Board's policy of using the business cycle to control the American economy. He vigorously used high interest rates to slow down the economy. (When he retired from the chairmanship, David Rockefeller awarded him with a membership on the Trilateral Commission.)

When Burns retired in January 1978, Carter appointed G. William Miller, an unknown whose only claim to the chairmanship was that he had served on David Rockefeller's International Advisory Committee of Chase Manhattan National Bank. After serving as Federal Reserve chairman for approximately sixteen months, Miller was made Secretary of the Treasury to make room for Paul Volcker, who was appointed by Carter on August 6, 1979.

Carter had the rare opportunity to appoint a chairman and four members—a strong working majority of the Board—and create a "Carter" Board, but instead he appointed a "Rockefeller" Board.

Ironically, Carter made this statement during his campaign, "It is important that throughout a president's term he have a chairman of the Federal Reserve whose economic views are compatible with his own." (Carter's Position Paper.) If Carter believed this, why did he appoint two chairmen whose economic views were diametrically opposed to his? Both Miller and Volcker advocated a high-interest policy. During the short time that Miller was chairman, we experienced one of the sharpest increases in interest rates in our history, and Volcker forced interest rates to the highest level in our history and has maintained a prime rate of over 15% for two years. If Volcker's economic views are compatible with Carter's, then Carter lied to us. It is difficult, if not impossible, to reconcile Carter's promise to help the working man by 'pursuing an expansionary monetary policy which encourages lower interest rates and more jobs' with his appointment of Volcker to the chairmanship of the Federal Reserve Board.

No one outside of the David Rockefeller Trilateral Commission was seriously considered for the chairmanship of the Federal Reserve Board, the most important banking position in the world. The five most highly touted candidates for the chairmanship of the Federal Reserve Board when G. William

Miller resigned in 1979 were all Trilateral members: Bruce K. Maclaury, President of the Brookings Institute; Paul Volcker; David Rockefeller; A.W. Clausen, Ex-Chairman of the Bank of America; and Robert Roosa, former Federal Reserve officer and partner in the investment banking firm of Brown Brothers. After David Rockefeller, A.W. Clausen and Robert Roosa removed themselves from consideration, Rockefeller and Roosa exerted strong influence on Carter to name Volcker as Chairman. (Sklar, p. 3.)

Why did David Rockefeller want Volcker as Chairman of the Fed's board? As a distinguished economist schooled in international monetary affairs and an expert at manipulating the international value of the dollar, Volcker was the perfect Trilateral choice. He was a member of the Federal Reserve Bank's fraternity and was beholden to the Chase Manhattan National Bank and to David Rockefeller personally—he was their man in the Federal Reserve System and the leader of the financial Junta. The practical reason why Paul Volcker was David Rockefeller's prime choice for Chairman of the Federal Reserve was that he had the 'firmest and loudest voice' for high interest rates on the Federal Open Market Committee.

The Trilateralists' political power that put Volcker into the chairmanship of the Fed also determines the success or failure of presidential candidates. In the last two elections, the American people have been programmed to elect a Trilateralist or a Trilateralist-influenced president.

Whether a candidate is a Republican or a Democrat is inconsequential to the Trilateralists who do not care about an issue unless it enhances their power and profits. The critical factor is not a candidate's party affiliation, but the strength of his commitment to their philosophy. The Trilateralists generally are not committed to any particular candidate. They have a better system: they support all acceptable candidates to be sure that the Commission wins, regardless. In the case of the Carter re-election campaign, Jimmy Carter was a candidate and a Trilateralist. Independent candidate John Anderson was also a Trilateralist. Though Reagan was not a member, he was surrounded by Trilateralists, chief of whom was his running mate, George Bush. There was considerable speculation at the time Reagan chose Bush as his vice president, particularly in light of Bush's moderate stance and his criticism of Reagan in the primary. But the choice of Bush brought massive Trilateral support for Reagan's presidential bid. If anything were to happen to President Reagan, Bush would become our second Trilateral president.

If Rockefeller can put a president in office, he can put him out, especially when, like Carter, he became expendable. In 1980, Reagan was personally supported by David Rockefeller, who had become disenchanted with Carter's injecting human rights into international affairs by imposing economic sanctions against offenders. "In my view," Rockefeller said, "the belief that trade can be an effective instrument to influence the social/environmental policies of other nations is ill-conceived, misguided and often counterproductive." Volcker's high-interest policy assured Carter's defeat. The economy could not recover and increasing unemployment and economic stagnation assured Reagan's victory.

In the 1980 presidential election, the American people had a choice of vanilla, vanilla, or vanilla since the Trilateralists owned all three candidates.

In the upcoming presidential election of 1984, we may once again be denied a choice since the Trilateralists are already preselecting the candidates. Every major Democratic hopeful with the exception of Senator Hart, is or was a member: Senator Cranston, Walter Mondale, and Senator John Glenn, who seems to have the strongest Trilateral backing. Senator Kennedy, who is not a Trilaterist, has already withdrawn from the 1984 presidential race.

Even though Reagan is not a member of the Trilateral Commission, his conservative views delight David Rockefeller. Besides having David Rockefeller's personal support, Reagan has attracted many influential backers from among the Trilateralists: David Packard, Chairman, Hewlett-Packard Company; Phillip M. Hawley, President, Carter/Hawley/Hale Stores, Inc.; Paul McCracken, Chairman, Nixon Council of Economic Advisors; George Weyerhaeuser, President, Weyerhaeuser Company; William A. Hewitt, Chairman, Deere & Company; Anne Armstrong, Co-Campaign Chairman and Former Ambassador to Britain; Senator William V. Roth, author, Kemp-Roth Tax Bill; Bill Brock, Chairman, Republican Party; Casper Weinberger, Vice President, Bechtel Corporation, now Secretary of Defense; George Bush, now Vice President. His economic advisor deserves special mention: Arthur Burns, Trilateralist and Ex-Chairman of the Federal Reserve Board.

We all hoped that Reagan would be different from Carter and would solve the real problem that plagues the American economy. Instead, he is only rearranging the furniture while the termites eat away the floor. Our basic problem is the unreasonably high interest rates that plagued our economy for the last five and a half years. Before our economy can return to normal, interest rates must return to normal, a prime rate of 2 to 4%. The high interest rates persist although the economy has been in a recession since Reagan took office. Like Carter, he accepted the high interest rates without challenging the Board. It is amazing how gracefully Reagan accepts and defends the policy of Volcker, a Democratic appointee. Instead of fighting high interest rates, Reagan has used the threat of continued high interest rates to black mail his "yes and no" Reaganomics through Congress. He told Congress that it must pass his $97 billion tax bill before interest rates can come down. There is considerable merit to cutting government spending, but it would be more beneficial if Reagan would cut interest rates, bureaucracy, and bureacrats, and not benefits.

The most important man in the Reagan Administration is Trilateralist Casper Weinberger, Secretary of Defense. His military budget is the "sacred cow" of the current administration and is thus above budget cutting. Reportedly, former Secretary of State Haig was "pushed out" due to Weinberger's pressure because Haig's pro-Israel stance transgressed the Trilateralists' Near-East foreign policy. While that may be conjecture, the choice of George Shultz as Secretary of State does not leave much to guesswork. Shultz was Weinberger's boss at Bechtel Corporation, one of the original financial backers of the formation of the Trilateral Commission and a company with a great interest in OPEC countries. Bechtel has contracts that amount to an estimated $30 billion in the Saudi-Arabian peninsula. The new secretary of state is 100% supportive of the Trilateral program. It will be interesting to watch his pro-Arab policy develop.

Though Republicans and Democrats alike had high hopes for Reagan, the reality of current American politics is that elections do not change anything. As Goldwater has commented, "When a new President comes on board, there is a great turnover in personnel, but no change in policy. For example, during the Nixon years, Henry Kissinger—Nelson Rockefeller's protégé—was in charge of foreign policy. When Jimmy Carter was elected, Kissinger was replaced by Zbigniew Brzezinski—David Rockefeller's protégé." (Goldwater, p. 279.) Reagan's prime movers are Casper Weinberger and George Shultz. The Trilateralists are still running our government, and the Federal Reserve Board is still ruining our economy. Despite his macho image, Reagan is on his way to becoming "Capon II"—a glorified errand boy for the Trilateralists.

* * * * *

The Shah of Iran's entering this country is an example of how David Rockefeller dominated the Carter Presidency.

After the Shah was overthrown, it was in our national interest to cooperate with Iran, our largest petroleum supplier. But the Rockefeller Syndicate had its own interest to serve, which was incompatible with that of the people of the United States and their government. When the Shah left Iran, the Chase Manhattan Bank was handling an estimated $2 to $15 billion of the Shah's personal wealth. Unfortunately, the Syndicate prevailed and America became embroiled in the fiasco of allowing the Shah of Iran to enter the United States.

When the Shah left Iran in his private Boeing 707 on January 16, 1979, and flew to Egypt, the State Department at first considered admitting him into the United States, and Henry Kissinger accordingly sought to find him a suitable home. Reportedly, he decided upon the Beverly Hills estate of Walter Annenberg, the former Ambassador to London. David Rockefeller assigned Joseph Reed, a vice president of Chase, to be in charge of the Shah's affairs.

In the meantime, the Carter Administration was attempting to improve relations with the Ayatollah's new revolutionary government. Because there was genuine concern about the problems that would result from allowing the Shah to come to America, the State Department asked Kissinger to discourage the Shah. Although Secretary of State Vance was personally involved in the request, Kissinger indignantly refused to comply. Then the State Department went directly to David Rockefeller and asked him to discourage the Shah. He refused. Kissinger approached the government five times and on two occasions talked to Secretary Vance on behalf of the Shah. In the meantime, Kissinger and Rockefeller received aid from the British government and found a temporary refuge for the Shah in the Bahamas. Then they arranged for the Shah to live in a private mansion in Mexico where they were financial advisors to that government.

Rockefeller and Kissinger, who was now the Chairman of the International Advisory Board of Chase Bank, enlisted the assistance of Jack McCoy, the Ex-Chairman of Chase, to help them pressure the State Department. They finally succeeded in obtaining approval to allow the Shah's children into the United States. Taking his cue from David Rockefeller, Brzezinski was firmly in favor of allowing the Shah to enter. When Brzezinski pressured Carter, Carter blew up. "---- the Shah! I'm not going to welcome him here when he has other places to go."

The American charge d'affairs, Bruce Laingen, urged the State Department not to admit the Shah into America because the embassy could not withstand the expected Iranian reaction.

We all know the results. After the Shah was admitted, the embassy in Tehran was stormed, and the American government faced fourteen months of international humiliation. David Rockefeller, Kissinger, and Brzezinski, all of whom are members of the Trilateral hierarchy, forced a change in the foreign policy of the United States to serve their own self-interest and the capon acquiesced — true to form.

When the Ayatollah took over the embassy, the American government's primary reaction was to save the assets of international banks by freezing Iranian bank assets in America and throughout the world. The move was designed to protect the international banks that had made loans to Iran, including Chase Manhattan, Citibank, and the Bank of America, which held some $2.8 billion of Iranian deposits in its London branch. Not only were many of the banks that held Iranian deposits closely related to the Trilateral Commission but almost all of the people who made the decision to freeze Iranian funds were Trilateralists themselves or closely tied to David Rockefeller through the Chase Manhattan Bank — President Carter, Chairman Volcker, Secretary of the Treasury Miller, and three Undersecretaries of the Treasury. Even though freezing Iranian assets was perhaps a good strategic move, this response was dictated by the Trilateralists to protect David Rockefeller's Chase Manhattan Bank and other banks affilated with the Trilateral group. When national policy is manipulated to serve a vested interest, the entire nation suffers.

But the Iranian experience was only one example of how the Trilaterals dominated the Carter presidency. In the case of appointing the chairman and members of the Federal Reserve Board, Carter's submission to the pressue of the "financial junta" cost the American people hundreds of billions of dollars.

Though it is difficult to have compassion for Jimmy Carter, part of his troubles arose from his naïveté and lack of understanding of what was going on around him. Once he had pledged his soul to the "financial junta" so that he could have the opportunity to become President of the United States, he was enmeshed in a calculated web of intrigue. There is no doubt that he was manipulated from all sides by sophisticated men who knew where they were going. Unfortunately, Carter did not.

Compared to Jimmy Carter's sellout of the American public, Watergate is peanuts. If we learn nothing else from our last three elected presidents, we should at least realize that "law and order," "I will not lie," "goody two-shoes" presidents can be dangerous to our freedom and to our pocketbooks.

The "Capon Presidency" has demonstrated dramatically that government officials cannot serve two masters. The embarrassing ineptitude of the Carter Administration and the inability of the Federal Reserve Board to legitimately handle the problem of inflation prove that point.

Historians and investigative reporters will write the final story of Jimmy Carter's presidency: his affiliation with Rockefeller's Trilateral Commission; his appointment of Trilateral members to major government positions; allowing the Shah into this country; his acquiescence to the Federal Reserve Board; and, most incriminating, his appointment of four illegal members to the Federal Reserve Board and nominating David Rockefeller's protégé as chairman.

The corruption of our presidency, the chairmanship of the Federal Reserve Bank, and top government officials have made bureaucratic whores of the most exalted officials of our land.

In one of his position papers, Jimmy "I-will-never-lie-to-you" Carter said, "We feel we've lost control of our own government, that it has become our master instead of our servant, that we are being ruled by special interests, and by politicians who don't care about us." Thanks to you, Jimmy, that is exactly what happened.

* This is the same Victor Lasky that Laurence Rockefeller paid $10,000 to write a derogatory book about ex-Supreme Court Justice Arthur J. Goldberg when he ran against Nelson Rockefeller in the 1970 New York Governor's race.

# CHAPTER 5

# *Board Of Governors*

*Give me the right to issue a Nation's money: then I do not care who makes the laws.*

*—Anslem Rothschild*

By passing the Federal Reserve Act, Congress conveyed to the Federal Reserve Bank the power to coin money and provide credit for the nation's commerce. The Federal Reserve Bank was established to perform the normal functions of a central bank and provide an elastic money supply to encourage the optimum performance of the economy. It was envisioned that the bank would be controlled by a public board that would respond to the credit needs of the economy. To ensure broad public representation on the Board, Congress mandated that the members be appointed from different sectors of the economy and be geographically disbursed. The president was so instructed by the law. He appoints the board members with the approval of the Senate. These qualifications were written in the law to restrict a president from appointing his bureaucratic flunkies or packing the Board with members chosen from the Federal Reserve Bank. Congress feared that the bank would become a self-perpetuating bureaucracy and the public would lose control of the Board.

That fear has come to pass.

The public has lost control of the Federal Reserve Bank. This chapter is about an autocratic Board packed with illegally appointed bureaucrats that thumb their noses at the President, the Congress and the public.

The Federal Reserve Board has a greated impact on the lives of American citizens than any branch of government created by the Constitution. Every facet of the American economy—stock prices, gold prices, inflation, investments, unemployment, bankruptcies, foreclosures, and national income are profoundly affected by the Board's decisions. By changing the interest rates, the Board creates and destroys wealth, modifies corporate and personal balance sheets instantaneously, and determines the level of investment for industry. Since the American dollar has become the international medium of exchange, the Board's decisions about the dollar affect everyone dealing in international commerce: the worker in Belgium, the expectant homeowner in Holland, the petroleum dealer in France, and the tourist vendor in Egypt. In some cases, the impact can be so drastic and extreme it can almost destroy the currency of another country, as has recently occurred in Mexico.

However, the Federal Reserve Board is rather modest about its position in the world's economy. If you were to inquire of the Federal Reserve Bank, you would receive the pamphlet that is reproduced below.

***The Federal Reserve System — the nation's central bank — was created by Act of Congress on December 23, 1913. The System consists of a seven-member Board of Governors, with headquarters in Washington, D.C., and a nationwide network of 12 Federal Reserve Banks and 25 branches.***

**Appointments to the Board**

Members of the Board of Governors are appointed by the President and confirmed by the Senate to serve fourteen-year terms of office. This length of service helps to insulate the decisions of Board members from day-to-day political pressure.

Terms are staggered, with one term expiring every two years. Upon death or resignation of a Board member, the President appoints a new Governor to fill the unexpired term of office. A Governor serving a partial term may be reappointed to a full term of office. A Governor serving a full term may not be reappointed. The President designates one member of the Board as Chairman and another as Vice-Chairman, for terms of four years.

**Representation**

Not more than one member of the Board may be selected from any one of the twelve Federal Reserve Districts. In making appointments, the President is directed by law to select a "fair representation to the financial, agricultural, industrial, and commercial interests and geographical divisions of the country." These aspects of selection are intended to ensure representation of regional interests, and of the interests of various sectors of the public. Governors have come to the Board from a variety of backgrounds, including the academic world, banking, government, business, and agriculture.

**Responsibilities of Board Members**

The prime responsibility of Board members is in the field of monetary policy. The seven Board members constitute a majority of the 12-member Federal Open Market Committee, the group which makes the key decisions affecting the cost and availability of money and credit. (The other five members are presidents of Federal Reserve Banks.) The Board also establishes reserve requirements—the percentage of deposits that depository institutions must maintain with the Federal Reserve or as vault cash. The Board issues rules concerning how and when the 12 Reserve Banks may make "discount" loans to depository institutions. Changes in the interest rate for such loans, proposed by the boards of directors of the Reserve Banks, are subject to the Board's approval. The Board also sets margin requirements for the use of credit in securities markets.

In addition to its money and credit responsibilities, the Board has broad supervisory and regulatory authority over the activities of its member banks, including their foreign activities. It also supervises the operations of the Federal Reserve Banks, and regulates all holding companies that control one or more banks.

The Board also has responsibility for implementing by regulation the major Federal consumer credit laws, such as Truth in Lending and Equal Credit Opportunity.

**Meetings**

The Board meets several times a week. Its meetings are conducted in compliance with the Government in the Sunshine Act. Certain meetings of the Board to consider such matters as confidential financial information are closed to public observation, but many meetings are open to the public. All consumer credit protection matters are discussed in public session.

**Reports**

The Board's monetary and other policies are designed to promote the nation's board economic goals, and the Board reports to and accounts to its actions to the Congress.

Twice a year, the Board submits a written report to Congress on the state of the economy and the course of monetary policy, and it may be called to consult with Congress on this report. The Chairman and other Governors also appear frequently before congressional committees to comment on the conditions of the banking system, on pending banking and economic legislation, and on budgetary and other economic matters.

An annual report on the Board's operations is also submitted to Congress. On a weekly, monthly, and quarterly basis, the Board makes available statistical reports on a broad range of economic subjects, including the money supply, interest rates, banking, industrial production, and consumer credit. Most of these reports are summarized in the monthly *Federal Reserve Bulletin.*

**Contacts Within Government**

As they carry out their duties, the Governors are in continuous contact with officials of other government agencies. For example, frequent meetings are held with the Treasury, the Council of Economic Advisers, and the Office of Management and Budget to help evaluate the economic climate and to discuss objectives. The Chairman is a voting member of the Depository Institutions Deregulation Committee, which is charged with phasing out limitations on the maximum rates of interest that may be paid on deposits. Governors also discuss the international monetary system with central bankers from other countries and are in close contact with the heads of the other U.S. agencies that make foreign loans or conduct foreign financial transactions.

This sterile description of the Federal Reserve Board of Governors serves its purpose of superficially informing the public about the Board. What the pamphlet does not say is that the members of the Board of Governors are the most powerful economic committee outside the Kremlin, with broad economic powers to control the economy of the United States and much of the free world. The pamphlet euphemistically refers to these powers in the fourth paragraph: "The prime responsibility of Board members is in the field on monetary policy."

Our current recession was programmed by the Federal Reserve Board. When the Board voted to restrict the money supply and cause the prime rate to soar to 20%, they also voted for 10% unemployment and a severely depressed economy. The thirteen million people who are now unemployed demonstrate the Board's power.

Despite the Board's power, surprisingly few Americans know who the Federal Reserve Board members are, where they came from, why they were chosen, or what their economic and social philosophies are. If you were quizzed today to name the Federal Reserve Board members, it is doubtful that you would be able to identify any of them. Probably you have never heard their names, nor were their appointment discussed prominently in the papers or on television. In view of their power to make decisions that significantly affect the lives of every American, they should be the most carefully chosen and widely publicized appointees in America, but they are not.

Because Board members control our money system and deal with great wealth, we should be certain that they are free from any involvement, commitment, or obligation to any vested interest group, particularly to the banking and financial industry.

In the original drafts of the Federal Reserve Act, the "banking interests" made a concerted attempt to gain control of the Federal Reserve Board by electing or appointing the members of the Board from their ranks. As a condition of his backing the bill, William Jennings Bryan demanded a revision of the section relating to appointment of the members of the Federal Reserve Board. He insisted that the proposed law be changed to require that members be appointed by the president from the public. The purpose of his amendment was to insure that the Federal Reserve Board would be a public body, chosen from the public and representing the public. The law stipulates two eligibility requirements for Board members. Section Ten of the Federal Reserve Act states that the members of the Board should constitute a "fair representation of the financial, agricultural, industrial, and commercial interest, and geographical divisions of the county." (Agricultural representation was specifically required in a 1922 amendment.) It further mandates that, "In selecting the members of the Board, not more than one of whom shall be selected from any one Federal Reserve District." As you read the following biographies, keep these legal requirements in mind.

As of January 1, 1982, the members of the Federal Reserve Board were:

Paul A. Volcker, Chairman
Frederick H. Schultz* — Henry C. Wallich
J. Charles Partee — Nancy H. Teeters
Emmitt J. Rice — Lyle E. Gramley

The chairman and most important member of the Board is Paul A. Volcker.

Who are these Board members who make such sweeping decisions about the American economy?

Frederick M. Schultz was appointed by Carter in July 1979. Although his appointment expires shortly, a brief resumé indicates that he was active in banking and holding company operations and investment services in Florida.

Henry C. Wallich was appointed to the Board in 1974 and will serve until January 1988. After immigrating from Germany, he became a citizen in 1944 and received a Ph.D. in economics from Harvard. He was with the Federal Reserve Bank in New York from 1941 to 1951, and from 1951 to 1970 he was a professor of economics at Yale University. He was a senior consultant to the Treasury Department from 1969 until appointed to the Board in 1974.

Charles J. Partee was appointed by President Ford to the Federal Reserve in 1976 and will serve until 1986. A graduate of Indiana University with a degree in business, specializing in finance, Mr. Partee has spent almost all of his adult life working as a bureaucrat for the Federal Reserve System, starting in Chicago in 1949. In 1962, after a brief association with the Chicago Trust Company, he became a member of the staff of the Board of Governors of the Federal Reserve. In November 1973, he became Managing Director for Research and Economic Policy, and he was appointed to the Board in 1976. As a man who spent most of his life as a researcher for economic policy and as a bureaucrat for the Federal Reserve, he is an unlikely "public member" of the Board, and under the qualifications set by the Federal Reserve Act, he should never have been appointed to the Board.

Nancy Hayes Teeters was appointed by President Carter in September 1978, and will serve until January 1992. Trained in economics at the University of Michigan, she joined the Federal Reserve Board's Division of Research and Statistics in 1957 and served until 1966. From 1962 to 1963, she was an economist for the President's Council of Economic Advisors. From 1966 to 1970, she was a fiscal economist with the Bureau of the Budget. In the next four years, she held positions at the Brookings Institute and the Library of Congress. From 1974 to 1978, when she was appointed to the Board, she was an economist with the Committee on Budget of the House of Representatives. She is a bureaucrat and does not qualify as a public member. Although Nancy H. Teeters is listed as being from the Chicago Federal Reserve District, her biography indicates that she has worked in Washington or New York since the 1960s. At the time of her appointment, she was in the Washington-Richmond District and was not eligible for Carter to appoint her.

Emmitt J. Rice was appointed by President Carter in 1979. Prior to his appointment, Mr. Rice was a banker who first worked for the Federal Reserve System in 1960-1962, and held other positions in the U.S. Treasury and/or the World Bank until 1970. In 1971, he became the vice president of the National Bank of Washington, which he left to become a member of the Federal Reserve in 1979. According to the law, Mr. Rice qualifies as a financial banker member of the Board. But Mr. Rice is represented as coming from the New York Federal Reserve District. His biography indicates that he was the vice president of the National Bank of Washington from 1971 to 1979. Again, Carter should not have appointed him.

Lyle E. Gramley was appointed by President Carter in May 1980, and will serve until 1994. An economist who received a Ph.D. in 1956 from Indiana University, he joined the Federal Reserve System in Kansas City in 1955 and remained there until 1962. In 1964, he became a senior economist with the Federal Reserve Board, heading up a division of Research and Statistics. From 1977 until 1980, he was a member of the President's Council of Economic Advisors. Carter appointed a Board member who is basically a research bureaucrat and patently unqualified as a "public" Board member. Once again, Carter should not have appointed Mr. Gramley because he is misrepresented as being from the Kansas City Federal Reserve District, while his biography shows that he left Kansas in 1962. Since 1964, he has worked in Washington, D.C., and had remained there until his appointment to the Board.

We are suffering serious economic problems because "illegal" bureaucrats manage our economy and because Jimmy Carter flagrantly disregarded the law's requirements for a broadly based "public board." No one would contend that our present Board constitutes a "fair representation of the financial, agricultural, industrial, and commercial interest and geographical divisions of the country." Where are the farmers? Where are the industrialists? Where are the merchants? Which member of the Board is proficient in agriculture? As for the bankers, they are represented twice.

All of the members of the Carter Board were bankers, economic researchers, or former employees of the Federal Reserve System, the Treasury, and other government-related agencies. A majority of the Board are bureaucrats from the Fed. There is not a single "public" member among them. And all of the members of the Carter Board are from the East Coast, primarily from the New York-Washington axis.

Despite the legal provisions of the Federal Reserve Act "that not more than one of whom shall be selected from any one Federal Reserve District," the Board is now composed of four members from the Richmond District according to their Federal Reserve biographies. If this is true, three of them are fraudulently listed as being from other districts:

| NAME | FRAUDULENT DISTRICT | ACTUAL DISTRICT |
|---|---|---|
| Nancy H. Teeters | Chicago | Washington |
| Emmett J. Rice | New York | Washington |
| Lyle E. Gramley | Kansas City | Washington |
| J. Charles Partee (Appointed by Ford) | | Washington |

Paul Volcker was not legally eligible to be appointed to the Board. Since the 1950s he was in New York or Washington, according to Federal Reserve biographical information. He served as president of the Federal Reserve Bank of New York from 1975 to his appointment as chairman in 1979. Because Emmett J. Rice represented the New York District, Volcker could not list his actual district, so he listed the Philadelphia District. Volcker's misstatement of his district was deceptive, fraudulent, and an intentional contravention of the law.

Take a good look and a deep breath. These are the people whom we ask, as fiduciary agents of the American public, to administer and operate the largest, most powerful bank in the world. The majority of them misrepresented their eligibility for office. If you lied while attempting to get a job for the government and was found out, it would be grounds for dismissal. If you lied about your qualifications to practice as a doctor, you could be dismissed from a hospital staff and prosecuted. If you lied about your eligibility to obtain admission to a college, you could be expelled from that college. If an uneducated alien lies on his immigration forms, he can be deported. But, in the case of the most sensitive banking positions in the world, blatant dishonesty is winked at by the President, by Congress, and by the Justice Department.

A majority of the Board of Governors are bureaucrats from the Federal Reserve System. This indicates that a clique of employees and ex-employees with the aid of the Trilateralist is perpetuating its control of the Federal Reserve Bank.

Paul A. Volcker was appointed chairman of the Federal Reserve Board by President Carter in August 1979. After graduating from Harvard in 1951, Volcker, who was basically trained as an economist, became a junior management assistant with the Treasury Department in Washington, D.C. On a leave of absence in 1951-1952, he went to England to study monetary policy at the London School of Economics under a Rotary Foundation Scholarship. When Volcker finished his stint with the Treasury in 1953, a friend of his father introduced him to Robert V. Roosa. Roosa was the Research Director of the Federal Reserve Bank of New York and he hired Volcker to work as an assistant in the bank's domestic research division. Roosa recalled later that he was impressed with Volcker because, "He asked swell questions, but was modest and humble, not in the manner of someone who expected to be Chairman of the Board in his first year."*

After a number of promotions, Volcker left the Federal Reserve Board and went to Chase Manhattan Bank, where, in addition to research duties, he acted as the representative of Chase Manhattan's president, David Rockefeller, at meetings of the Commission on Money Credit. He remained with Chase until 1962, when his benefactor, Robert V. Roosa, now the Treasury Department's Undersecretary of Monetary Affairs, brought Volcker to Washington. Volcker was made the Director of the Treasury's Office of Financial Analysis, and in November 1963, again upon the recommendation of Robert V. Roosa, he was appointed Deputy Undersecretary for Monetary Affairs by John F. Kennedy.

During the Johnson presidency, Volcker worked directly under Roosa, dealing with foreign and domestic monetary problems, and was the supervisor in the Office of Financial Analysis, the Office of Debt Analysis, and the Office of Domestic Gold and Silver Operations. In 1965, Volcker again resigned from the government and took a position with Chase Manhattan in New York as vice president and director of Forward Planning and as David Rockefeller's representative on a select committee to advise President Johnson in financial matters. Volcker remained with David Rockefeller and Chase Manhattan until January 1969, when President Nixon appointed him to be Undersecretary of the Treasury of Monetary Affairs with the special responsibility for international money matters. By this time, he had established himself as an economist whose conservative, orthodox views on monetary policy were compatible with those of the Nixon Administration.

Paul Volcker was Robert Roosa's protégé. Robert Roosa is an international banker and close business associate of David Rockefeller. His experience in the Treasury and on the New York Reserve Board was a springboard to a partnership in the international banking firm of Brown Bros., Harriman & Co.

Roosa's relationship with David Rockefeller is "tight." He served the Rockefellers as Vice Chairman of the Rockefeller Fund, a Trustee of the Rockefeller Foundation, and Chairman of Brookings Institute and the Brookings Trust. He holds directorships in a number of super multinational corporations associated with the Rockefellers Syndicates. He is one of David Rockefeller's most able lieutenants. David chose him as a charter member of the Trilateral Commission. Since then, Roosa has been a watchdog developing and guiding Volcker.

On August 1, 1975, after being recommended by Rockefeller and Roosa, Volcker became the president of the New York Reserve Bank and a member of the Federal Open Market Committee (FOMC). As the second most important man in the Fed, next to Chairman Burns, he advocated an increasingly "activist" role for the Fed and became known as the strongest advocate of a tight-money, high-interest policy for the Board.

Among the organizations that Volcker belonged to and served on was the Overseas Private Investment Corporation. He also served on the Board of Directors of the Council on Foreign Relations.

Financial observer Edward Cowan of *The New York Times* regarded Volcker as "essentially an eastern money man, one of the New York banking crowd that has been shaping the United States' monetary policies since Alexander Hamilton." It is important to note that Volcker built his reputation by specializing in international monetary affairs. He has even been described as "The Henry A. Kissinger of monetary diplomacy," a reputation that resulted from his manipulating the value of the dollar on the international market. Volcker became "known from London to Tokyo as chief architect of, and traveling salesman for U.S. international monetary policy." (Edward Cowan, *N.Y. Times* 9/24/72)

When Carter appointed Volcker chairman of the Fed in 1979, our country needed a domestic specialist, not an international globe-trotter. But Volcker had the important qualification, he was a Trilateralist and the choice of David Rockefeller. In his campaign, Carter argued that tight money and high interest rates could not stop inflation, but he appointed the leader of the "tight money" advocates to the chairmanship, an act which caused one critic to comment that it would have been better if Carter named brother Billy rather than Volcker.

Instead of appointing an economic statesman to implement his policies and lead the nation to better times, Carter appointed a technician who advocated a simplistic policy of high interest rates to fight inflation. His only credentials were that he had developed a reputation for manipulating the international value of the dollar and he was the banker's choice.

Volcker used tight money and high interest rates to enrich the financial community. He knew that increasing the nation's interest rates would increase the value of the international dollar, a policy that greatly benefitted international banks.

The close relationship between Paul Volcker and international banker David Rockefeller should alarm the American public.

All Americans should be concerned that the head of our most important economic agency, the Federal Reserve Bank, is beholden to the most important international banker in the world. By his acts as chairman of the Fed, Paul Volcker has demonstrated his gratitude to his benefactor.

Because corruption is inherent in the concept of "conflict of interest," a basic rubric of American political ethics is that no "conflict of interest" can be tolerated in positions of public trust. We require public officials to divulge financial holdings or vested interests that may taint their objectivity in matter that come before them. How can we ignore the obvious conflict of interest that arises through co-mingling of Volcker's public trust with the profit strategy of the most powerful consortium of bankers and financiers in the world?

If an athlete is consorting with known gamblers, he suffers severe penalties. Football star Joe Namath was forced to give up his share in a night club because he could have been influenced by some of the patrons. Willie Mays and Mickey Mantle were forced out of organized baseball because they were "greeters" at Atlantic City casinos. Why, then, do we allow the highest official of the most sensitive national financial agency—the chairman of the Federal Reserve Board—to be beholden to financial leaders who obviously seek to prostitute him? The chairman of the Federal Reserve Board should have only the most guarded and sterile relationship with men like David Rockefeller and other members of the Trilateral Commission, and then only in full public view. But we find that Volcker and Rockefeller are "Den Brothers," members of the Trilateral Commission, an elitist lobby committed to the Chase Manhattan monetary policy.

After Volcker's appointment, it did not take him long to assert his dominance over the Board and to firmly establish his policy of relentlessly increasing interest rates. Shortly after being sworn in, on Friday, October 5, 1979, a majority of the Board were against his move to tighten the money supply. Volcker threatened to resign if he could not raise the discount rate. His coercion paid off, for three members changed their positions and rates were raised.

Since the chairman of the Federal Reserve Board is the primary force in determining Federal Reserve policy, Volcker is in reality the most powerful government official in the United States. Sherman J. Maisel (no relation to the author), a member of the Federal Reserve Board from 1965-1972, provides one of the few inside stories as to how the Federal Reserve Board operates. In speaking of his experience on the Board, he commented: "No one would question that the Chairman of the Board of Directors holds the most monetary power." (Maisel, p. 111) In a chart, he indicates that the chairman of the Board exerted as much as 45% influence on policy decision. In second place was the staff of the Board and the Federal Open Market Committee (who are very responsive to the chairman's wishes) with a 25% influence. The other six governors were relatively unimportant and given credit for only a 20% influence, almost a negligible contribution to Board policy. The influence of the twelve District Reserve Banks was even less significant, with only a 10% influence. Maisel also indicates that the Board was not subjected to a dominant outside influence in determining policy matters. He theorizes that the administration commands only 35% of the outside influence, a percentage that varies according to the power of the president and his officials. Congress has only 25% influence, and the public a paltry 20%.

Because the Board is relatively free from effective outside influence, the chairman can run the bank without any real opposition, even from the majority of the Board. Volcker is a particularly strong chairman who runs the Board and determines its policies according to his own viewpoints. The chairman of the Board of Governors of the Federal Reserve Bank is powerful because the bank is independent of political control. No elected official can control him.

The 1913 Congress attempted to keep the Board free from the pressures of vested interests. The objective was a bank responsive to the welfare of all people, not just to special factions. But the result of the bank's independence is that it has become the object of control of the financial elite. To cunning men with billions of dollars to gain, the problem of controlling an independent Fed was not that difficult. By controlling the chairman and perhaps a few other members of the Board, they could manipulate the nation's money supply and earn monumental returns for their efforts. An independent Fed was an invitation for a takeover by David Rockefeller and the Trilateralists. As a Trilateral collaborator, Chairman Volcker has been able to subvert the bank to serve the profit strategy of the Rockefeller Syndicate, while the Fed's traditional independent status precludes effective congressional intervention to correct matters. The Board's independence acts as a shield to shelter its corruption.

DEGREE OF MONETARY POWER 1965-1973

| THE FEDERAL RESERVE SYSTEM | |
|---|---|
| The Chairman | 45% |
| The staff of the Board and FOMC | 25% |
| The other governors | 20% |
| Federal Reserve Banks | 10% |
| OUTSIDE INFLUENCES | |
| The Administration | 35% |
| The Congress | 25% |
| The public directly | 20% |
| The financial interests | 10% |
| Foreign interests | 5% |
| Other regulatory agencies | 5% |

(Maisel , Sherman Managing the Dollar)

As a result, the independence of the Federal Reserve Board is the critical political-economic problem facing America. Though Congress intended for the Federal Reserve Bank to be a separate "entity" with a measure of autonomy, the legislature never intended to elevate the Fed's Board above the democratic authority of the president, Congress, and the Constitution. The Board, however, cleverly parlayed its autonomy and its control of the nation's money supply into a position of absolute power over our economy that it can ignore Congress, the president, and the people. The Board operates on the premise that it knows what is best for the public and is better qualified than the president and Congress to determine national economic policy—a dangerous, arrogant, and autocratic viewpoint that constitutes an imminent threat to our democracy.

Congressman Wright Patman understood what the Federal Reserve Board was up to and has long recognized the danger of the Board's independence:

> On the political side, independence means that the Federal Reserve is not accountable to anyone for its actions. As the situation now stands, there is no mechanism by which the Federal Reserve can be made to change a policy it has chosen to follow. The members of the Federal Reserve do not come up for election as do members of Congress or the president. Though an arm of Congress, the Federal

> Reserve is not responsible to it. . . . The Congressional power of the purse — the historic source of the legislature's power — does not apply to the Federal Reserve, which provides its own revenue. The System is not even subject to audit control of the General Accounting Office. . . . In the normal course of events, these men cannot be removed from office and because of their long tenures they do not reflect any single President's ideas.

Federal Reserve critic Martin A. Larson agreed with Patman about the undemocratic nature of the Federal Reserve's independence. In writing in *Our Manipulated Dollar*, he commented,

> Thus, while Congress has no control over the Fed, this agency can overrule Congress instantly in any economic action it may take, Our Federal Legislature has, therefore, not only farmed out to a privately-controlled entity what is probably its most important constitutional function and power — it has even placed itself in subjection to the rule of this irresponsible agency.
>
> We must, then, conclude that we are ruled primarily not by elected representatives, but by a consortium of international financiers who use their position to manipulate our currency for their agrandisement to a degree, probably without parallel in the history of civilization. (Larson, pp. 78-79)

According to Sherman Maisel, "The independence of the Board is based on the fact that it has convinced the public that it is concerned with the national interest. It has budgetary freedom, long terms for the members, immunity to removal, the right to appoint, and control of its staff free from any supervision. Even the President has no authority over the Board." (Maisel, p. 136)

Even though a president's plan to promote economic activity is enacted into law by Congress, the Federal Reserve Board can veto the law simply by decreeing contrary monetary policies that defeat the purpose of the president's plan. For example, if Congress votes to encourage business activity, the Board can override the action by raising interest rates high enough to discourage it. If the president proposes and Congress approves a "make work" program for a half a million jobs, the Fed can raise interest rates 2 or 3% and put two million people out of work. The record is clear that the Federal Reserve Board, not Congress, is determining the economic policy of the United States. The president and Congress are subject to the Fed's veto, but no one can effectively veto the Fed's policy. Sometimes called the "fourth branch of government," it is unique because it is free from the checks and balances of the constitutional branches of government. Anslem Rothschild was right, Give the board the right to issue the nation's money: then they do not care who makes the laws.

Although great care was taken to keep politics out of the Fed, not enough was taken to keep the Fed out of politics. Because of its independent power to manipulate the economy, the Fed's Board exerts a powerful influence on the course of presidential and congressional politics. The Fed has used its monetary policy to influence elections through what has been called the Board's "political cycle," that is, manipulating the economy by design to influence elections.

The Federal Reserve Board also has tremendous influence on the performance of our presidents once they are in office. If the Fed chooses to intimidate or refuses to cooperate with a president, the Board has powerful economic tools to create problems for an administration and to jeopardize its re-election. It can manipulate the money supply in a manner to make a president look very good or very, very bad. Sometimes to demonstrate its power, the Federal Reserve Board just flexes its financial muscles. The Eisenhower Administration was marred by three unnecessary recessions because the Board chairman, William McChesney Martin, wanted to assert his control over the money supply after having been restricted until 1951 by Roosevelt's Treasury Plan. Truman, Kennedy, and Johnson complained that the monetary policy of the Federal Reserve Board was developed in opposition to the economic and fiscal policies of their Administrations. (Ellias, p. 85)

President Johnson, who had the problem of building his Great Society while providing guns to fight the Vietnam War, was subjected to a severe monetary crunch. The "tight-money" policy was originated by Federal Reserve Board Chairman William McChesney Martin, who disagreed with Johnson's economic policies. Although President Roosevelt was able to force the Federal Reserve Board to fund World War II by keeping interest rates low and steady, Johnson had the misfortune of experiencing rapidly escalating interest rates throughout his term of office. In 1967, there was one brief respite in the upward climb of interest rates, but after a few months, they resumed their ascent. During the Kennedy-Johnson presidencies, the prime rate tripled, increasing from 2.7% to nearly 8.25%. In a report, Johnson pleaded with the Federal Reserve Board, asking them not to veto his efforts for full employment by raising the interest rates. Interest rates were still climbing rapidly when Johnson made his decision not to run for re-election. The domestic economic problems caused by the rapidly increasing interest rates undoubtedly contributed to that decision.

Nixon was one of the few presidents who did not suffer at the hands of the Federal Reserve Board because he seemed to have had a strong and positive relationship with Chairman Arthur Burns, whom he appointed. In his first term, Nixon had the benefit of two years of declining interest rates before his re-election campaign, a fact that explains to a great degree the tremendous re-election vote that he received.

Sherman Maisel, who was on the Board during the Nixon re-election campaign, related how the Secretary of the Treasury, George Shultz (now Secretary of State) encouraged an increase in the money supply to aid the re-election campaign. "The rule of gradualism no longer satisfied George Shultz, Director of the Office of Management and Budget and the strongest economic voice in the Administration. He now espoused an activist monetary policy. Money would determine spending. If an election were to be won, the Federal Reserve would have to increase the money supply at far more than the 4.2% average of

1969-1970. In his words, "The 'real juice' for the expanding economy had to come from monetary policy." (Maisel, p. 268) Shultz's message was clear: Ease the money supply, stimulate the economy, and re-elect Nixon.

There is no doubt that the Federal Reserve Board can influence the outcome of presidential elections as well as congressional and senatorial contests. If the Federal Reserve Board creates or maintains intolerably high interest rates, the American public will elect new representatives, thinking that they will improve the economy. If the Reserve Board manipulates the economy so that good economic conditions prevail before an election, the incumbent will have smooth sailing, e.g., Nixon's re-election in 1972.

President Carter's administration was the victim of the most damaging and intense manipulation of interest rates in the history of the presidency. Because of the growing unemployment, inflation, and high interest rates, Carter could not possible have been re-elected. Economic power is the most virulent form of political power. And today the president and Congress are the captives of the economic power wielded by the Federal Reserve Board.

In the final analysis, the key to the Board's independence is in its power to restrict the money supply. If the Board performed within the word and intent of the Federal Reserve Act and provided an "adequate" money supply, it would be just another bureaucracy administering to the credit needs of business, commerce, industry, and government.

Nowhere in the Reserve Act or its amendments is the Board authorized to restrict the money supply. It has assumed that power. As a matter of fact, the preamble of the Reserve Act states: "To establish an elastic currency" . . . one that expanded with need of the economy and contracted when not needed. Section 11 of the Federal Reserve Act enumerates the specific powers granted to the Federal Reserve Board under the law; none of its fifteen sub-sections grants the Board the power to restrict the money supply. The all-important monetary control was assumed by the Board under its authority to regulate discount rates, set reserve ratios, and operate the Federal Reserve Open Market Committee. But this authority was specifically granted with definitive guidelines set forth in the law. Section 14 of the Federal Reserve Act specifically stipulates that the governing principle for setting the discount rate "shall be fixed with a view of *accommodating* business and commerce." Furthermore, the law states that the Open Market operation "should be governed with a view to *accommodate* commerce and business. . . ." The Board has consistently ignored these clauses. Since 1951, the Board has distorted the currency system, making it an economic control device, a practice never contemplated by the Congress that created the Federal Reserve Bank.

In 1977, Congress passed an amendment to the Federal Reserve Act entitled "The Federal Reserve Reform Act of 1977." Congress directed that "the Federal Reserve System and the Federal Open Market Committee shall maintain long-run growth of the monetary and credit aggregates commensurate with the economy's long-run potential to increase production, so as to promote effectively the goals of maximum employment, stable prices, and moderate long-term interest rates." Since 1977 the Fed has followed the opposite policy: restricting the growth of money. As a result, their policy caused production to sink to 67% of capacity; unemployment to increase to 10.8%; prices to inflate to 16.8%; and interest to skyrocket to 22%.

*The Reserve Act does not give the Board the authority to restrict the money supply.* Unfortunately, an intimidated Congress has not challenged the Board's usurpation of power, preferring instead to ignore the Board's transgressions.

The Board has usurped the exclusive right of Congress to tax. It has levied a heavy unauthorized tax on the nation. Every time the Federal Reserve Board forces interest rates up 1%, they levy a 1% tax on every credit transaction. Every individual and business must pay the unauthorized tax for any goods or services they finance. If the Board increases interest rates 15%, it levies a 15% tax. If you bought a car recently on time payments, or if you borrowed money to send a child through school, you are paying a penalty —a levy that can amount to thousands of dollars a year per family. If a family bought a $100,000 home during this period of artificially high interest rates, they will pay an additional $6,000 to $10,000 a year as a result of the Board's unauthorized tax. The burden of this tax is heaviest on our harried middle class, our poor, and our young.

To keep taxation close to the will and control of the people, the Constitution specified that every tax bill must originate in the House of Representatives. Yet, the Federal Reserve Board has arbitrarily levied a tax on the use of credit by the people, its businesses, and its government without any public hearings, without any testimony or objections from dissenting members of society, without congressional approval, without the checks and balances of a legislated tax, and without the possibility of a presidential veto. Congress, which has the constitutional duty to legislate all federal taxes, has never authorized the Federal Reserve to levy a tax on credit transactions.

The Federal Reserve Tax is the most flagrant abuse of "taxation without representation" in the history of constitutional government in the United States. In 1981, the average tax for each family was approximately $5,000. We were taxed by the Federal Reserve Board for the priviledge of using our credit system, and we did not even have an opportunity to voice our objections!

We all pay the tax; even the federal government pays it since borrowing to finance the federal debt is taxed just like personal or corporate borrowing. Paying just the interest on the national debt will cost the American government an estimated $112.5 billion in 1983, $90 billion of which is the unauthorized tax the Fed levies on government borrowing!

The $64 billion question is: What happens to the hundreds of billions of dollars of revenue that are generated each year by the Board's unauthorized tax? Who gets the money and benefits from the proceeds of this unauthorized tax? The revenue created is fantastic: A 10% increase in interest results in an estimated revenue of over $200 billion per year! In 1981 it is estimated that the unauthorized tax amounted to $320 billion! The financial institutions, not the government, are the tax collectors and beneficiaries of this credit tax.

Did you know that as an independent institution the Federal Reserve Board has operated in secrecy since 1913 and that no other branch of the government has reviewed its performance in detail? Not even the Government Accounting Office. The Fed issues and destroys billions of dollars of our currency and sets the interest rate on $4 trillion of credit, and yet *it has never been audited by an outside auditing agency*. This is a serious problem because secrecy allows the Board to conceal mistakes, poor judgment, favoritism, and malfeasance.

Prudent public policy dictates that safeguards and constant vigilance be used to protect the public from government agencies that have the opportunity to favor their "friends" at the expense of the public.

Wright Patman, long-time chairman of the House Committee on Banking and Currency and critic of the bank's secrecy, commented:

> Then there are these seven members of the Federal Reserve Board who are supposed to represent the public interest on the Open Market Committee. Those fellows meet in closed-door sessions, secret sessions. They don't make the minutes public for years. And, incidentally, that's after all statutes of limitations have run out on any crime that they have committed, you know. They're practically safe. So they determine how much interest shall be paid and they determine the volume of money. Now, two or three thousand bankers know that instantly. They can capitalize on that knowledge and information. But other people don't know about it.

Since its creation, the Federal Reserve Board has operated in secrecy, shielding from Congress and the public important information on its performance. Goldwater commented on the failure to audit the Fed.:

> The Federal Reserve is a bank of monetary issue. It is empowered to establish a national discount rate and to authorize the printing of the currency of the United States. The accounts of the Federal Reserve System have never been audited. (Goldwater, p. 282)

The bank has been conducting in secrecy the most critical aspect of its operation—Federal Open Market Committee (FOMC), its most powerful monetary tool.

The FOMC is influential in determining the supply of money and, thus, interest rates. Nevertheless, the committee does not allow public participation, preferring instead to pursue its policy-making in cloistered secrecy. Without a legitimate public forum and with only the FOMC members' limited personal experiences and sterile statistics, this non-representative body makes decisions that control and direct America's economy and our lives.

The staff of the Fed is under the direction of the chairman and is also covered by the blanket of secrecy. The public has no way to obtain information about the ethics or honesty of the personnel of the Fed. It is a reasonable assumption that with all the money they handle, some of them would succumb to temptation, but have you ever heard of the Federal Reserve Board firing someone for malfeasance or dishonesty? In the first thirty-six years of operation, only one officer was removed according to information made public, and when questioned about it, the Board simply stated that it was "for cause."

Refusing to release any other details as to who or why, the Board contended that it was a "private concern" between the individual and the Board.

The fact that the Board and the officers of the Federal Reserve System are practically immune from prosecution is upsetting. Even if we were to pierce the veil of secrecy and determine that a Board member were guilty of a felony, it would be almost impossible to obtain an indictment, much less an conviction. Wright Patman stated it succinctly when questioning William McChesney Martin, chairman of the Federal Reserve Board of Governors, in August 1965: ". . .we cannot punish you. Even if your acts are equal to high crimes and misdemeanors, we cannot do anything about it."

Are all of the Board members and staff of the Federal Reserve System totally honest? If not, what have been their transgressions against the American people to date? How can the American people protect themselves from the mismanagement of their currency? How can we know? Only by full public disclosure.

Outright felonious acts are not the only public concern. Whenever an agency's operation is hidden from the public's scrutiny, there is a high potential for subtle acts and covert deeds contrary to the public interest. Without violating any laws, the members of the Board of Governors are in a position to create vast financial windfall profits and inequities within the financial community by sophisticated manipulation of policies. Without full disclosure and open public meetings, the people and the press are denied their right to judge the legitimacy of the Board's acts.

Sherman Maisel (pp. 173-174) discussed the Board's secrecy:

> To most people, the Federal Reserve is mysterious. It is not the Delphic Oracle, but it may not be far removed. It fights inflation with unseen, but powerful tools. It may make mistakes, but they are hard to document. As long as policy statements remain cryptic, no one can keep score or record its errors. There is no batting average published for the Fed.
>
> A strong, self-protective society exists within the Federal Reserve System. When under attack, its officials tend to stick together. In any discussion of improving quantification and making operations more open, someone will always ask why the enemies of the System should be given more information-that is to say, more weapons — to attack it.

Maisel sums up his comments with, "It cannot be denied that, with more specific policies, the opposition might become fiercer and more successful."

The public's right to know must be paramount. If we had full disclosure and public and media scrutiny of the Federal Reserve Board's actions for the last twelve years, it is a good bet we would not be in our present economic quagmire and I would not be writing this book.

All aspects of our social and cultural lives reflect the consequences of the decisions of the Federal Reserve Board. The Board's monetary policy is effectively *pushing back* the social gains of the last fifty years. America's commitment and dedication to a humane social policy for the needy, handicapped, and aged are being bent by the force of the tight-money policy of the Federal Reserve. As a direct consequence of the Fed's high-interest policy, in the 1983 budget year the government must pay over $112.5 billion in interest. To compensate for this interest, Reaganomics has embarked on a budget-cutting program that curtails aid and welfare to the aged, the infirm, an the needy. Simply put, our government is paying a $100 billion windfall income to the wealthy by increasing the misery of the helpless. The consequence of high interest rates is a social tragedy and a regressive consequence of the policy of the Federal Reserve Board.

We do not deny that the welfare system needs revising and updating. What is being challenged is the wisdom of the changes being forced by budget pressures of high interest rates from the Federal Reserve Board. A better approach to cut budget deficits is to force government interest rates back to a normal 1 to 2.5%, cut bureaucratic welfare administration costs, cut bureaucrats not benefits, and perhaps there would be enough left to enact a fair and equitable tax cut.

The legacy of the Volcker Board to the American public is the sickest economy since the Great Depression. If allowed to continue, the Board offers more distorted economic policies and continued economic problems. By their own acts, they have indicted the Federal Reserve Board. As the disillusioned co-author of the Federal Reserve Act, Senator Robert Owen, observed: "I make no charge against them on which they do not stand self-convicted."

* Roosa made this statement about the time the Trilateral Commission was being formed (1972). This reference to the chairmanship was prophetic.

* Frederick H. Schultz has since retired, and a new appointment has been made by President Reagan. But even with this change, the basic comments in this chapter about the majority of the Board are still valid.

# CHAPTER 6

# *Federal Reserve Policy Part 1*

***Those who glibly talk about controlling inflation by monetary policy, have failed to consider that moderate monetary measures by themselves alone are relatively ineffective, while drastic measures may easily turn the economy into a tailspin.***

***—Alvin Hansen, Economist.***

Like all massive conglomerates, the Rockefeller Syndicate has a carefully designed plan to maximize profits and expand its dominion of power. The Syndicate is a $500 billion combination of large domestic and international banks, gigantic insurance companies, and multinational financial institutions that derive a large part of their income from interest. When Carter appointed Rockefeller's aide, Paul Volcker, to the chairmanship in 1979 and four "friendly" members to the Board, Rockefeller's profit strategy became the standard operating procedure for the Federal Reserve Board. The following is an outline of the salient points of the Syndicate's profit strategy:

1. The primary objective is to control the Board of the Federal Reserve Bank, and thereby increase interest rates as high as possible for as long as possible. For a ten-year period, the prime rate has averaged above 10% and reached an unprecedented 21.5% in 1981!

2. The second objective is to encourage high federal budget deficits. As the federal debt grows, the Syndicate's income grows. As interest rates to service the debt increases, the Syndicate's income increases accordingly. During the Burns/Volcker chairmanship, the national debt doubled, and interest rates have quadrupled. Government interest payments have multiplied tremendously, increasing from $20 billion in 1972 to $112 (est.) billion in 1983 (an increase of nearly 500% in nine years).

3. The third objective is to increase the income of the international banking sector of the Syndicate by maintaining a high international value of the American dollar. In the last ten years, the international loans to developing countries by American banks has increased sixfold, much of it arranged by David Rockefeller and his Syndicate.

4. The fourth objective is periodic recessions. By using their cash, the

Syndicate can take advantage of the Federal Reserve Board's programmed recessions to scavenge the economy and increase their wealth at bargain prices at the expense of smaller firms weakened by "tight money," high interest rates, and the recession.

The Board's policies are spectacularly successful in increasing profits for the Syndicate. Chase Manhattan Bank earned $105 million in 1976, during the Carter administration its profits increased to $443.9 million in 1981, more than fourfold. However, the Board's policy did not work as well for the public; the economy was in a deep recession in 1981.

**SHORT-TERM INTEREST RATES**
**Business Borrowing**

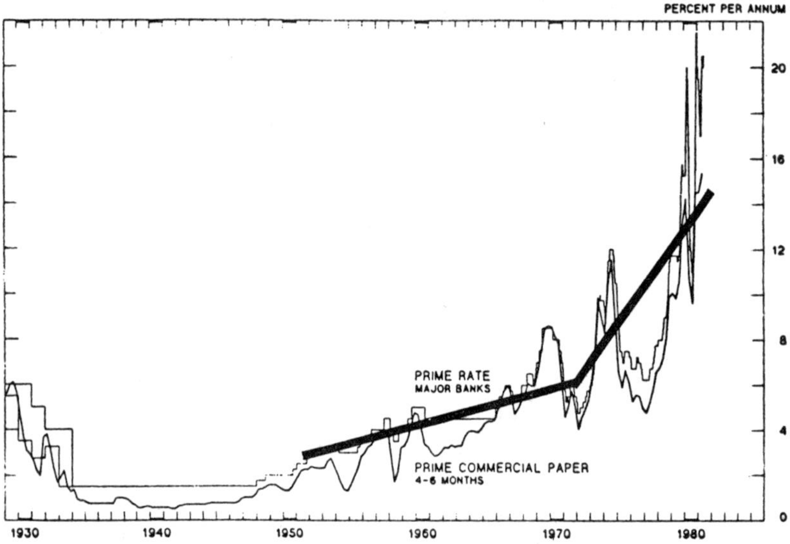


**RECORD OF INTEREST RATES**

This chart shows the result of Federal Reserve Board manipulation of interest rates since World War II. Interest rates increased astronomically. For example, Prime Commercial paper rates increased 3000% – an average annual increase of 80%! The extreme swings in interest rates caused constant economic instability and uncertainty. The trend line shows the rapid increase of interest rates during the Burns-Volcker chairmanship.

If you doubt David Rockefeller's commitment to high interest rates, reflect on his remarks in a speech to the New York State Bankers' Association in Tarrytown, New York, on June 1, 1980. Rockefeller vehemently argued against usury laws that set legal limits on interest rates, "The very term itself – usury – is enough to make a banker's blood boil." He went on to say, "The elimination of consumer credit usury ceilings is a critical challenge for our industry and our association in the decade of the 1980s . . . And that means – repealing, overriding, and eliminating existing state usury laws on banks' consumer credit."* Rockefeller's viewpoint is clear: interest rates should be allowed to rise as high as Paul Volcker could force them.

The Federal Reserve Board has justified its high interest policy on the basis that it was the most effective economic tool to control inflation. The underlying theory is that inflation is a monetary phenomenon involving too many dollars chasing too few goods, thereby bidding up prices. So, if the Board restricts the money supply or its growth to the proper level, it will counteract the inflationary force resulting in stable prices. So the key to halting inflation is simply to decrease the supply of money. They reason that with less money there will be a corresponding decrease in the demand for goods and services. The Fed's theory is that if interest rates are increased to a point where a consumer cannot afford to buy a commodity and pay the interest rates, he will forego the purchase. Likewise, if an investor cannot make a return that allows him to pay the interest rates, he will forego borrowing money to make the investment. As a result, the demand for money declines as well as the demand for goods and services, and presto – inflation is abated.

The Board uses the Money Supply Index as its major inflation indicator. When, by its formula, the money supply is growing too rapidly, the Board uses one of its monetary controls to tighten credit.

This simple process does not work. Like most economic theories, although based on logic, this policy does not work in the real world. To have an effect on inflation, monetary policy must be used so drastically that it inevitably forces the economy into a recession. Since World War II, the Board has interceded by increasing interest rates six times, resulting in six recessions – each more severe than the previous one.

Before analyzing the anti-inflation policy of the Federal Reserve Board, a brief history is in order. During World War II, Franklin D. Roosevelt forced the Federal Reserve Board into an agreement with the Treasury in an attempt to force the Federal Reserve to supply an adequate amount of money to fight the war at a low interest rate. Government bonds were pegged at .375%, with the Fed underwriting the market to guarantee a return of 2.5%. After the end of the war, the agreement remained in effect until 1951. Throughout this period, the members of the Federal Reserve Board chaffed under the restrictions on their control of the money supply and warned that serious inflation would result unless they were free to manipulate the money supply. In 1951, during the Truman Administration, an accord releasing the Fed from its restrictive agreement with the Treasury was signed. The Fed rapidly re-established its monopoly of money by attacking an almost nonexistent "inflation."

"Inflation" is the Fed's battle cry, the cornerstone of the Board's economic policy and the propaganda ploy to sell it. Since World War II, the Fed's single-minded battle against inflation has dominated the course of economic developments in the United States. The Fed made "inflation an economic buzz-word, a propaganda device that elicits an automatic and irrational mental knee-jerk reaction. "Inflation" has become a dirty word: "like sin, everyone is against it." (Maisel, p. 11) Over the years, economists and think tanks dominated by the financial elite have joined in the chorus of shouting the evils of inflation. They have been so effective that the American people have naively accepted the Fed's policy of "tight money high interest" as though it were economic salvation.

Unfortunately, the fear of inflation diverts our attention from the real economic problems. We have been involved in a Quixotic war on inflation while ignoring the real economic problems of the nation: assuring economic growth, job security, preparing for the new technological revolution and a better life for our citizens in an improving environment.

In the case of the Fed, it was "overkill." Ex-Fed Governor, Sherman Maisel, noted: "The Federal Reserve has never accepted the idea that minor sin should be winked at, that a little inflation could be a good thing." (Maisel, p. 16) Although the Fed believed that all inflation, whatever the cause, could be managed by its high-interest policy, its self-confidence outreached its ability.

Inflation of the late 1960s and early 1970s was partially due to the extraneous forces that could not be controlled by monetary policy. These forces—the Vietnam War, oil prices, environmental costs, the impact on food prices (i.e., exporting grains, increased fertilizer costs, fuel costs, transport costs, etc.), and accelerated foreign investments in America—are inflationary, but not responsive to monetary management. The Fed should have allowed them to run their course. By intervening with high-interest rates, the Board increased and prolonged their inflationary impact.

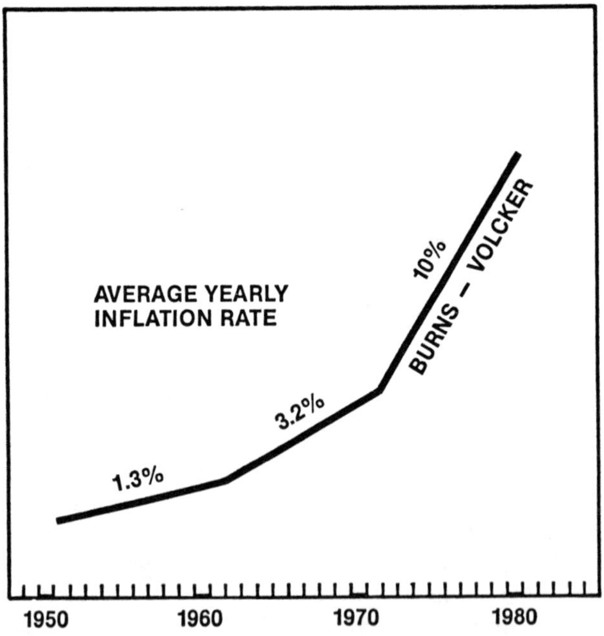


**COMPARATIVE PERIODS OF INFLATION**

The "high interest" policy of the Fed did not work. The higher the board forced interest rates, the higher the inflation. Ten years of record interest rates by Burns and Volcker tripled the inflation rate of the previous decade.

For the last decade, the Burns/Volcker Board applied vigorous monetary restraints on the economy. But inflation did not slow down, it accelerated at an extraordinarily rapid rate, averaging almost 10% a year (from 1972 to 1982), compared to an annual inflation rate of 1.3% in the period from 1952 to 1962, and 3.2% from 1962 to 1972. The Burns/Volcker anti-inflation policy multiplied inflation three times that of the 1962-1972 period, and eight times that of the 1952-1972 period! Why do you think that happened? Here is a clue: the prime rate increased by a factor of eight in the same period.

The obvious conclusion is that the Board's increasing interest rates during the last twelve years has been the major cause of inflation, but this common-sense approach to economics seems to elude the members of the Federal Reserve Board. Sherman Maisel realized that increasing interest rates increased prices: "Whatever their indirect impact, the direct effects of interest rate rises are inflationary. Interest plays a major role in the consumer price index." (Maisel, p. 17) The Fed's vote to increase interest rates is a vote to increase prices throughout the economy. In the course of business activity, interest is considered a cost of doing business and is added to the price of goods and services. In addition, there is an "amplifying factor" that is responsible for the increase in price to be greater than the increase in interest. The "amplifying factor" is a result of the fact that products are financed a number of times during the course of their manufacture, and each step along the way an increment of cost due to higher interest is added. Overhead, administrative costs, and profit are increased in proportion to the increase in the price of the commodity. Therefore, an increase in interest typically causes a larger increase in the price of the product than the magnitude of the increase in interest itself.

Another factor that amplifies the effect of an increase in the interest rate is the practice of banks to charge larger lending fees during times of tight money. Because of multiple loans during the course of manufacturing a product, these cumulative additional fees are also added to the price of the goods.

*The inflationary effect of increasing interest rates is inherent in the Federal Reserve Board's policy.* The only way for it not to happen is if the increased cost of money is absorbed by profits. Considering the present low level of profits, this is not likely to happen voluntarily. When the manufacturer has no choice but to cut profits to absorb high interest costs, it can and has bankrupted many businesses.

In an article in *The New York Times* on October 7, 1979, Henry Kaufman, a partner in Salomon Brothers, commented that the increase in oil prices was not the primary cause of inflation. He pointed out that "In the past year, the Consumer Price Index has risen 11.5%. Excluding high energy costs, the Index has gone up 9.4%." In effect, the increase in inflation caused by petroleum can only account for 2%. Wages were not responsible for inflation, according to Secretary of State George Shultz, who was previously the United States Director of the Office of Management and Budget and Secretary of Treasury in the Nixon Administration: "Certainly you cannot make any case that what happened to wage income is responsible for inflation . . . fiscal and monetary forces produced the inflation." Mr. Shultz put his finger on the cause when he mentioned the monetary forces since fiscal policy has almost been nonoperational since the Kennedy-Johnson years.

Let's analyze one year, 1978, and see if we can estimate interest's impact on inflation. In 1978, the inflation rate was 9% and the prime interest rate increased almost 4%. Considering the residual impact of the previous year's interest increase and the amplifying factor of interest increases, the Board's anti-inflation policy was responsible for 6 to 8% of the inflation of 1978.

The following chart shows that thirty years of increasing interest rates failed to control inflation, but that higher interest rates caused the Consumer Price Index to rise in proportion. Much of the long-term inflation since World War II can be attributed to the Board's anti-inflation policy!

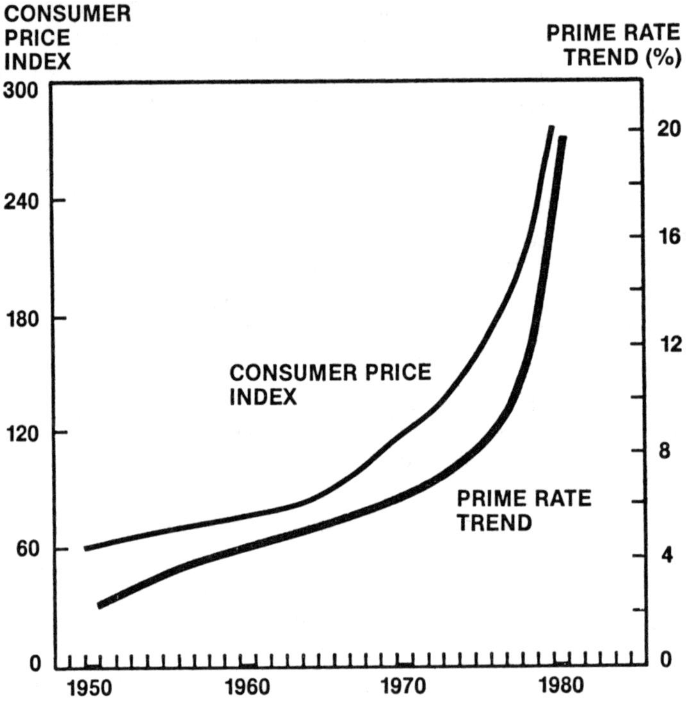


**CONSUMER PRICE INDEX INCREASES COMPARED TO PRIME RATE INCREASES**

For thirty years, the Federal Reserve Board increased interest rates to keep inflation down. But this chart shows that increasing interest rates forces prices higher. It demonstrates beyond a doubt that inflation increases as interest rates increase!

The evidence is clear that the Board's anti-inflation policy does not work. It does not retard inflation, rather, interest rates act on prices to force inflation up in direct relation to the increase in interest rates. The Board created the dragon they vowed to slay.

The money supply does not respond to interest rates as the Federal Reserve Board assumes. Rather, the reverse is true: high interest rates tend to increase the money supply. Raising the interest rates increases pressure to expand the money supply. The following chart indicates that high interest rates have little long-term restraint on the growth of the money supply and that, as a matter of fact, the money supply grows in response to high interest rates.

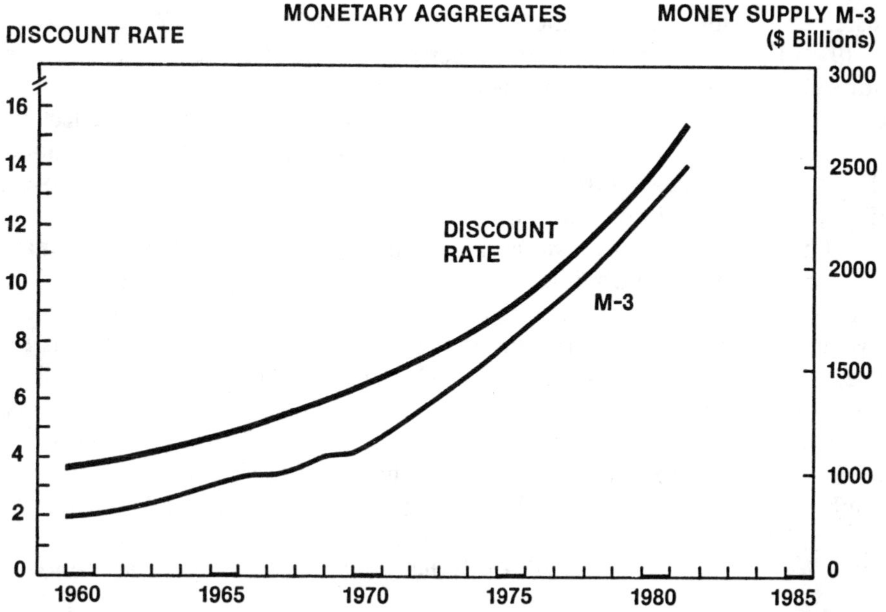


**INCREASES IN DISCOUNT RATE VS. MONEY SUPPLY INCREASES**

This chart disproves a Federal Reserve myth. The Board argued that high interest rates restricts the money supply. The facts prove that it has the opposite effect, the money supply *increases* in the same proportion as the interest rates increases.

Money analyst Henry Kaufman summed it up, "The real story behind our severely aggravated inflation is that the growth of credit has been proliferating while the Federal Reserve has been focusing on the M1 and M2 supplies." (M1 and M2 is an index of the money supply.) (Henry Kaufman, *The New York Times*)

It is only common sense to deduce that high interest rates encourage banks to make loans. For example, if interest rates are low, a bank will be very selective about the quality of the borrower and will tend to reject many loan requests and make more conservative loans. But when a banker is enticed by 25 or 26% interest, a reasonably well-qualified borrower is very attractive to the bankers since at those percentages, the bank has a large risk factor built into the rate. And, if the bank secures its loans properly with sufficient amounts of collateral from the borrower, it stands to gain either way. If the loan is paid off, the bank has made a fantastic return, and if it is not paid off, the bank is in a position to claim the collateral. Like all other businesses, the desire to increase profits compels banks to make loans when interest rates are high, and thus increase the money supply. Chart 6 proves this observation. As interest rates increased, the money supply increased at almost the same ratio.

Kaufman sums up the problem by explaining that the Federal Reserve has failed to understand the problem of credit growth: "If it had done so, the Federal Reserve would have perceived long ago that its monetary and interest rates policies were incorrect because they favored borrowing and consumption instead of saving and investment." (Kaufman, *The New York Times*, October 7, 1979) Furthermore, Kaufman argues that the Federal Reserve Board does not follow proper indicators of the money supply; the aggregate money supply can increase considerably while the Board's indicators may not reflect the change. (There are other significant factors that affect the supply of money that are not reflected in the Board's statistics such as credit creation between firms, credit extension, trades, and money substitutes.)

Furthermore, it is not axiomatic that high interest discourages the demand for money. There are often circumstances when money is desperately needed and the borrower must pay the higher rate of interest. Also, there is a speculative aspect that affects borrowers; if they feel that interest rates are going to rise, they rush to the banks for loans. The banks feel the pressure and will up the rate of interest and the higher interest rates will induce bankers to make loans. A banker's bragging quotient is determined by the average interest rate of his loan portfolio. The higher the rate, the louder the bragging.* There is no doubt that high interest rates increase the propensity for bankers to create money. While there may be an instantaneous adjustment to M1 due to interest rates, it is rapidly compensated for in the economy by the use of near-money, or "street money."

The inescapable fact is that the money supply is not effectively controlled by increasing interest rates except when it becomes so excessive as to diminish economic activity by causing a recession.

There is an automatic pressure on the money supply when interest rates increase: there is a direct devaluation of the dollar when interest rates are increased. When money is borrowed at a higher-than-normal interest rate, it is immediately deflated. For example, when the Federal Reserve doubled the interest rates from 10 to 20%, a hundred dollar loan is worth only ninety dollars to the borrower because there is a ten dollar surcharge for the loan caused by the higher interest rates; therefore, if the borrower needs one hundred dollars, he must ask for one hundred and ten dollars.

Despite the facts and our unsuccessful experiences, the Board continued to use tight money as a deterrent to inflation. The recent experience of Japan where a large increase in money supply significantly diminished inflation, indicates that the Board should have eased monetary controls. From 1970 to 1975 the average annual increase in the price level was 11.7% in Japan. During that period, to combat the inflation the Japanese increased their money supply a monumental average of 19.4% per year. Between 1975 and 1980, the price level decreased to a 6.6% average increase, diminishing to a comfortable 2% in 1982. Now compare this with the Fed's record in the United States. From 1970 to 1975 the average annual increase of inflation was 6.8%, and the Fed followed a very restrictive monetary policy allowing a modest average yearly increase of 6% in the money supply. Between 1975 and 1980, the Fed was even more restrictive, and inflation soared to 16.8% in January 1980. At the end of 1982, after two years of deep recession and five years of very tight money, our inflation rate is three times that of the Japanese. Clearly, the Fed's unrealistic restriction of the money supply increased and extended the inflation.

A valid test of the Board's policy of tight money, high interest is to compare the performance of our economy with others that have had the benefit of an adequate money supply and relatively low interest rates for the last few years. For example, Switzerland, which has more money per capita than any other capitalist economy, has had one of the lowest inflation rates. The Japanese Central Bank discount rate decreased to 5.5% in 1981, while in the United States it was increasing to 14% in 1981 (*United Nations Monthly Bulletin of Statistics*, November 1981). Let's compare the difference in economic growth, unemployment, and inflation for 1982 between the United States and Japan.*

| | JAPAN | UNITED STATES |
|---|---|---|
| Economic Growth | 3.0% | -1.9% |
| Unemployment | 2.5% | 10.5% |
| Inflation | 2.0% | 6.2% |

*Time's Pacific Board of Economists (1982) *Time*, November, 29, 1982.

The Japanese maintained significant economic growth and low unemployment with low interest rates. Why can't the United States? Let's compare the United States with Japan as of 1982. In Japan with lower interest rates, unemployment is 2.5%. In the United States with high interest rates, unemployment is 10.5%. Despite the full employment in Japan, inflation is only 2%, whereas in the United States with 10.5% unemployment, inflation is still at 6.2%. Japan, with its low interest rates, was able to post a gain in economic growth of 3%. In the United States with high interest rates, growth declined by nearly 2%. The difference between the growth in Japan and that in the United States is 4.9 percentage points. This is upsetting. Are we becoming a second-class nation? You must have asked yourself, why has Japan advanced so rapidly and effectively in the new technological era while we seem to be bumbling, stumbling, and falling all over ourselves? Forget Theory Z. It is purely and simply a case of money. Japanese industry has the advantage of an adequate flow of investment capital at relatively low interest rates. American industry has been handicapped by tight money and exorbitant interest rates.

Another test for the effectiveness of the Fed's monetary policy is whether the tight money, high interest rates discouraged the American public from going into debt. The answer again is no. Total debt in the United States grew as the interest rates increased. The result was that we were paying higher interest rates on more debt. The cost of interest to the American people skyrocketed but that was about all.

Paul Volcker, chairman of the Fed, has criticized the federal government for deficit spending, arguing that the large government deficits are a major cause of inflation. How accurate is that accusation? The charge is not justified.

While it is true that government spending can have an inflationary impact in departments such as Defense, where cost-plus contracts are frequent and other noncompetitive practices encourage "buddy" contracts. The deficit spending of the government would only be inflationary if the private sector were fully employed. But we have not had that circumstance during the last decade—the reverse has been true. We have had idle plants, idle men, and a surfeit of inventories.

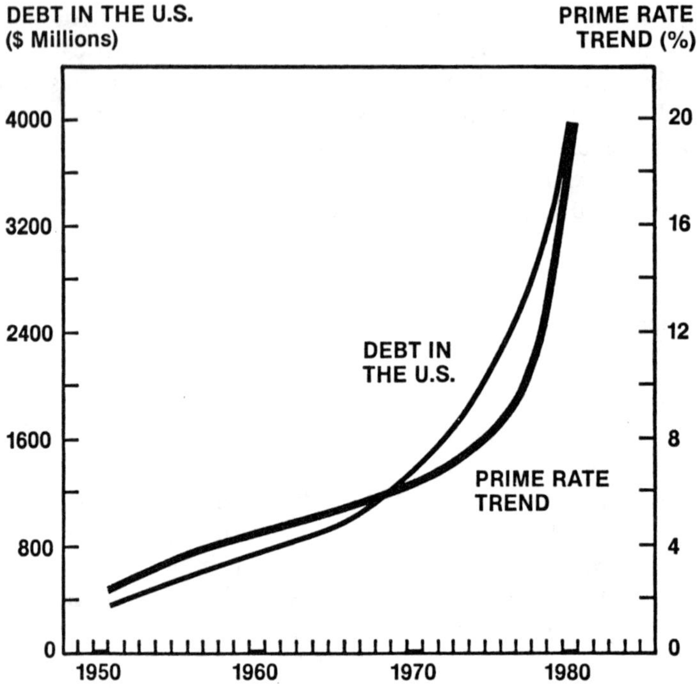


**GROWTH IN DEBT IN THE U.S. COMPARED TO PRIME RATE INCREASES**

This chart disproves another Federal Reserve myth. The Board defended the use of high interest rates on the promise that they discourage borrowing. Not so, debt in the United States grew in proportion to the rapid increase in interest rates.

In recent years, budget deficits have been a direct result of the inflated interest rates that the Board has force government to pay to service the national debt. The chapter on The Federal Debt offers a strong argument that the growth of the federal debt from $425 billion in 1972 to over $1 trillion in 1982 was the direct consequence of the Board's anti-inflation policy during the Burns and Volcker chairmanships.

The facts speak for themselves. There is a cause-and-effect relationship between the Board increasing the discount rate and the skyrocketing of the federal debt. Every time the Fed voted to increase its discount rate, it was also voting to increase the federal debt by the additional increment of interest required to service the debt.

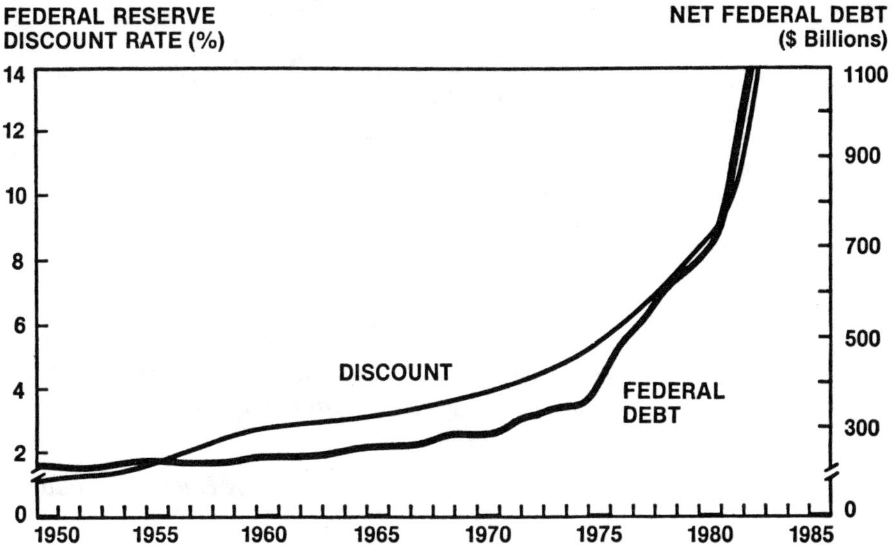


**THE GROWTH OF THE NATIONAL DEBT RELATED TO THE INCREASES IN THE DISCOUNT RATE**

This chart demonstrates that the growth of the National Debt is the result of the Fed's increase in interest rates. For the last five years, the debt has grown in porportion to increases in the Discount rate. The surge in interest rates was a primary cause of doubling the national debt.

* President Carter accommodated his fellow Trilateralist and signed into law the Monetary Control Act of 1980, which in effect nullified state usury laws in the field of home mortgages and some business and agricultural loans.

* I recall an occasion when I was meeting with the president of a large western bank a few days before Christmas. It was twilight and we were looking down on a Christmas bedecked Los Angeles. He commented to me with pride that his loan portfolio averaged over 18%. Santa and the Federal Reserve Board had been good to him.

# CHAPTER 7

# *Federal Reserve Policy Part II*

***Raising the rate of interest either: (a) has very serious consequences which could not be tolerated, or (b) is not an effective way of combating temporary, inflationary tendencies.***

***—Alvin Hansen, Economist***

A critical criterion of any economic policy designed to help the economy is time-effectiveness. If a policy does not produce positive results after a reasonable length of time, it should be abandoned and something else should be tried.

Was the Board's anti-inflation policy time-effective? Did the Board cure inflation in a reasonable length of time? The answer is no! The Fed's cure for inflation never worked. The consumer price level increased by a multiple of four from 1951 to the end of 1981. Thirty years is too long to wait for a policy to prove its effectiveness.

Despite the Board's vigorous anti-inflation program, since 1972 unacceptable high inflation has dominated our economy and the threat of inflation is ever present. If the Board's tight-money policies were going to work, the results should have been evident when Chairman Burns forced interest rates skyward. From 1972 to 1974, the Burns' Board tripled the prime rate in an effort to control inflation, but during that period inflation increased from 3.4% in 1972 to 12.2% in 1974! The recession of 1975 slowed down inflation, but in 1977 the Fed resumed its high-interest policy and inflation started up again, reaching 16.8% in January 1980.

Most economic reforms, including many welfare programs, were enacted to buffer the negative effects of economic downturns. Despite government efforts to eliminate depressions, recessions, and economic instability, the Federal Reserve Board has programmed six recessions since 1951 when it regained control of the money supply. Congressman Charles Lindberg, Sr., who fought against the Federal Reserve Act, warned that the Federal Reserve Board would have the power "to create depressions scientifically," He was right. Look at the record:

| Periods of Board-Created Tight-Money, High-Interest | Followed by the Recession of |
|---|---|
| 1951–1953 | 1953–1954 |
| 1954–1957 | 1957–1958 |
| 1958–1960 | 1960–1961 |
| 1962–1969 | 1969–1970 |
| 1972–1974 | 1975 |
| 1977–1981 | 1980–? |

Every time the Board applied its tight-money high-interest policy, it caused a recession. Of the members of Congress in 1913 that passed the Federal Reserve Act, Charles Lindberg, Sr., was the only one who fully realized the bill's potential for misuse of power and how the Board could control the U.S. economy. As Lindberg prophesized, the Board has manufactured an economic cycle of its own design—the "Federal Reserve Cycle," an engineered business cycle that has amplified and perpetuated inflation.

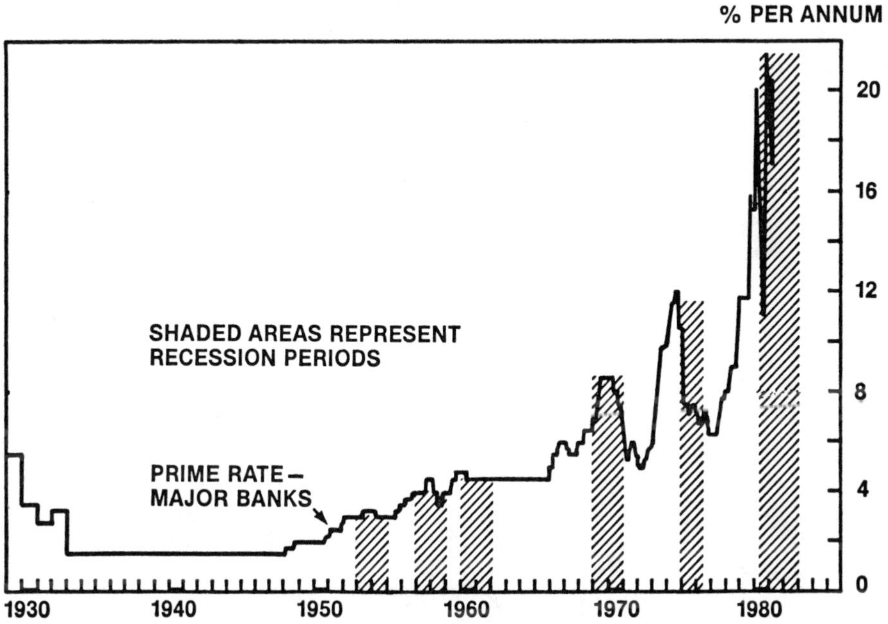


**THE FEDERAL RESERVE CYCLE**
This chart shows the six Federal Reserve Cycles since 1951. Each recession (shaded areas) was intentionally programmed by the Board increasing interest rates to restrict economic activity until there was a recession.

The Federal Reserve Cycle is periods of Federal-Reserve-Board-created inflation followed by periods of recession. Briefly, this is how the sequence works: The Federal Reserve fuels inflation with it increases interest rates which are reflected in higher prices of goods and services. The Fed continues to increase the interest rates until the economy is strangled, causing a recession.

Business slacks off, unemployment increases, and bankruptcies increase. In answer to public pressure to ameliorate the effects of the recession, the Board then allows interest rates to decline, and the pent-up demand for commodities (those purchasers who postponed buying until interest rates decline) is manifested. This surge of demand seeks to be satisfied in a short time, and since the recession has curtailed production, there is a short-term disruption in the flow of goods. The result is an inflationary force on the economy. The cycle begins again when the Federal Reserve Board notices the new inflationary pressure and again forces interest rates up. We have suffered through six Federal Reserve cycles since 1951.

The amplitude of the cycle has increased dramatically during the Burns and Volcker chairmanships. Greater inflation followed by deeper recessions for each succeeding Federal Reserve Cycle. Since prime interest rates reached 21.5%, inflation reached 13.3%, and unemployment exceeded 10.8% during the current cycle, the question has to be asked—How high will interest rates climb and how high will unemployment go in the next cycle?

The following chart shows the amplitude of each Federal Reserve Cycle since 1950.

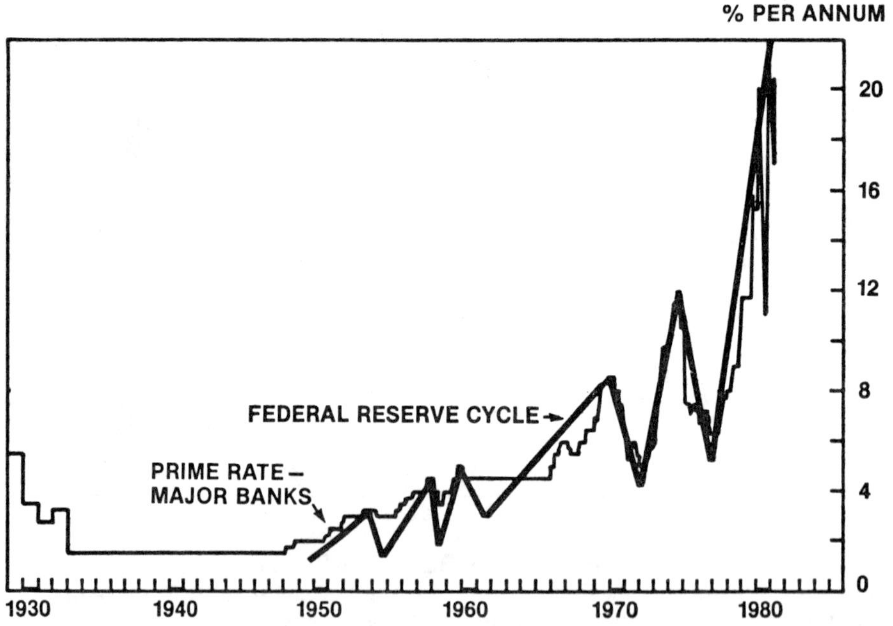


**AMPLITUDE OF FEDERAL RESERVE CYCLE**

This chart demonstrates four facts: (1) the amplitude of the Federal Reserve Cycle is increasing; (2) Interest rates lost their effectiveness as an economic tool. Higher and higher interest rates are necessary to precipitate a recession; (3) The Federal Reserve Cycle is forcing the trend of interest rates upward. Notice, they never return to their previous low; (4) The Federal Reserve Cycle is out of control.

A dramatic example of the Federal Reserve Cycle and the inflationary effect of the Board's tight money, high interest policy can be seen in the housing market. From 1972 to 1975, the Fed tightened the money supply, setting the stage for the real estate inflation of 1977 to 1980. Many people who qualified as legitimate home buyers from 1972 to 1975 could not buy new homes because of the artificially high interest rates. When the interest rates fell after the recession of 1975, these buyers entered the market en masse. The supply of new homes was inadequate since the tight money market and the following recession diminished the home building industry's capacity to provide an adequate supply of homes. Home buyers then turned to lower priced, owner-occupied homes. The demand was so great that it forced existing homes prices to increase significantly. Many of the families who sold their smaller homes re-entered the market to buy new and larger homes, thereby adding to the upward pressure on the price of new homes. Speculation in the housing market added an additional inflationary movement to prices.

As this example illustrates, the key element in the Federal Reserve Cycle is "pent-up demand." When interest rates go down, the pent-up demand is added to the normal demand and results in an abnormally high demand for goods, thus creating a sellers' market. The normal demand, plus pent-up demand, creates a peak demand that seeks to be satisfied in a short time, thereby rekindling the inflationary pressure and starting the cycle anew.

Our economy is faced with a very serious problem — the Federal Reserve Board cannot break the inflation cycle with its monetary policy, for when the Board intercedes to stop inflation with high interest rates, it plants the seeds for the next round of inflation.

Economist Alvin Hansen noted another problem in using high interest rates as a regulatory device. It is much easier for the Fed to cause a recession than to cure one. He anticipated the Board's problem of ending our current recession — the difficulty of reducing interest rates to encourage recovery:

> Once the interest rate structure has been raised sufficiently to check the boom, it is no easy matter to lower the interest rate structure in the ensuing depression and thereby permit recovery. The difficulty of getting the rate down once it has been raised in the boom period and the deterrent effects which a high rate on recovery presents a strong argument against the use of this device as a regulatory mechanism.

He accurately anticipated the dilemma of the Federal Reserve Board. For the last three years, we have suffered a recession along with extraordinarily high interest rates. The Board claims that to lower interest rates would rekindle inflation. This is the dilemma of the Board's policy. The only alternative is for the Fed to keep interest rates high and to keep the economy in a prolonged recession — an alternative that is too costly and damaging to be acceptable.

The devastating long-term economic instability created by the Federal Reserve Cycle and the continuous use of a tight-money policy by the Fed has forced the economy into an economic quagmire of "stagflation."

Stagflation threatens the very basis of our economic system with its underproduction, underemployment, and continuing inflation. Stagflation is an economic cancer. If, to avoid inflation, we must suffer chronic stagflation, a rapidly growing national debt, continuous high interest rates, and periodic programmed recession, the capitalistic system is in danger. The Federal Reserve policy has caused serious structural damage to our economy and, if allowed to continue, will jeopardize our private enterprise system.

George Brockway, philosopher and economist, commented on the Board's policy with dramatic wit:

> What a way to win a war . . . destroying the economy in order to save it.
>
> If war is too important to leave to the generals, money is too important to leave to the bankers . . . Some politicians believed that bankers—especially the political bankers of whom Federal Reserve Chairman Paul Volcker, is chief-muylah are sacrosanct, and that we should follow them uncritically into war on inflation, much as we were once expected to follow the generals into Vietnam. My guess is that the outcome is going to be very similar.
>
> . . . I can see that Mr. Volcker stands tall in the saddle, but so did George Armstrong Custer. My fear is that even if Mr. Volcker finds a way to win his war—that is, to reduce inflation, at least temporarily—many of the ordinary foot soldiers like me will be too dead to feel grateful . . . the political bankers attack inflation by raising the interest rate. This was done, they said, to restrict the amount of money in circulation. Why should we do that? Well, something had to be done, and everyone knows that inflation is at least partly the result of too much money chasing too few goods.
>
> Was that really happening? Did you go into a store at any time in the past several months—any kind of store—hardware or supermarket, discount department store or specialty boutique? What did you find there? Was anything in short supply? Anything at all—even plastics and other petroleum products? What is this nonsense about 'too few goods'?
>
> Anyone who encounters the real world on a regular basis might be tempted to conclude that the political bankers had things inside-out. In the real world, there's too little money in circulation—where it counts. (George Brockway, *Washington Monthly*, June 1980, p. 48)

The classical economic doctrine of inflation assumes that the reason for scarcity of goods is that the factors of production are at full capacity. Therefore, excess money in the economy results in bidding prices up. Under these conditions it assumes that the labor force is fully employed. Bidding for labor's services during full employment would result in an inflationary increase in the price of labor and would not lead to the production of any additional goods or services. Therefore, according to the theory, restricting the money supply would limit demand and avoid bidding up prices.

This classical theory used by the Board to set policy does not apply to the recent inflation since our factors of production for years have suffered from underutilization. For the last decade, our manufacturing capacity, especially that of heavy industry like the steel mills, has been woefully below capacity operating at less than 50% capacity. The mills are capable and anxious to produce additional tons of steel and could do so without bidding up the production costs. Our ailing auto industry could produce additional cars without increasing manufacturing costs per unit. Conceivably, the cost of autos would go down if fixed costs were distributed over more automobiles.

The American home building industry is an unemployed giant with historically high inventories. It is difficult to imagine that building homes would be inflationary. Unemployment has been above 5% since 1970, and now it is over 10%. There would be no inflationary pressure putting most of the unemployed to work. By any measure of common sense, the Board's policies do not make any economic sense.

The Fed's anti-inflation policy works against itself. Our best protection from inflation is to maintain an adequate and constant flow of goods for the economy. But during the Fed's tight-money period, high interest rates discouraged new investment in plants and equipment and factories became obsolete. The cumulative effect of the tight money and the recession diminishes the resilience of the economy to accommodate the up-turn in demand with an adequate and even flow of goods competitively produced. When interest rates are lowered, the purchasers move back into the market, and their pent-up demand exerts inflationary force on the economy due to temporary shortages of inventories. In reality, the Federal Reserve policy diminishes our supply of goods as well as our capacity to produce goods. This is just the opposite of what an intelligent anti-inflation program should seek to achieve; namely, the production of an abundance of goods so that they could compete for the buyer on a free market and thus keep prices down.

One of the strongest arguments against the Board's monetary policy is the fact that by repeated use of interest rates as a device to control inflation, they become less effective. Sherman Maisel, saw the pattern:

> The effectiveness of any policy tends to diminish the more often and more intensively it is used. If money is tight, people create substitutes. When credit rationing threatens, business make certain that they are not caught with their liquidity down the second time around. If interest rate policy is used, the patterns of borrowing and lending change. It took much higher interest rates in 1969 than in 1966 before spending was cut back. Now still higher rates, with a greated disruption of financial markets, may be needed if monetary policy is depended upon as the primary tool to curtail prices. With time and the ability of the economy to plan, there is less bang for the buck of monetary restraint. (Maisel, p. 312)

For many years, interest rates above 4% were considered high; however, after interest rates went to 21%, a new benchmark for "high" was established. Thus, to have any negative effect on the money supply, the Board must force interest rates higher than before because the economy has adjusted to the previous "high" interest rate.

The result is that the Board has found it necessary to use higher and higher interest rates each time it has tightened the money supply to cause a recession. For example, the Board had to force the prime interest rate to 4% in 1960, then to 8% in 1970, and then to 12% in 1975. In 1980, it had to force the prime to 22%. Since 1960 the Board found it necessary to increase the interest rates by a magnitude of 500%! (An average increase of 25% per year—that's inflation!) How high must the interest be forced next time?

The conclusion to be drawn is that interest rates, no matter how high they were forced, did not stop inflation. It took a recession every time to achieve that, but it required higher interest rates each time to precipitate the recession.

The essence of the Board's policy is that it must make the economy sick before making it well. This is witch doctor's mumbo-jumbo rather than an intelligent, pragmatic economic program to solve a national economic problem rapidly with a minimum of negative side effects.

For thirty years the greatest productive organization the world has ever seen, the American economy, has been forced on six occasions to perform far below its capacity by the Federal Reserve Board on the premise that it was good for the economy! As a result, our economy has lost its competitive edge and has started a slide to become a second-class economic power. Neither the double-digit inflation nor the double-digit recessions, which were caused by double-digit interest rates of a corrupt Board, were necessary. The Federal Reserve Policy of controlling inflation by one parameter—the money supply—is a simplistic solution to a very complex problem, in a very complex economy. Subjecting our national economic welfare to a policy that uses one variable, the supply of money, to control inflation is folly.

Economist Alvin H. Hansen argued against the use of interest rates to control the economy:

> Can raising the rate of interest effectively control a speculative boom? Both on the grounds of experience and general theoretical analysis, it is now widely accepted that the interest rate is a very poor instrument of control for the purpose envisaged. In a pronounced boom, it is the speculative activities which ought to be clubbed down—not the ordinary run of stable industries—an increase in the rate of interest hits the vital industries; but affects hardly at all the high-profit speculative ventures. It is not denied the credit restriction and increase in the pressure of interest rates can check the boom. But they do so by undermining the sound basis of prosperity and employment until the whole economy turns into a dangerous tailspin. (Homan, p. 250)

Milton Friedman, one of the most noted monetary authorities in the world, has been a constant critic of the Federal Reserve System, even to the point on one occasion of advocating that it be abolished. In Friedman's case, the criticism results not because of the Fed's use of monetary policies, but because of its misuse of monetary policy. As a monetarist, Friedman has been particularly critical of the Federal Reserve Board's failure to cope with inflation: "The Fed has given its heart not to controlling the quantity of money, but to controlling interest rates; something that it does not have the power to do. The result has been a failure on both parts: wide swings in both money and interest rates. These swings, too, had an inflationary bias." (Friedman and Rose, p. 255)

Friedman further commented that since World War II, the Federal Reserve has put the American economy on a roller coaster with "alternate rises and falls in inflation and decreases and increases in unemployment. Each inflationary peak and each temporary inflationary trough have been at a higher and higher level and the average level of unemployment has gradually increased." (Friedman and Rose, p. 8)

In what appears to be abject exasperation, he wrote, "In one respect the system has remained completely consistent throughout. It blames all problems on external influences beyond its control and takes credit for any and all favorable occurrences. (p. 81)

Sherman Maisel, also an internationally respected monetary authority who can be described as a pragmatic economist with leanings toward fiscal economics, made this assessment of the Board after his retirement:

> In my judgment, the techniques used over the past twenty years have tended to over-emphasize monetary policy and under-utilize fiscal and incomes policy. . . . Meanwhile, inflation has become a more pervasive and difficult problem. The Federal Reserve itself has sometimes been guilty of promising more than it can deliver through monetary policy, while minimizing the costs involved.

On a number of occasions Maisel warned that any monetary policy that depends on high interest rates as an anti-inflation tool should be used sparingly and carefully and that monetary policy had severe consequences, it must be monitored carefully, while simultaneously and sensitively evaluating the problems of inflation versus the problems of recession and unemployment. In 1973, he made this assessment of Board policy:

> There is a trade-off between idle men and a more stable value for the dollar. A conscious decision must be made as to how much unemployment and losses of output is acceptable in order to get smaller price rises. A major depression, however, with its severe losses of output and jobs and other untold hardships, is unacceptable as a primary anti-inflation weapon. Monetary policy has to ease its pressure when a crisis threatens. (Maisel, p. 14)

Even as early as 1960 President Kennedy (then senator), opposed the Fed's high interest policy on *Meet the Press* (October 16), noted that high interest rates had induced a recession but had not stopped inflation. In his talk, he indicated that he understood the Federal Reserve Cycle and the danger of stagflation.

> . . . each successive valley in the economy has ended with higher and higher rates — with the result that paradoxically high rates accompanied heavy unemployment, low production and a slack economy. (Harris, Seymour: *Economics of The Kennedy Years*, Harper & Row, 1964)

Kennedy warned the Fed against interfering with growth by restrictive monetary policies and encouraged the development of new economic tools to contend with inflation.

> As Arthur Okun of the Brookings Institute wrote recently, any anti-inflationary policy relying on balancing the budget and tightening money — as is now in place in the United States — should carry a truth-in-packaging label revealing that is probable contents are 90% production losses and job losses and only about 10% inflation saving. (*The New York Times*, Ann Critenden, August 17, 1979)

The Federal Reserve Board's anti-inflation policy could not have worked and did not work. It seriously damaged the economy and caused unnecessary periods of great personal suffering. It intentionally made the public victims of programmed recessions.

# CHAPTER 8

# *The Chairman of the Board*

> ***Practical men, who believe themselves quite exempt from any intellectual influences, are usually the slaves of some defunct economist.***
>
> ***– John Maynard Keynes***

Today America stands at a crossroads. We can deteriorate into a nation that looks back on its Golden Age or we can scale new technological heights. To move forward we must unburden ourselves from the albatross of high interest rates artificially maintained by the Federal Reserve Board.

From 1950 to 1965 the prime rate averaged 4.3%. Since Burns became chairman in 1970, the average for twelve years was 9.5%. From 1979, when Volcker became chairman, through 1982 the average was an unconscionable 15.5%! Even during three years of recession, the prime rate has averaged 15%. How can the Board justify these excessively high interest rates for this long a period while the economy suffers? They cannot. Every time interest rates decline 1% it costs the financial industry $20 billion. If they came down, as they should, another 7%, it would cost bankers $140 billion. That is the reason for high interest rates.

During the anguish of this current recession, the Rockefeller Syndicate's Volcker is trying to maintain a floor of 10% for the prime. If they succeed, imagine how high interest rates will be forced during the next period of inflation, 27, 30, or 33%?

By now the American people must be wondering how much they must sacrifice to reduce inflation a few percentage points. How much loss of production, how much unemployment, and how long must we suffer to obtain even a brief respite from inflation?

In March 1981, the inflation rate was 8.5% for the year. By the end of 1982, eighteen months later, inflation was still at an estimated annual rate of 5 to 6%, only a 2.5 to 3.5% reduction in inflation. Eighteen months of high interest and severe recession to achieve a 2.5 percent decrease in inflation is an expensive price to pay especially when some of the decrease can be attributed to external factors such as lower petroleum prices. The Board obtained that 2.5 to 3.5% decrease by forcing unemployment from 6.2% at the beginning of 1980 to 10.8% at the end of 1982. Measured in terms of human misery, it costs a 4.25% increase in unemployment to gain a 2.5 to 3.5% reduction in inflation. This means that over five million people lost their jobs. In addition, the Board forced an additional 12% of our production capacity to become idle to achieve this goal.

All creditable sources acknowledge that our current (1980–1983) recession was Volcker/Federal Reserve-created; intentinally planned by Volcker, a sophisticated economist who acted with full understanding of the consequences of his acts. We must face economic reality: programmed recessions are an integral part of the financial junta's profit strategy. The Rockefeller Syndicate wants the best of both worlds. They benefited from mammoth increases in income from the Board's programmed high interest rates. Now the Board's programmed and continuing tight money has created a bonanza of firms who are vulnerable to takeovers at bargain-basement prices. During recessions the Syndicate expands its powers, wealth, and control of the economy.

The phenomenon of Volcker is paradoxical. He has done more than any public official since Hoover to disrupt the nation's economy and our lives, yet he is looked upon as "necessary" — America's "Conscience." This image is the result of a propaganda plan to make him indispensable. His good press is led by *TIME Magazine* and echoed by the rest of the Trilateral press. Volcker has been sold to us like a mouthwash: create the need — supply the product.

How necessary and how good has Volcker been for the American public — about like mouthwash, it doesn't work and we do not need it. But you be the judge.

How good a chairman has Volcker been? Measured by his performance for the Rockefeller Syndicate, he has been terrific. Everything has gone their way. But, measured by his performance on behalf of the American people, he has been terrible. History will record that the Volcker era of super high interest rates was the apex of bureaucratic malfunctioning of an "outlaw" institution led by an illegal chairman that did violence to the American community.

Let us look at Volckers's record:

(1) He forced interest rates to record highs.

(2) He has kept interest rates higher for a longer period of time than has any previous chairman.

(3) He forced the worst recession since the Great Depression.

(4) He has prolonged the recession. He could have ended the recession in 1980 simply by lowering interest rates sufficiently, but he chose to extend the recession. Recovery may require four or five years — or the economy may never recover completely.

(5) He has caused the highest inflation peak in our history by forcing interest rates to record highs.

Measured by any legitimate criteria, Volcker is one of the worst officials to serve this nation.

On October 18, 1979, shortly after Volcker became chairman, the *New York Times* quoted him as saying, "The standard of living of the average American has to decline."

That was an ominous statement. Our lifestyle should be determined by the products of our labor in a free enterprise system, not by an autocratic bureaucrat. His policies made his prediction come true. His recession made his point.

On October 6, 1979, Volcker announced that the Board would regulate the money supply by shifting its emphasis from controlling interest rates to controlling the amount of bank reserves. Obviously this did not work effectively because a year and a half later we still had double-digit inflation, double-digit interest rates, plus a recession.

On October 17, 1979, in a statement to the Joint Economic Committee, Volcker explained his reasons for increasing the discount rate. The increase would, he claimed, lead to a "more profitable and productive America, a strong dollar, and a sense of stability and coherence in a world economy."

Three years later: Is this a more profitable and productive America with deep recession, the highest unemployment, the highest bankruptcy rate, the highest foreclosure rate, and the most farm failures since the Great Depresion?

Is there stability and coherence in the world economy that is suffering from the worst recession since World War II? We are facing the potential collapse of the international money market with defaults by Poland, Mexico, Brazil and serious economic and social problems throughout the Third World.

A strong dollar? This is the only commitment that Volcker delivered. There is a good reason: A strong dollar is necessary for David Rockefeller's ambitious international banking strategy. The fantastic increase in the international debt coupled with Volcker's high interest rates produced a bonanza for the international bankers.

This is the reason that Volcker maintained a strong dollar. In two years the value of the dollar rose 40 points on the Argus International Currency Index. This did not benefit the American public, they have paid a heavy price for the strong dollar. Our exports are too expensive for the rest of the world and foreign exporters see the American market as a gigantic dumping ground for their products.

In the fall of 1979 *The New York Times* reported that Volcker predicted that increasing interest rates would not have a significant adverse impact on jobs.

Since 1951, every peak in unemployment was preceded by a period of increasing interest rates. Chairman Volcker knew that his prediction was false. Predictably, his vigorous increase in interest rates in October 1979 resulted in a 44% increase is unemployment in a six-month period (from 5.4% to 7.8% in July 1980). Then after another round of drastic interest increases (from July 1980 to September 1981, prime increased from 11% to 20.5%), unemployment increased to 10.8%. Simply stated: Volcker doubled interest rates and forced unemployment to double. If Volcker really believed that increasing interest rates would not affect the level of unemployment, his expertise as an economist is questionable. And if he purposely misled the public, his integrity is questionable.

Should Volcker receive credit for lowering the inflation rate? Look at the real causes of the decline. First, mortgage rates declined more than 7 percentage points, a fact that is reflected in the price index as a substantial decrease in the cost of housing. However, this is a hollow achievement because the Fed forced those rates up in the first place, and no accolades are due for correcting mistakes. Second, the decline in the inflation rate represents the general weakness of the economy: panic selling of inventory, selling without profit to meet overhead, selling at a loss out of desperation, forced selling of bankrupt merchandise to meet creditors' demands, selling foreclosed homes, etc. It was the recession that forced these price reductions. Should the Fed take bows for this questionable accomplishment? Third, part of the decline in inflation is due to the "dumping" by foreign countries of their over production at low prices (oftentimes below cost) and compete unfairly with domestic productions. Fourth, part of the decline in inflation resulted from the decrease in petroleum prices. In 1982 the price of gas in many areas declined by as much as 15%. It would be far-fetched to credit the Board's tight-money policy for this deflationary serendipity.

Volcker and the Trilateral press erroneously interprets the decline in inflation as a vindication of his tight-money, high-interest policy. It is absurd to give credit to Volcker for controlling inflation when all he did was stop doing the thing that was responsible for the inflation—increasing interest rates. Volcker is like an assailant who plunges a six-inch knife into your chest, then pulls it out two inches, and says, "There, doesn't that feel better?"

Should Chairman Volcker take credit for the beginnings of a recovery? No one admits it but Reagan has outdone every Democratic president in his "priming the pump" fiscal policies. Reagan has a massive recovery program underway. In the past the Democrats' recession-recovery policy was deficit spending and tax cuts. Now we have "Mr. Conservative" with the biggest deficit spending program in history and he forced through Congress the biggest tax cut in history. (Although it was for the rich, he claimed that it would trickle down to the poor.) In addition, the Reagan Administration has generated record benefit payments.

Reagan's fiscal policies aside, the factor that has contributed significantly to the incipient recovery is the normal operation of the inventory cycle. Inventories were low so there was a cautious restocking of the shelves and retail sales were bolstered by attractive new products that induce more consumer spending. The question is: why has the recovery taken so long? Low interest rates could have cured the recession in 1980. But the recession is still with us and thirty million Americans are suffering the trauma of unemployment.

Volcker deserves no credit, he has retarded economic recovery. We have been in a recession for over three years, and Volcker has maintained the prime rate above 15%. It boggles the mind to realize that at the end of 1982, in the deepest recession since the 1930s, the prime rate remains ten times higher than the rate during the Great Depression, World War II, and the post-war period.

Volcker's continuing high interest rates poses a serious problem to recovery. If he forces the economy to remain in the recession too long it may lose its resiliency and fail to bounce back. Too long a recession will extinguish pent-up demand and precipitate a severe crisis because Reagan has exhausted most of the fiscal policies to "prime the pump."

I do not believe that Volcker was or is concerned with the problems of the American people. Volcker's subverting the chairmanship of the people's bank has cost each and every American thousands of dollars and untold suffering. The facts indicate that at all times he acts to benefit the Rockefeller Syndicate. It must be clear to every reasonable person that David Rockefeller wanted Volcker for a purpose. Volcker knew that high interest rates were inflationary, and they were a subsidy to the bankers. He was paying his obligation to his benefactors.

Volcker's demeanor as chairman is chilling. He operates like a Gengis Kahn of the money market. His policies are responsible for worldwide suffering. In times of starvation, the dollar is mightier than the sword. Yet, he shows no concern for the victims of his policy. The unemployed are merely statistics. He led the financial assault that put seven to eight million people out of work and ruined the lives of countless others. Bankruptcies, foreclosures, and farm failures are just the price of inflation. He performs his role as the junta's hit man with such indifference as to make the mafia seem like sentimentalists. Perhaps he has insulated himself from the stark reality that he is responsible for the tragic course of events in our economy and the world economy.

A major problem in American government today is the "revolving door" which allows government officials to switch between private industry and government. In the Department of Defense high-ranking admirals and generals become affiliated with defense industries and receive high salaries for procurement or lobbying. This interplay between private industry and government officials inevitably develops into a conflict of interest that is costly to the government. Government officials realize that "friendly relations" with prospective employers while on government payrolls will earn them attractive salaries in private industry. By granting favors to the right people they use their government position as a springboard for a lucrative salary in private industries.

Many officials have left the Fed to go into high paying positions in the financial industry. But our concern is one particular man. Paul Volcker has already been through "the revolving door" on a number of occasions. As stated before, between stints at the Treasury and the Federal Reserve he worked as personal aide for David Rockefeller at Chase Manhattan Bank on two occasions. *Time* magazine reports that when Volcker leaves the Fed (if he does) and goes to work for the private sector (it was rumored that he would become President or Chairman of Chase Manhattan Bank) he would receive compensation of at least $500,000 a year. (*Time*, January 1, 1983, p. 41) Since Volcker was not worth $500,000 prior to becoming chairman of the Fed, why has the experience of being the public's chief banker now made him worth that much to the industry he supervised? There is an explanation. It is Rockefeller's payment for a job well done while he was chairman. It must concern us that the man who controls our national bank will be worth ten times what the government has paid him, once he leaves that position. There is no doubting that David Rockefeller and other bankers are highly pleased with Volcker's performance as chairman and are eager to show their appreciation. The fact that Paul Volcker is worth $500,000 a year demonstrates his success in promoting the profit strategy of the Rockefeller Syndicate. This is a case of putting a fox in charge of the hen house-and the fox getting fat.

President Reagan, like Carter before him, is not in control of the economic policy of our nation. Reagan argues that he is not responsible for the economic troubles that pervade America today, and he is right. Our current recession is a product of the Federal Reserve policy. But Reagan is culpable because he has done nothing to pressure the Fed to significantly lower interest rates and cure the recession. Until he does, Reaganomics is only a bubble floating on the fickle policies of the Federal Reserve Board.

Reagan has successfully carried his battle with Congress to the people. If he took the issue of interest rates to the people, he could force Volcker to reduce them significantly. Instead he has embraced Volcker and his high interest policies.

Does it not seem curious that Reagan would allow a Carter appointee to dominate his domestic economic policy? He sneered at everything about Carter except Volcker – Why? Simple, accepting Volcker and his policies was one of the conditions of Rockefeller-trilateral support for his presidency. Reagan understands that you do not tamper with the income of the Syndicate without getting hurt. For insurance, the backup man, Vice President Bush, is a Trilateralist member. If Reagan reappoints Volcker, it will indicate that he is firmly in their pocket.

We have paid a terrible price by tolerating the Federal Reserve Board's control over interest rates: the corruption of our presidency, the subversion of our monetary system, and the continuous economic instability that has caused a severe decline of our economy. By serving a covert master, the Volcker Board has defrauded the American public. In 1981, the average middle-class family paid a penalty of over $8,000 in excess interest illegally levied on the American economy by the Federal Reserve Board. In addition, the Federal Reserve recession costs the public $200 to $300 billion a year in lost production ($3,600–$5,000 per family). In their game of financial extortion, the American public was the "mark," victimized by its own national bank.

Volcker exploited the sting to the hilt. Using inflation as the diversion, in one year the Volcker Board ripped off $300 billion from the public. The scam was so artfully done that the American people acted as though Volcker had done them a favor. Like all con games, he made it seem natural, as though it was supposed to happen to us – the consequence of an economic malfunctioning of the free enterprise system.

But it was not our free enterprise system that caused the problem. It was not our economy that malfunctioned. It was not the ineptness of American businessmen. It was not the unbridled greed of consumers that caused the problem. It was a subverted Federal Reserve Board with autocratic powers operating in secrecy that orchestrated the rip-off by following the profit strategy of David Rockefeller and his financial Syndicate.

We cannot reclaim our government until we make it impossible for the "Rockefellers" et al. to control the Federal Reserve Bank. The profits to the Rockefeller Syndicate is so great that spending $100 to $200 million to control the Federal Reserve Board, the President, and intimidate Congress, is peanuts. Corruption pays big dividends, the annual windfall profits from controlling the Fed amounts to hundreds of billions of dollars.

Rockefeller and his international financial elite plan for power and profit by treating the world as a chess board and the heads of states as pawns. Laws, human rights, fair play, political parties, public trust, and national allegiance have no meaning in their game. And we, the people, are the spoils of victory.

Congressman Lawrence P. McDonald wrote in November 1975: "No one has dared reveal the most vital part of the Rockefeller story: that the Rockefellers and their allies have, for at least 50 years, been following a plan to use their economic power to gain political power of first America, and then the rest of the world." (*Rockefeller File*, Gary Allen)

Sensationalism? Alarmist? Or a Paul Revere's cry to defend our democracy and our pocketbook – you be the Judge.

# CHAPTER 9

# *The National Debt*

The rapid growth of our national debt from $425 billion in 1972 to $1 trillion plus in 1982, was the direct consequence of Federal Reserve Board policy. The inflated interest rates that the government was forced to pay and the decrease in revenue resulting from two deliberate recessions explains the meteoric increases in federal debt. It began with the appointment of Trilateralist Arthur Burns to Chairman of the Fed in 1970, and accelerated since 1979 by fellow Trilateralist Chairman Paul Volcker.

The following table shows the relationship between the budget deficits and the interest paid by government. If there were no interest payments, there would be no deficits.

| *YEAR* | *DEFICIT* | *INTEREST PAID* |
|---|---|---|
| 1972 | $ 23,373 (Billions) | $ 20,563 (Billions) |
| 1973 | 14,849 | 22,782 |
| 1974 | 4,688 | 28,032 |
| 1975 | 45,154 | 30,911 |
| 1976 | 66,413 | 34,511 |
| adj. | 12,945 | 7,216 |
| 1977 | 44,948 | 38,009 |
| 1978 | 48,807 | 43,966 |
| 1979 | 27,694 | 52,556 |
| 1980 | 59,563 | 64,504 |
| 1981 | 57,932 | 82,537 |
| 1982 | 98,578* | 99,537* |
| Total | $504,955 | $524,682 |

*Estimates S/B 504.955

If we add up the deficits from 1972 to 1982, they amount to $505 billion. The total interest paid during that period was $524 billion. Now, let us recalculate the growth of the national debt using a 2% rate (from 1929 to 1960, U.S. short-term Treasury bills averaged less than 2% interest). The interest cost to the government from 1972 to 1982 would have totaled only $93.5 billion, saving the government $431.5 billion. The national debt would have increased a mere $73.5 billion during those eleven years.

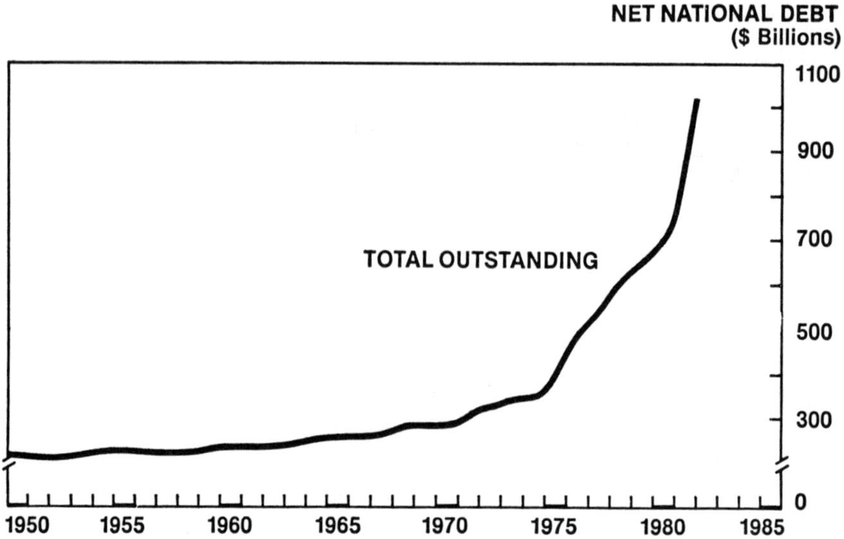


**THE NATIONAL DEBT**

The National Debt doubled in the last ten years, the result of Federal Reserve Board's high interest rates and two programmed recessions. A double blow to budgets that forced the Debt above $1 trillion.

| | | BILLION DOLLARS |
|---|---|---|
| Increase in federal debt (1972-1982) | | $505 |
| Actual interest paid this period | $525 | |
| Interest that should have been paid (at 2%) | 92.5 | |
| Debt caused by the Fed's excessive interest rates | | $431.5 |
| National debt increase if the Fed had *not* raised interest rates | | $ 73.5 |

By using high interest rates as a monetary policy to fight inflation, the Federal Reserve Board created the major part of our national debt.

The reader can comprehend the impact of high interest rates on our current budget deficits with the following comparison: In the 1945 budget, $3.70 out of every $100 was paid for interest (one out of every $27): in 1981, 14.40 was paid (one out of every $7). The interest portion of the budget is four times greater today than in 1945. This is why we hear so much about cutting the budget. Other budget items must be cut to make room for the additional 10% interest portion.

Economists may disagree on almost everything, but across the board they do agree that the recessions of 1975 and 1980 were caused by the high interest rates of Burns and Volcker. Because they cut deeply into government revenues, these recessions were a major cause of the federal deficits that Volcker now deplores.

Citing the recession of 1970, the *Congressional Quarterly* observed that "The Budget in 1971 and 1972 would have been in balance if the economy had been at full output and employment. The actual deficits represented the loss of Federal revenues caused by economic performance below potential." ("Congress The Nation 1971-1972," Vol. III, *Congressional Quarterly, Inc.*)

In the case of the 1975 recession, the revenue receipts dropped dramatically and did not recover until mid-1978. President Carter's economists estimated that because of the Fed's 1975 recession, $200 billion income per year was lost. This represented a loss in government revenue in 1975 of approximately $40 billion. Since the deficit was $45 billion, the loss of $40 billion revenue explains most of the deficit.

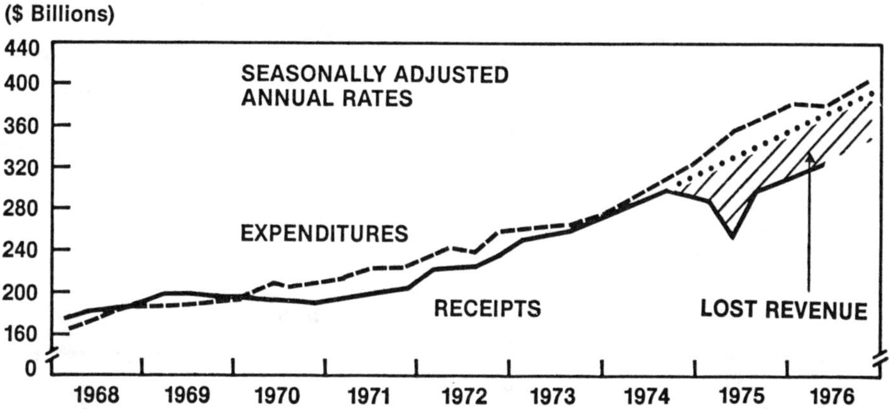


This chart shows how dramatically the Federal Reserve recession of 1975 reduced government revenue. As the dotted line projection shows, there would have been little if any deficit if the Fed had not forced the recession on the economy.

1980 was a re-run. Because of the severity of the 1980–? recession, the loss of projected revenue may amount to $100 billion to $200 billion per year. The result will be massive deficits.

If the Fed had not increased interest rates in a fruitless effort to control inflation and had not precipitated two recessions, there would have been a significant budget surplus!

The following chart shows the relationship between the increase in interest rates and the size of federal deficits. As interest rates increased, the size of the deficit increased accordingly. Three-month Treasury bills increased fourfold (1972-1982) and the size of the budget deficits increased by the same magnitude.

The interest payment on the federal debt cost each family $1,875.00. It should have been less than $200.00. The Board's high interest rates costs us dearly.

The following chart shows an amazing correlation between the growth of the federal debt and the increase in interest rates. The national debt increased as the Federal Reserve Board increased interest rates.

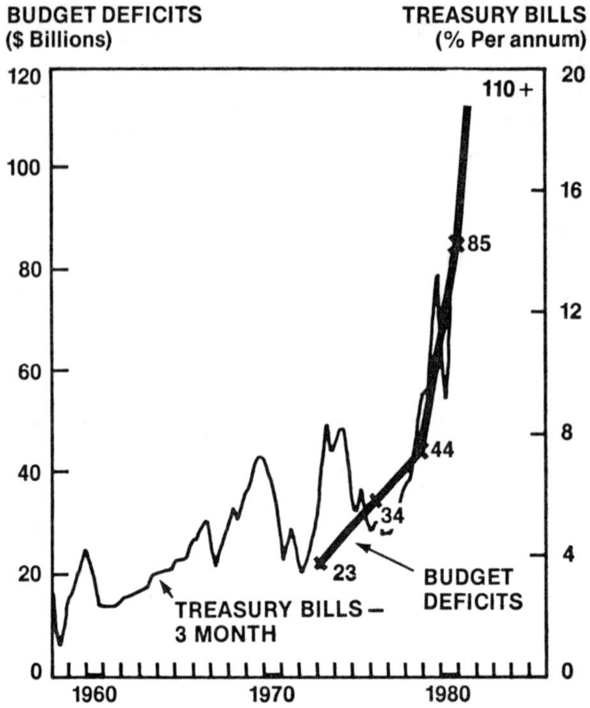


**RELATIONSHIP OF BUDGET DEFICITS AND INCREASING INTEREST RATES**
This chart demonstrates the correlation between budget deficits and the increases in interest rates. As the Federal Reserve Board increases interest rates, it also increases budget deficits.

The phenomenal acceleration of the national debt appeared planned, a consequence of Burns and Volcker's violent increase in interest rates. Each deficit represents a guaranteed income to the money-lenders. It is axiomatic that a large federal debt at the highest possible interest rate increases the Rockefeller Syndicate's income.

Congress intended that the Federal Reserve Board assist the Treasury in funding the debt of government. It was anticipated that the Fed would act as a fiduciary agent for the government providing funds at the lowest possible rate of interest. The Board used the Accord of 1951 to progressively ignore its mandatory agency to the government. Now the Board sets interest rates as high as possible and forces the government to pay them irrespective of how outrageous they may be. Recent interest rates for the U.S. government exceeded 15%, a ridiculously high rate to pay for U.S. securities.

It is an economic distortion that the strongest economic power with the most sophisticated and highly organized money market in history should be paying our current astronomical rates of interest.

By any measure of proper underwriting based on risk, our government's interest rate should be about 1 to 2.5% and the cost of servicing the debt

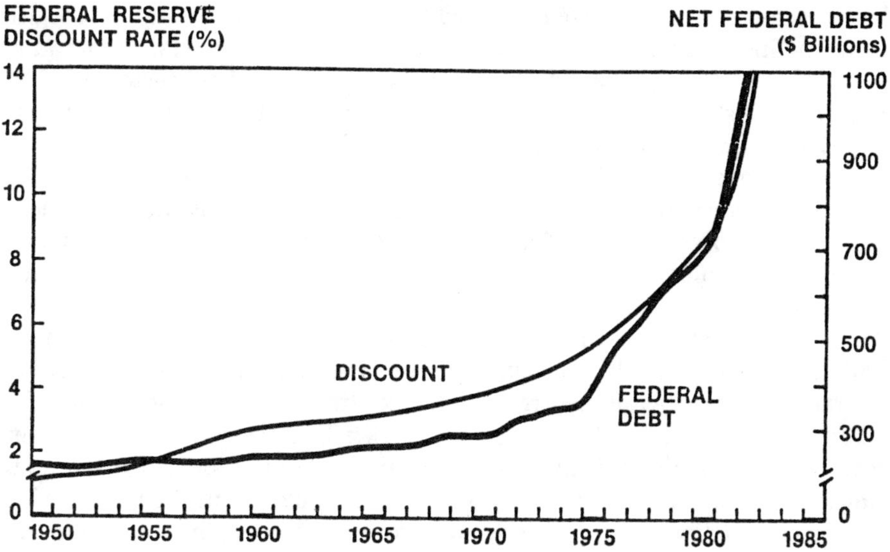


**THE GROWTH OF THE NATIONAL DEBT RELATED TO THE INCREASES IN THE DISCOUNT RATE**

This chart demonstrates that the growth of the National Debt is the result of the Fed's increase in interest rates. For the last five years, the debt has grown in porportion to increases in the Discount rate. The surge in interest rates was a primary cause of doubling the national debt.

should be less than $30 billion annually. Countries of less financial quality than the United States are paying significantly less interest. Japan is paying 5%; Switzerland, 4%. Before the birth of Christ, the Greek city-states financed their governments at 7%; in the sixteenth century, Genoa's exploration of the New World was financed at 2%; and, England in the eighteenth and nineteenth centuries financed government projects at 3.5%. For two hundred years British Government Bonds were low, relatively steady, and well below 5% except for two brief periods.

Government Bonds (sometimes referred to as "govt's") issued by the American Government are the best securities ever offered in the history of finance. A claim against the American Government is a claim against all of us — the total wealth and resources of the wealthiest political entity that has ever existed. Because of America's economic strength, our monetary system is the value standard for the rest of the world. The value of gold is quoted in dollars; international commerce is conducted in dollars; the value of all currencies of the world are quoted in dollars; the monetary reserves of many countries are established in dollars. A promise to pay by the American Government is the best secured financial instrument in the world, and the most risk-free. Therefore, it should command a very low interest rate.

Why are we paying outrageous rates of interest? Why is our national debt increasing so rapidly? Senator Goldwater explained the reason: "International bankers make money by extending credit to governments. The greater the debt of the political state, the larger the interest return to the lenders." (Goldwater, *With No Apologies*) The American government is the best customer of the banking industry because of our large national debt. In 1972 the government paid 20 billion in interest. After a decade of Burns and Volcker we paid 5.5 times that amount. In 1983, the government will pay the bankers et al., $112.5 billion in interest! By increasing the debt, the bankers increase their income. If our federal debt were paid off tomorrow, there would be panic in the financial world, $112+ billion of income would disappear and bank assets would diminish dramatically.

The Rockefeller Syndicate profits handsomely on income from the national debt. Predictably, Volcker increased the national debt with high interest rates and a programmed recession. Spouting his Bre'r Rabbit duplicity, "Don't throw me to the high deficits," Volcker lulls the people into believing that he is against the deficits. Yet, he has the power to reduce the deficits by simply lowering interest rates, why does he not do it? Simple, he would reduce interest throughout the domestic economy and ultimately throughout the world. This would be a serious blow to the Syndicate's profits.

> Not long ago, Federal Reserve Board Chairman Paul Volcker delivered another of his finger-wagging lectures. Unless the Reagan Administration trims its $100 billion+ federal deficit this year, Volcker warned, Americans can expect no relief from staggering interest rates. Coming from Volcker, I am afraid, such talk is as welcome as a lecture on home security from a burglar. (Howard J. Samuels, *Los Angeles Times,* February 5, 1982)

High interest rates attract the international banker and investors to the American "give-away." The Fed has created a plush haven for foreign funds. In 1970, the foreign ownership of the federal debt was miniscule, around $10 billion; by 1980, foreign ownership approximated $150 billion and cost our government about $18 billion in interest. Measured by the quality of the security of U.S. bonds, the payments to foreign investors should have been less than $3 billion. But, because of the policies of the Federal Reserve, the American government will enrich foreign investors with a premium of $15 billion in interest payments and will cost every American family $300 in taxes.

Most foreign investments in the United States are handled by gigantic banks such as Chase Manhattan, an international bank with international allegiance and commitments. International banks do what is prudent and profitable for them; they have no national commitment.

The people of the United States have a national commitment: the national debt. The question is how can we reduce or eliminate it?

I have a plan.

If Congress would create a commission that would levy a tax on credit transactions by the same magnitude as the Fed's increases in interest, we could pay the Fed deb off in a few years.

The program would work like this: when the Federal Reserve Board wants to discourage demand and investment, instead of increasing interest rates it would notify the commission, which would levy a tax on credit at the same rate. The effect on the demand is the same, but to the Treasury there is a big difference. The revenue would accrue to the U.S. government and the revenue is large. In 1981 it would have amounted to over $300 billion! With this extra income, the debt would be paid off at a rapid rate.

Sounds far fetched? This is what the Federal Reserve Board has been doing for years. As a government bureau, it has levied a tax on all credit transactions, but the banks collect and keep the tax—over a trillion dollars in the last decade. What would your reaction be if the government allowed merchants to keep the sales tax they charge?

Controlling our national debt is a difficult, almost impossible task. It brings up the question: Why do we have a national debt? The government could pay its bills each year simply by issuing currency. There would be no debt, and there would be no interest to pay on the debt. But the monetary experts reasoned that it would put too much money in circulation, and government must be penalized for its capricious spending by paying interest on its deficits. Instead of issuing cash, the government issues government bonds. In reality, the government has issued currency, but a special kind of currency called "Government Securities" that bear interest.

The creation of government debt is simple. When the United States Treasury needs 1 billion in dollars, a billion dollars of U.S. bonds are printed and the Federal Reserve Bank is notified, who in turn advises the Bureau of Engraving to print $1 billion Federal Reserve notes (dollar bills). The Treasury delivers the United States bonds to the Federal Reserve, which then issues the Federal Reserve notes to the Treasury. By this simply process, the Federal Reserve Board has created $1 billion in Government Securities for its portfolio, and a $1 billion debt for the American people on which they must pay interest. If you analyze this sequence carefully, you will realize that the same amount of money is printed, but the government ends up owing the Federal Reserve Bank and its assignees $1 billion, plus interest.

This exchange between Congressman Wright Patman (Democrat-Texas) and Marriner S. Eccles (Chairman of the Federal Reserve Board) may shed some light on the process.

Mr. Patman: "How did you get the money to buy these $2 billion of government bonds?"

Mr. Eccles: "We created it."

Mr. Patman: "Out of what?"

Mr. Eccles: "Out of the *right* to create credit money."

The point should be made that high deficits are not exclusively from Democratic administrations. The Republicans are contributing more than their share. Senator Goldwater noted, "During the six years of Nixon, the increase in the Federal debt was more than twice what it had been in the eight Kennedy-

Johnson years." (Goldwater, p. 273) Reagan's vociferous attack on high deficits made him the man who carried the big ax. But, when he became president, Reagan introduced us to the largest deficits in history.

Banks hold a significant portion of their portfolio in Government Securities. The risk is nonexistent and the return is excellent. As the Federal Reserve Board tightens the money supply and forces the interest rates up, government securities become more attractive to banks. Commercial banks' investment in the United States Treasury notes and bills had been constant since 1950, leaped almost fourfold from 1974 to 1981 as the interest rates on the three-month Treasury bills rose from 4 to 15%.

Increasing the dollar's international value has dominated the policy of the Federal Reserve Board since Volcker became chairman. It was part of the Trilateral plan: the spectacular plunge of David Rockefeller into international banking. In a short time he became the most important international banker in the world. He adroitly used the strength of the dollar to force other currencies off the international market. By keeping U.S. interest rates high with the help of fellow Trilateralist Paul Volcker, the dollar became the international medium of exchange. Almost all international transactions took place in dollars. The buying and selling of gold, petroleum, and other currencies; and Rockefeller controlled the supply of dollars.

The high interest rates generated by Volcker on the American market echoed throughout the world. The high interest Chase Manhattan Bank charged other governments was the result of the high rates Volcker forced on the American Government. David Rockefeller and other international bankers, many of whom were Trilateralists, loaned $600 billion to Third World countries at horrendously high interest rates. The income to international bankers from loans to Third World countries has increased more than 18-fold since 1972.

Our government was used by David Rockefeller. Volcker increased domestic interest rates to enhance the profitability of the Rockefeller-Trilateral international banking operation. They parlayed high American interest rates into a $100 billion annual income at the expense of our economy and poverty-ridden Third World countries.

Secondly, most of the $600 billion loans were made without proper caution. Example, Mexico was extended $80 billion in loans. To pay the interest on its debt, the Mexican government must pay more than the profits it receives from its developing oil industry. Servicing the loan may be too heavy a burden on a weak Mexican economy. There is a real and imminent danger of default en masse on Third World loans. This is a threat to the stability of the American banking system because the top ten banks have loaned many times their net worth on questionable foreign loans.

The problem for the American people and government is that we find it necessary to underwrite those loans. Our government intervened in the loans to Poland, Brazil, and Mexico. Others are sure to follow. Consider the impact on the American government and banking systems if the debtor nations decided in unison to dishonor their debts. The United States government may bear the burden of avoiding defaults on many of these loans. Our national debt may increase considerably to save the mistakes of greedy international bankers. "The international debt crisis can be boiled down to a problem of four countries, ten U.S. banks and the Federal Reserve," Salomon Brothers' Bruce Brittain observed.

"If things got out of hand," explains a U.S. administration official, "and inflation grew as the result of Federal Reserve action, everyone in effect would be paying a share. It would be a tax to save the system." (*Time,* January 10, 1983)

In summary, the high interest rate policy of the Fed's Board plus the loss of income from programmed recessions are responsible for our high budget deficits and the skyrocketing of the national debt. If the Fed had not intervened, we would have experienced a net decrease in the national debt during the last decade!

Future deficits could be avoided if the Board lowered interest rates immediately. The interest portion of the budget would be reduced to the $30 billion level, and the economy would recover and increase its level of activity and generate healthy revenues for all levels of government.

There is something the Fed should do immediately. It holds over $125 billion of the national debt, paid for with our money. It collects interest on that debt. The Board should return to the Treasury its entire portfolio of Government Securities and cancel that much of the national debt. It would save us about $12 billion in interest payments per year.

# CHAPTER 10

## *"The Economy Is In A Hell Of A Mess"*

***Ronald Reagan, November 20, 1982***

For once, we have heard a politician speak the truth. Of course, he didn't intend for us to hear it, but it is the truth, an honest appraisal of the culmination of twelve years of mismanagement of our economy by the Federal Reserve Board.

The following story recently appeared in the newspaper:

> They are sleeping on a riverbank in San Jose. Underneath freeway bridges in Florida. In tents pitched outside Houston. In parks throughout the country.
>
> They are this winter's homeless, in numbers not seen for half a century. Rescue missions are pressed beyond limits. City warehouses and church basements are open for overnight guests. And vacationers share camp grounds with those who have nowhere else to go.
>
> Some are the derelicts and bag ladies chronically on the streets. But a third or more have tumbled from the middle-class, many taking their families with them. (Scott Kraft, The Associated Press, January 1983)

Is this really happening in America, the land of democracy and free private enterprise? For two centuries we have prided ourselves on our great democracy and the superiority of our free private enterprise system where everyone has an equal right under law to be as successful as his talents allow. This is the American dream, an equal chance for upward mobility. What has happened to it?

Howard J. Samuels, a member of the Johnson Administration, made these comments recently:

> Our monetary policy has created the current fiscal crisis. Not only the 1980 and 1981 recessions were created by an onset of monetary tightness and soaring interest rates; the recessions of 1970–1971 and 1974–1975 were, too. For virtually the entire past twelve years we have been either in the trough of recession or climbing out of one, with barely any normal times in between. There is no doubt that the problems in the American economy fit squarely on the shoulders of the Federal Reserve Board.

> The cumulative effect of thirteen years of economic self-strangulation has undermined our economy and worsened every national problem. It has impoverished our state and local governments, damaging the essential infrastructure of public facilities on which our economy depends. It has wasted our human capital in needless unemployment. It has reduced real income and fostered increases in crime. Most important, it has weakened our stature as the leader of the West. (Los Angeles *Times*, February 5, 1982)

He went on to say that the underlying causes of inflation have been worsened by the Fed's policy and noted that the current easing of inflation is due not to the Fed's monetary policy but to other factors such as the oil glut and rich harvests. Mr. Samuels makes a strong argument that one of the major causes of long-term inflation is falling productivity. The Fed's high interest rates have discouraged investments that were necessary to increase industrial productivity. In addition to the short-run inflation that the Board causes directly with increased interest rates, the high rates contribute to a long-term inflationary trend by reducing productivity and the ability of labor to produce commodities at a lower cost per unit.

In a recent article *Time* magazine reported the results of a study by Time's Board of Economists. Paul Eckstein, a Harvard Professor and Chairman of the Data Resource Consulting Firm, said, the economy is probably in the worst shape that it has been for nearly half a century. Walter Heller, Professor of Economics at Minnesota and Ex-Chairman of the Council of the Economic Advisors under Presidents Kennedy and Johnson, said, "This is the deepest and most dangerous recession of the post-war period." Rimmer D. Vries, economist for Morgan Guaranty Trust Company, stated flatly, "We are sitting here in the midst of a major depression." Heller cited statistics indicating that about 20% of all households are directly affected by unemployment and that another 40% feel threatened by mounting layoffs.

"Most ominous, the U.S. slump is only part of a world-wide pattern of malaise. In the European Community, more than 11 million people, or 10.3% of the work force, are unemployed. Developing nations from Africa and Asia to Latin America are staggering under a $626 billion foreign debt load. A string of near defaults on loans to Mexico, Argentina and now Brazil has rocked the international monetary system." (*Time,* December 27, 1982)

This is the "Volcker Recession." The current worldwide recession was planned by the Federal Reserve Board and sold to the public as necessary to stop inflation. It resulted from enormous increases in interest rates purposely inflicted upon the nation by the Volcker Board.

The recession is the worst since the Great Depression. Unemployment is above 10.8% with thirteen million people unemployed, while more than 2.5 million have become discouraged and have stopped looking for work. And more than thirty million people will be displaced by unemployment in 1983 and suffer the hardships of financial uncertainty. These statistics, however, do not tell the real story of the employment problem because services are not hit as hard as manufacturing. Unemployment is higher in industrial areas such as

Michigan, where unemployment is 16%. Minorities suffer most, with 18% of all blacks unemployed and with 50% of all black youths unemployed. Unemployment is also much higher among young job seekers, and while it is difficult to ascertain accurately, it is approximately 20%. While unemployment is at its highest rate in forty-two years, plant capacity is at a low point, with almost one third idle, and factories closing daily. Foreclosures on homes have set a record. The Mortgage Bankers' Association estimated recently that 0.55% of the nation's twenty-seven million home loans were in the process of foreclosure and that another 5.35%, or 1.5 million homes, were past due. The foreclosure rate is an index of the trauma of the American family in times of recession. An index of the trauma of small business is the bankruptcy rate. Dunn and Bradstreet Corporation recently reported that bankruptcies are the highest since the depression of 1933. By September 1982, bankruptcies had reached 17,052. Even major corporations have felt the impact, and it is not unusual to hear of a billion dollar loss, for example, of National Harvestor, Ford Motor Company, and other major corporations.

One loss that cannot be expressed in dollars is the abandonment of humanistic goals—an important dimension of the quality of American life, i.e., concern and compassion for the aged, the infirm, the destitute, and those whose accidents of birth have rendered them incapable of adjusting to a competitive economic society. Government's commitment to human decency is being sacrificed to enable the government to pay the high interest rates decreed by the Federal Reserve Board.

There has been a tremendous increase in human suffering as the consequence of the economic stress induced by the Board's policy. B.M. Brenner, a Johns Hopkins sociologist, was quoted recently as saying that 35,000 to 36,000 people die for each percentage point increase in the unemployment rate. This means that since Mr. Volcker has been chairman of the Fed, 175,000 people have died because of his policies. Volcker's monetary policy has been more catastrophic than a nuclear plant meltdown!

But the effect of unemployment is not simply limited to a higher mortality rate. It is related to the increase in child abuse—one of the most tragic of human experiences. The number of child-abuse cases has climbed dramatically, and a relationship between the increase in child-abuse cases and the rate of unemployment has been documented. In Oregon alone, child-abuse cases have jumped 41%. One social worker commented that most parents try to avoid abusing their offspring, but under severe stress, they regress, lose control, and take their financial frustration out on their children. Economic stress is further evidenced by the fact that 62% of the mental health centers polled in 1982 reported an increase in the number of clients who needed help because of problems related to unemployment. Seventy-four percent of the family service centers that responded to a survey indicated that the number of family violence cases has increased, a surge that was generally blamed on unemployment and sour economic conditions.

Professor Brenner's studies showed some other appalling relations between unemployment and personal problems. The study indicated that a 1%

increase in unemployment leads to 4.1% more suicides, 3.4% more state mental hospital admissions, 4% more state prison admissions, 5.7% more murders, 1.9% more deaths from cirrhosis of the liver, 1.9% more deaths from heart and kidney diseases, and 1.9% more deaths of all kinds.

This sounds like the casualty list of a Civil War; it represents the human side of the money-index that Volcker and the Board chose to ignore. This litany of human misery and degradation is the result of greed and financial gluttony. Our common sense must tell us that this is not a legitimate by-product of a prudent economic policy. I wonder what the ultimate cost in human misery must be to convince Volcker and the Board that this recession is too high a price to pay for a temporary lull in inflation?

Not only have the needy suffered. The Volcker policies of the Federal Reserve Board are an attack on the middle-class, the bulwark of the American economic system. They are the vast majority of borrowers, who buy homes, finance cars, and finance their businesses. They must pay the major portion of the Fed's high interest rates.

It is unfortunate that the middle-class must bear the burden for the care of the poor, but it is unconscionable for them to bear the burden of a scam to enrich the wealthy.

An alarming example of how the Board has legislated social policy is the redistribution of wealth by increasing interest rates. The personal "interest income" portion of "national income" increased from 3.1% in 1948 to 13% in 1981. This means that during this period, the share of "personal income" received by interest recipients quadrupled. Lending money at higher interest rates does not contribute to productivity; therefore, during this period interest recipients unjustly received a windfall. The 13% represents a 10% parasitic drain on other sectors of the economy. "Capital Incomes" declined: "Proprietors Income" declined by 50%; and "Personal Dividend Income" declined by 40%. The distressing message is that those who were actively participating in the economic process by owning a business or by investing in "risks" would have been better off it they had sat back and collected interest without making any contributions to the economy. For every six dollars paid for a man's labor in 1981, one dollar was paid to an interest recipient for remaining idle!

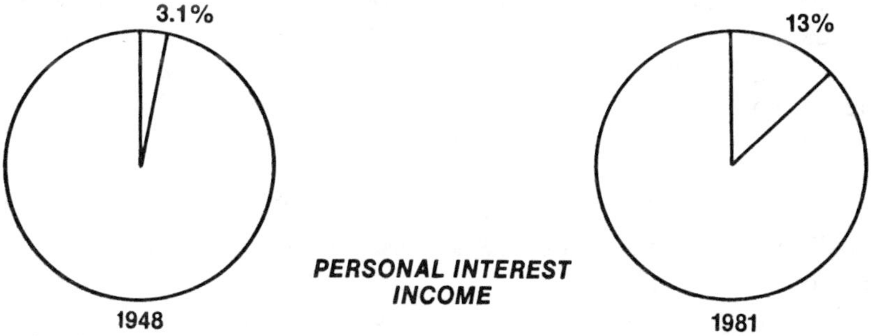


This chart shows the dramatic increase in personal interest income. In 1981, it was 4.5 times larger than it had been in 1948. (Economic Report of the President, 1982, p. 255)

In addition to redistributing the nation's income, the Board's policies are responsible for the concentration of corporate economic power in the last decade. It would be inconceivable for Congress to enact legislation that encouraged the concentration of economic power into super corporations. There would be a tremendous outcry if they attempted such a move, but the Federal Reserve Board has accomplished this without any public hearings or legislative due process.

The inordinate growth of conglomerates has been encouraged by the monetary policies of the Fed. When money is tight, there is more competition among borrowers for funds, and banks make loans to clients with strong qualifications. Since the strongest qualification is massive financial size, the financial wizards who control American corporations use acquisitions and mergers to enhance their bargaining power on the financial market. As a result, in today's market financial qualifications are more important to corporate survival than are productivity and efficiency. The urge-to-merge pressure is indicated by the fact that "$100 million mergers" in 1980 were consummated at nine times the 1975 rate. (George Brockway, *Washington Monthly,* June 1980, p. 52)

It is regretable that in recent years many viable small and medium businesses have succumbed to the necessity to merge because they cannot finance their operations. They found that the terms of financing were so onerous that to accept them would be to operate the business for the benefit of the bank. The only other alternative was to merge with a financially powerful corporation.

Since the Federal Reserve Board's policy discriminates against and penalizes the small borrowers, financial cliques have developed between large corporations and large banks. Giant conglomerates, multinational corporations, and fair-haired friends of the banking elite will receive adequate funds in times of tight money. But if you are the average bankable entrepreneur, the chances are that you will receive insufficient financing, if any. The purse strings of America are bank-controlled. When money is tight, the banks determine who will survive and who will not. The clique of wealthy, privileged people who direct the operations of super corporations is always privy to a bountiful supply of money. As a consequence, they have a significant competitive advantage.

The challenge on the American economic scene today is to guess not what the economy will do but what the Federal Reserve Board will do. Neither businessmen nor consumers can intelligently plan their economic future when subjected to volatile interest rate increases. From January 1980 to January 1981, the prime interest rate increased six points from 13.86 to 19.97%, a 43% increase in one year.

A consumer, who saves to buy a new car or home, may find that when he is qualified to make the purchase, interest rates have forced the monthly payments out of reach.

Prudent business planning is negated by fluctuations in interest rates. Profit margins disappear or become losses. A firm's solvency is often threatened, not by poor management but by tight-money and high-interest rates.

Uncertainty is particularly treacherous for the businessman who needs considerable lead time to plan new factories, or re-tool old ones. Extended business planning can best be undertaken during times of relative economic stability. Interest rates are an important parameter in business planning. How can a businessman plan rationally when he is subject to a spastic money market? Will the Fed raise interest rates to 6, 12, 22, or 30%? There are no objective criteria, it depends on the subjective decisions of the Board.

The Board's legacy to the 1980s is an obsolescent, underemployed industrial system that has lost its world leadership at a time when a new technological revolution is spawning. America's challenge is to aggressively and vigorously move into the twenty-first century industrialization of robots, computers, and sophisticated control systems. To achieve this will require liberal financing and low interest rates. This is the American industrial imperative: an adequate supply of money at low, steady interest rates of 2 to 4%. The question is will Volcker allow the nation the benefit of low interest rates?

If there is any doubt about Volcker's autocracy, reflect on his power over the presidency, the Congress, and our individual lives for the last three years. Think of the difficulty of lowering interest rates in the depths of a recession when there was no rational reason for them to remain so high. Congressmen demand that Volcker reduce interest rates, but interest rates remain where Chairman Volcker wants them. It is Volcker's decision, not the President's, not Congress', and not the public's.

The profit strategy of the Rockefeller Syndicate has become our national monetary policy and that, Mr. President, is why "the economy is in a hell of a mess," the victim of financial gluttony, the kind defined by Harvard anthropologist Melvin Konner: "The dangerous gluttons are the ones who blindly stuff themselves with land, with money, with power, with other people's happiness and other people's safety." (Melvin Konner, "The Roots of Gluttony," *Science Digest,* September 1982, p. 32)

# CHAPTER 11

# *A Return To Economic Sanity*

***The economy has paid heavily to ease the inflation nightmares of the independent monetary authorities. Using tight monetary policy, presumably to stop inflation, while the economy was actually stagnating, is positive proof that something is basically wrong with the theory and practices of Federal Reserve monetary policy. It indicates that Federal Reserve policy has arrived at the point where it is willing to make the economy pay a calamitous price for a dubious safeguard.***

***Congressman Wright Patman***
***Congressional Record***

While there are no easy answers to economic problems, there are some that are better than others. The Federal Reserve Board had one economic tool that they repeatedly used against inflation: "Tight-money, high-interest rates." Every time it was used since 1951, it increased inflation and then produced a recession. If this is the best way to control inflation, capitalism has an achilles heel and is doomed to constant underproduction, underemployment and long term inflation—pervasive stagflation.*

On six occasions the Board bet our money on that policy. Six times we have lost. There must be a better way. There must be some economic tools that can rescue us from the uncertainty of the roller-coaster economics of the Federal Reserve Cycle. And there are.

I have outlined two programs that control inflation with low interest rates. The first is a program of forcing interest rates down and keeping them low and steady by monetary policy. I do not recommend this policy except for emergencies, but I have included it to demonstrate that if the Fed really wants to control inflation by limiting the supply of money, this is the best way to do it.

I endorse a combination of policies outlined in paragraphs 2 and 3. Policy 2 uses credit requirements to control demand and investments when necessary. Policy 3 is a return to a free money market and allows interest rates to decline by competition and keeps them low and steady with an elastic money supply.

A word of caution: there are no static answers to serious economic problems. A free economy is innovative and dynamic. As soon as a policy is announced, the economy begins to adjust to the policy in a manner that assimilates and neutralizes it. In time it will be necessary to replace the policies suggested with new pragmatic policies that will fit the circumstances and problems of the future, but for the present, they offer a fresh and hopeful beginning.

1. Manage the growth of the money supply from the supply side by discouraging banks from creating credit. Since banks are responsible for creating too much credit, it is more effective and certainly more equitable if the Board attacked the problems of curtailing credit at the source by discouraging banks from making loans. If the prime rates were lowered to 2%, banks would make fewer loans because they could only make "riskless" loans. In this range of interest rates, every fractional decrease exerts a restraint on credit creation. Lowering interest rates is a very effective way to restrict the supply of money.

If the Board had used low instead of high interest rates for the last 30 years, the results would have been spectacularly beneficial to the economy, the public, and the government. Low interest rates are a better inflation fighter because they are deflationary and do not add to the cost of goods and services. The American family would have saved thousands of dollars in interest payments. The government would have saved hundreds of billions of dollars in interest payments, and our national debt would be manageable or non-existent.

There is no question that the Board has the ability to maintain low interest rates. After all, that is the reason that the Federal Reserve Bank was created.

> The period from late 1939 to 1951 was as violent and catastrophic as any in the entire history of the United States. At the beginning of this period, millions were still unemployed from the Great Depression. A short time later, we were shooting away $250 million every day on the battlefield. Then the war ended and we reconverted to a peacetime economy with tremendous pent-up purchasing power and inflation. Then came the Korean conflict.
>
> Yet, during this entire period of economic stress and turmoil the interest rate on long-term Government bonds never exceeded 2½%. And these bonds never sold below par. This proves that the Fed can restrain higher interest rates, when and if it wants to. The Fed has the ability to set the interest rate at 2½% and keep it there. (Wright Patman, *Congressional Record*)

There was a period in our history when programmed low interest rates produced spectacular results. This was the Roosevelt program during World War II and the post-war years. To facilitate the financing of World War II, Roosevelt ordered the Federal Reserve Board to assist the Treasury in providing ample funds at a low, steady rate of interest. He accomplished this objective by requiring the Federal Reserve System to "peg" the Government Security Market at 2.5% yield. The program was doubly successful: it supplied adequate money to the government to fight an extremely expensive war, and it facilitated the conversion to a peacetime economy at a low, steady rate of interest. During this period, other interest rates, such as Prime Commercial Paper, remained low. During the War, the prime rate remained at 1.5%. From 1939 to 1949, the prime rate increased only 0.5%.

The Roosevelt policy of adequate money at a constant, low rate of interest was an effective way to control long-term inflation. World War II and its heavy deficit spending, post-war recovery, conversion to a peacetime economy, and the Korean action were all accomplished without the intervention or meddling of the Federal Reserve Board. And even though the inevitable post-war inflation was sharp and lasted about two and one-half years, it ran its course. After the inflation subsided in 1948, the money supply diminished normally, and a stable price level (less than a 1.8% annual inflation rate) was maintained for almost *twenty years.* The economy grew rapidly, and the United States became the most impressive economic phenomenon in the history of the world, a standard for other nations to emulate and envy.

If low interest rates are so terrific, why didn't the Board use them as an anti-inflationary policy? Simple, they have one flaw: low interest rates would have denied the financial industry the windfall income that high interest rates generate.

There is another reason that the Fed's Board was not interested in using a "low interest rate policy." The "tight-money policy" confers great power on the Board: power to control the economy, the presidency, the Congress, and our lives. By tightening the nation's purse strings the Board becomes an economic Czar, it can force millions of people into the ranks of the unemployed, cause a recession, defeat a president or veto the acts of Congress. If the Board were to make credit plentiful, they would become just another service agency.

2. A policy of manipulating consumer and investment credit controls (minimum down payments, terms of loans, etc.) to control excess demand. It is a relatively simple matter to control demand by manipulating the terms for credit. For example, to slow down the demand for homes, automobiles, or appliances, rapidly and effectively, increase the percent of down payment and shorten the period of loan repayment (i.e., increasing the monthly payments). This will decrease demand significantly. If mortgage rates were lowered to 7%, millions of potential home buyers would enter the market. This mass demand would inflate the prices of houses because of a limited supply. By increasing down payments from 10 to 20%, about 50% of the potential purchasers could not buy. If the down payment was increased to 30%, relatively few potential buyers would have enough money for the down payment. Conversely, if supply exceeds demand, reducing the down payment brings additional purchasers into the market.

Most credit-card purchases can be controlled by increasing the minimum monthly payment schedule. By requiring full payment at the end of every month, the creation of credit through credit cards can be eliminated. Credit controls are effective, immediate, and specific. To enforce the regulations, a national credit board may be needed. Compare this program with the Fed's control of consumer credit with high interest rates:

(A) The Fed discouraged the purchase of homes by making interest rates so high that purchasers can not afford the monthly payments. However, if a purchaser buys a home, he is obligated to a high interest rate long-term mortgage that may require him to pay for his home five times. On a $100,000 mortgage at 18%, the buyer would pay approximately $500,000 during the term of the loan. If interest rates were 5 to 7%, and demand was discouraged by increasing down payments, the buyer would save almost $300,000!

(B) The Fed's policy is counter-productive; as interest rates start to rise, it induces potential purchasers to rush into buying before rates become too high.

(C) Credit controls work immediately and can be modified quickly to achieve the desired results. The Fed's high interest policy works erratically and slowly.

(D) The credit control program is specific in its application. For example, if the inflationary pressure is only on automobile prices, credit restraints can be applied only to that industry. Interest rate increases effect the whole economy and inflate the price of all commodities; yet they may be ineffective controlling demand in the industry that needs restraint.

(E) High interest rates are a damaging, inequitable financial burden on the public. In 1981 excess interest payments averaged $5,000 per family, and an unearned windfall to the bankers of $320 billion.

(F) The high-interest policy of the Fed has serious undesirable effects that distort the free market economy, creating extensive economic instability that ultimately leads to recessions in the short run and stagflation in the long run.

Credit controls work effectively to control the national level of investments in factories and equipment by requiring that banks demand that investors place a specified percentage of their cash into the loan fund. The ratio can vary from 0 to 100% to fit the economic circumstances and the inflation threat. In the past, the Fed's Board has used a similar method to control speculative inflation on the stock market. They call it margin requirements.

3. The third policy for inflation control is to require the Fed to provide the economy with low and steady interest rates with an "elastic currency" that expands with the needs of the economy and let the market determine the interest rate. This is similar to the first alternative since both programs are based on low interest rates. The difference is that in the Roosevelt program, interest rates were kept low by edict. This is the preferred plan. I am suggesting that interest rates will remain low and steady by the operation of a free money market with the Fed standing ready to provide reserves necessary to service an expanding economy as the Federal Reserve Act mandated. This policy is simply integrating the banking system into the free enterprise system by removing the Board's monopolistic power to tighten the money supply. It recognizes the government's obligation to "assure an adequate currency to transact the business of the nation." Professor O.M.W. Sprague, Harvard University economist, wrote in the *Quarterly Journal of Economics,* February 1914:

> The primary purpose of the Federal Reserve Act is to make sure that there will always be an available supply of money and credit in this country to meet unusual banking requirements.

The Federal Reserve was created by Congress to provide the economy with a neutral money supply—that which expands and contracts according to the needs of the economy.

The American money market is the best organized with the lowest risk factor in history. Under the conditions of a free market, interest rates should be near historical lows, reflecting the cost to orginate and service credit, a risk factor and a fair profit. Until it is proven that a free money market does not work, the amount of credit and interest rates should be determined by the free money market mechanism. If intervention by the Fed is necessary, it should be initiated by elected officials, suggested by the president and approved by Congress, and then on behalf of the public, not the bankers.

With an adequate supply of credit, we will benefit from low and steady interest rates which are a prerequisite for a stable economy. Let's evaluate the effects of low interest rates on our economy:

(A) Low rates are noninflationary;

(B) Low rates, set by a free market, are a legitimate price for the use of money—high interest rates are a monopolistic rip-off that rewards a nonproductive sector of the economy;

(C) Credit is the life blood of our system, and low interest would encourage competition and allow a freer flow of goods and services. High interest rates restricts economic activity;

(D) Low interest rates are more conducive to greater productivity and a more efficient economy. On a free money market, products and services compete fairly and generally the most efficiently produced product will gain greater acceptance. On the other hand, tight-money and high-interest rates encourage quasi-monopoly situations where survival depends on the ability to obtain financing. If a manufacturer has an inside track on financing, his product will survive whether it is the best or not.

High interest rates discourage productivity in another way. A 1% gain in productivity is insignificant when it can be wiped out by a 6% increase in interest cost. Productivity becomes relatively inconsequential when the cost of money dictates price.

(E) Low interest rates encourage investment in plants and equipment. This stabilizes prices by improving productivity. High interest rates encourage investments in sterile money instruments, such as Money Market Accounts, and denies capital investments in the modernization of industry and improved industrial productivity.

(F) Balancing the budget would become a possibility. The extraordinarily high interest rates the government has had to pay to service the federal debt has made high deficits inevitable. The net result would be to slow or reverse the growth of the federal debt.

(G) The American people would be wealthier and our economy healthier. We would not be subjected to the uncertainty that high interest creates. We would free ourselves from the cyclical gyrations of the Federal Reserve Cycle, thus enabling us to emerge from our crippling stagflation.

(H) The social benefits are too numerous to mention; economic democracy would be restored.

(I) We would be able to compete on the international market with vigor and unfettered American ingenuity.

To implement this program of low interest rates and "easy" credit, a word of caution is in order. Inflation potential is built into the Fed's policy, a type of kinetic inflation. Even though we are in a recession, if an economic upturn occurs, inflation will return. The Fed's tight-money policy is similar to price controls; when eased, inflation inevitably starts in. However, it can be ameliorated, but a transition period is necessary. One suggestion is to schedule the reduction of interest rates in such a manner as to reward those who wait to buy or invest. The reward is automatic. For example, if an investor plans to build a factory and interest rates are 9%, if he waits nine months to a year he would have an advantage of a 5% rate. The schedule of reduction of interest rates can be adjusted to fit the circumstances. Concurrently, credit controls should be applied as an auxiliary deterrent to spending and investing. Through experience, we may discover other economic tools to assist during the transition period.

We have suffered so long from 10, 15, or even 25% interest rates that we have forgotten the advantages of 1, 3, or 5% rates. We have become accustomed to high interest rates because the money changers led by Paul Volcker are brainwashing us into believing that 10% interest rates are normal. This is an abomination. Interest rates today should be the lowest in history. The U.S. government should pay no more than 2% for its financing. Prime rate should range from 2 to 4%; mortages from 4 to 6%, and consumer credit up to 7%.

*Stagflation has predominated our economy since the recession of 1970. Unemployment has averaged 6.9% and the trend is upward.

# CHAPTER 12

# *A Plan For Economic Democracy*

Our country is in a crisis, the victim of the Federal Reserve Board's high interest rates. Our free enterprise system is stagnant; our competitive edge has been lost; and we are becoming a second-class economic power. Industry sputters, a victim of long-term capital shortages. Almost all Americans have suffered. The monetary assault of the Federal Reserve Board is an attack on all classes, particularly the middle class, for they pay the price for high interest rates. Unfortunately, the needs of the poor, the feeble, the handicapped, and the aged are sacrificed to pay the inflated interest on the national debt.

The threat to the American economy is not from the left or the right, but from within the system itself. Capitalism is failing because the "Money Changers" became too powerful and converted our National Bank into a private money machine. It happened because David Rockefeller's financial strategy was brilliant: he made the right moves and recruited the right cast of characters who played their parts with ruthless dedication. It happened because the Federal Reserve Bank was corruptable and was easily controlled. It happened because the American public behaved like lambs, passively and naively allowing the Federal Reserve Board to chart our economic destiny. Congress was intimidated, acted willy-nilly, and ignored the issues when it should have demanded bare-knuckle debates on Board policy. Presidents cooperated, and the public followed like sheep to the shearing, led by the Pied Piper of Money.

But the American people are the ultimate democratic force, and if we understand the problem and public opinion solidifies, we are capable of achieving impressive goals. When the people understood the futility of the Vietnam War and expressed their convictions, it soon ended. When the people of California were fed up with excessive property taxes and would not take them any more, they passed Proposition 13. Now there is a new public move afoot in America to establish a sense of reality in a crazy world of atomic bombs. Ground Zero is an organization formed to send a message to Congress and the president. Ground Zero received considerable attention from our "leaders" in the last national election and as a result the nuclear freeze issue is now on the floor of Congress.

Our economic survival is at stake, we must be effective! At issue is the survival of our democracy and the American way of life. If the American people have the resolve and the will to fight, we shall prevail, and the outcome will be a strong nation, ready and able to enter the 21st century with renewed economic strength and dedication.

We must regain control of the presidency and the Congress for our democracy to survive. Every voter must be made aware that any candidate having any connection with the Trilateral Commission or David Rockefeller should be voted down. David Rockefeller and the Trilateralist have vested interest directly opposed to the public. Remember, if they retain high interest rates they collect them – you pay them. Republican or Democrat makes no difference if the candidate is in Rockefeller's pocket.

This book was written as a call to action: to arouse public interest by educating people to what has been happening and to provide a viable economic program. Because we cannot expect any help from a neutered Congress, we must do the job ourselves. Our priorities must be clear and specific.

First, the Federal Reserve Board must be limited to function as a central bank. Its self-designated authority to tighten the money supply must be revoked, and its mandate to supply an adequate supply of credit for the needs of American government, commerce, industry, and consumers must be reaffirmed.

Second, we must put Americans back to work by immediately increasing production and employment with steady low interest rates and other incentives if necessary.

Third, we must develop a program to alleviate the suffering of the victims of the Fed's tight-money and recession policy. Many families suffered financial hardships because they were forced to accept high interest rates when financing their homes, businesses, and farms. They are now facing the loss of everything they own. Because this recession was intentionally created by the Volcker Board, these people are in a real sense the victims of government action, sacrificed in the Fed's fraudelent war on inflation. The government has done nothing to alleviate their hardships and protect them from the unfair consequences of its own policy.

I suggest the following program to help victimized businessmen, farmers, and homeowners save their property. Congress should vote a moratorium on any farm, business, or home mortgage that bears interest rates higher than 8%, with the stipulation that the borrower-mortgagee pay interest of only 8% during the moratorium and that they have the right to refinance at lower interest rates without penalty. Even Hammurabi's Code protected the farmer against "unreasonable" foreclosures caused by acts of nature. We should protect our farmers against "unreasonable" acts of the Federal Reserve Board, Today's loan and mortgage defaults are as much the fault of the lender as of the borrower, perhaps more so. In many cases, farmers who were especially vulnerable to the Fed's tight-money policy were forced to accept loans at ridiculously high interest rates, and the bankers took advantage of them. Senator Talmadge reported that in 1980, over 50% of farm loans were denied because of local shortages of funds. The farmers under financial duress had no alternatives but to accept loans at scandalous rates. Many farmers could not meet payments because the Fed programmed our current recession that forced farm income down. In some places in the Midwest, defaults on farm loans were as high as 25%. The farmers, businessmen, and homeowners are victims of government actions. They should receive government protection from foreclosure to survive the catastrophies brought upon them by the ruthless monetary policy of the Fed.

Fourth, we must develop a program to encourage savings. The residents of Peking save proportionately more per worker than do the residents of Los Angeles because the Communist government rewards the savers with a variety of benefits. We should adopt their capitalistic incentive program and make it attractive for all Americans to save. Enacting tax advantages is one method. For instance, instead of taxing savings income, Congress should create a tax preference by not taxing savings (it may be necessary to set an upper limit) or by giving tax deductions for yearly net increases in savings by individuals. A schedule could be devised that rewarded each $1,000 net yearly/increase in savings with a $100 to $200 tax credit. Whatever method we use, encouraging the habit of family saving is important to the long-term health of the economy.

Fifth, we must develop an intelligent inflation policy. A maturing economy such as ours will suffer periods of inflation, particularly when extraneous factors such as wars, OPEC, and environmental reform force higher prices on the economy. In such cases it is wise to allow the marketplace to adjust freely to the inflation. The best long-term anti-inflation policy is to keep the cost of money low enough to encourage investments in the production of goods and services. A new technological revolution is taking place and the American economy must retool to supply 21st century products. Short-run inflation can be moderated with credit controls that are not inflationary and do not financially penalize purchasers. (Such policies have additional advantages—they encourage national savings.)

It must be pointed out that no economic reform is forever. As soon as a reform is enacted, the nature of the system is such that forces will find ways to neutralize its effectiveness. No economic policy can be used consistently for an indefinite period. We must make adjustments to solve today's problems and in a few years see what additional adjustments must be made to update policy.

The transgressions of Trilateral Commission members must be scrutinized with a view towards correcting the abuse of our monetary system and instituting legal or criminal action against them whenever warranted. To conduct this investigation, I suggest that a blue-ribbon citizens' committee be appointed to look into the operation of the Federal Reserve Bank during the last twelve years.

Specifically, this panel should probe the activities of David Rockefeller, Arthur Burns, Paul Volcker, and other members of the Trilateral Commission to determine the extent that conflict of interest influenced the performance of the Federal Reserve Board. In San Diego County, California, a county fair official was indicted and convicted for accepting favors from a concessionaire at the fair. Shouldn't the same standards apply to David Rockefeller and his Syndicate?

Supreme Court Justice Abe Fortas was forced to resign in 1969 because of a conflict of interest for accepting $20,000 from the Wolfson Foundation of Louis E. Wolfson, who was a convicted financier. There exists today a more damaging and corrupt conflict of interest between Paul Volcker, chairman of the Fed, and David Rockefeller, chairman of the Trilateral Commission. Rockefeller's vested interest is antithetical to the public interest. Ask yourself this question: why was David Rockefeller interested in who became chairman of the Fed? The answer is obvious: everytime the Fed increases interest rates his Syndicate's income increases proportionately—the higher the interest rate, the higher their income. Volcker was the strongest advocate of high interest rates in the Fed and David Rockefeller wanted a chairman who would increase the Syndicate's income.

The four years of the Capon Presidency are a national disgrace. The Carter presidency should be probed extensively. As was previously pointed out, the Trilateralists groomed and elected Jimmy Carter to the highest office of our land and he appointed twenty-five trilateralists to key government posts. He appointed four ineligible, illegal, unqualified members to the Federal Reserve Board. Each of these appointments should be investigated, especially Paul Volcker's appointment as chairman.

The investigators should demand an explanation of why Carter allowed the Shah to come to the United States when he knew the problems that would result.

The most expedient manner of inquiry is for the Congress of the United States to appoint a special investigator with the power of subpoena to investigate the Federal Reserve Board. However, it is doubtful that an incisive, objective inquiry will be undertaken by Congress. David Rockefeller and the Trilateral Commission has intimidated Senators and Congressmen. That is why I suggest that a public board of inquiry made up of courageous blue-ribbon citizens dedicated to America's welfare undertake the probe.

My next recommendation is for a class-action suit on behalf of the American public be filed against the Federal Reserve Board seeking (1) a writ of injunction restraining the Federal Reserve Board from any further acts; (2) a claim of damages on behalf of the public for $1 trillion; (3) the removal of all unqualified board members; and (4) a complete audit of the Federal Reserve System. The basis of the action that the Board is illegally constituted; it has acted beyond its authority; and it has failed to fulfill its legal mandate.

The law specifically states, "In selecting the members of this Board, not more than one of whom shall be selected from any one Federal Reserve District." (Section 10, Federal Reserve Act) Four of the current seven Board members come from one district: Richmond, Virginia, Federal Reserve District (Washington, D.C.). The law further states, "The President shall have due regard to a fair representation of the financial, agricultural, and commercial interest and geographical divisions of the country." There is no fair representation—no members represent commerce or agriculture. The majority of the Board are bureaucrats from within the Federal Reserve System, the Treasury, or the Department of the Budget.

Only the East Coast was represented on the Carter Board. Eighty percent of the geographical divisions of the country had no representation on a board that was making decisions that critically affected their lives. The eligibility requirements for Board members were enacted into law to insure that the Federal Reserve Board would be a public Board run by legitimate public members. Carter not only ignored these fundamental public safeguards but removed the Board from public control and delivered it to David Rockefeller.

Furthermore, the Federal Reserve Board has acted beyond its legal authorization. There is no mandate in the Federal Reserve Act granting the Board the power to arbitrarily restrict credit. Every guideline in the law that alludes to the supply of money refers to an "adequate money supply:" the Board and the Federal Open Market Committee "shall be governed with a view to accommodate commerce and business . . ."

In view of the power and the resources of the Trilateralists, we cannot be optimistic about the results of the legal challenge, but we must try.

We must demand and obtain a complete and thorough audit of the Federal Reserve System. The Federal Reserve Board has mismanaged our money in secrecy. The Federal Reserve System has never been audited in its entirety by an outside agency. The Board denies us, the public, the right to inspect their records to determine for ourselves their integrity and the quality of their public service. The Board members maintain that they alone have the right to judge themselves. There is something drastically wrong. The Board controls trillions of our dollars but denies us the right to audit what has happened to it! As citizens we have a duty to be suspicious about the integrity of the Board in view of their Rockefeller-Trilateral connection, their public-be-damned attitude, and their subservience to the Syndicate's profit strategy. It is our prerogative, our right, and our duty to determine for ourselves how good or how bad the Board has performed.

Because powerful financial interests have many ways to award corrupt public officials who serve their purpose, every current and future member of the Federal Reserve Board should be audited before and after serving in office. Corrupters pay their colleagues in government service before they serve (as in the case of the Rockefellers paying Henry Kissinger $50,000) or after their service by appointing them to important boards and committees (appointed Ex-Chairman of the Fed William McChesney Martin to trustee of Rockefeller Brothers Fund and appointed Ex-Chairman of the Fed Arthur Burns to the Trilaterial Commission). By giving them positions at inflated salaries in the private sectors (appointing Kissinger Chairman of Chase's international committee and director of Rockefeller Fund). By rewarding them with academic grants for research and appointments to lucrative positions in foundations and think tanks (appointed Arthur Burns Chairman of the committee to fight inflation). The public must make it illegal for Federal Reserve Board members to compromise their public obligation and integrity by accepting favors or gratuities from the financial industry before, during, and after their service with the Fed. The Federal Reserve Bank must be insulated from the influence and corruption of the industry it regulates.

My third recommendation is that for the protection of the American public, we must establish a National Usury Law by an amendment to the Constitution. The exact rates are debatable. However, I suggest for maximums: federal government, 2%; prime rate, 4%; mortgages, 6%; consumer credit, 7%. A constitutional amendment that specifies maximum interest rates will remove a major temptation for the self-serving financial industry to control our central bank by corrupting Congress and the presidency. The incorporation of a usury article in the Constitution is a key reform in my proposals. This usury proposal strikes a powerful blow at the banking elite because it destroys their money machine. Needless to say, they will attack it with vigor.

My fourth recommendation to achieve this goal and persue necessary legal action, I suggest that we form a citizen's Committee for Economic Democracy. Because the federal government does not allow a referendum, it will be the committee's job to develop strategy to enact the amendment. One powerful device to demonstrate public approval is a national petition signed by all who are opposed to, or have been victimized by, high interest rates. A mammoth briefcase lunch-pail march on Federal Reserve headquarters is an effective way to solidify public opinion and gain national attention.

My fifth recommendation is to restructure our constitutional government. I propose a constitutional amendment creating an Economic Congress for the United States. If democracy and the free enterprise system are to survive in the United States, we must end the autocracy of powerful men and strip the Federal Reserve Board of its power over our money supply. Policy decisions that affect the nation's economy should be the responsibility of a diversified congress elected by the people and charged with these priorities: (1) optimum economic production and employment; (2) an improving standard of living; and (3) low and steady interest rates by providing a "neutral" money supply for the economic welfare of all citizens. This Economic Congress should have the power to legislate and administrate credit controls to provide a reasonably stable price level.

The scope of legislation has grown too broad for Congress. Matters of abortion, public works, and international affairs preclude consideration of matters of economic and monetary policy. For almost two decades, Congress has deferred its responsibility for the nation's economic well-being to the Federal Reserve Board. The timidity with which Congress approaches the Board and chairman in matters that affect the public interest is embarrassing evidence of how much Congress fears a confrontation with the Chairman. The Board and its lobby obviously has tremendous influence in the halls of Congress.

Therefore, if we are to accept the challenge to insure stable economic prosperity for the future, we must create an Economic Congress by a constitutional amendment. The purpose and function of an economic congress would be to act as a legislative body dealing with the problems and policies of the currency system, the Treasury, and the federal debt.

This economic congress should consist of a minimum of one hundred and fifty geographically dispersed public members, none of whom belong to the financial industry, are associated with the financial industry, or receive compensation from the financial industry in any manner (except interest, normal fees, and "like payments"). The members will serve four-year staggered terms and cannot be reelected. They cannot accept contributions from the financial sector in any form. An additional ten members will be chosen from the financial community. The financial community cannot participate in the election of public members, only in the election of financial members. The Economic Congress will make policy concerning the operation of the Treasury and the Federal Reserve System. It will be charged with controlling the magnitude of the national debt, servicing the debt, retiring the debt, and encouraging balanced budgets. The Federal Reserve Board will be demoted to serve as technical body to implement policies of the Economic Congress.

This is a far-reaching proposal with a major impact on our basic constitutional government. At the time of the framing of the Constitution, the authors could not have possibly anticipated the complex economic structure that has developed in the United States. Now is the time to establish a separate legislative body to democratically deal with the economic problems of the nation. This proposal will necessitate a great deal of study, criticism, and evaluation to measure its workability. Now is the time for vigorous economic debate to improve the American system. Perhaps this book will supply an impetus to that debate. If my proposals are viable, they will survive.

We should anticipate that the junta will develop a strategy to counter this attack on their power structure. Their tactics will be varied, potent, and possibly vicious. They have access to the propaganda power of the Trilateral media, government officials, professional men of repute (and ill repute), economists, and moral assassins. The tactic that concerns me most is that after two years of extending the recession, Volcker may develop a social conscious in response to this and other attacks and resign or end the recession.

Volcker has the option to allow the economy to recover and enhance Reagan's reelectability by simply lowering interest rates sufficiently. This would lull us back into our complacency. That is the danger. Even though this recession abates and an economic upturn begins, the underlying problem still exists and will threaten our future. The problem is the control of our government by the financial junta. On that score we cannot compromise. The government and the Federal Reserve Bank must be returned to the people. We must be wary and not allow a temporary "economic bone" or change in personnel to deter us from that goal. A return to a high interest policy will once again cause economic disaster. Wright Patman made a cogent argument for low, steady interest rates when he commented that if we could finance World War II and maintain full employment at 2.5% interest, we certainly should be able to finance peace and prosperity at 2.5%. Patman is right and we could if the Fed would allow it.

When I look at my country today, I see it suffering from open wounds, like a trusting child maimed by a butcher who passed himself off as a surgeon. Almost all Americans are hurting today, victims of crimes of greed, personal immorality, and public corruption. The legacy of the leaders of the Federal Reserve Bank whom we trusted, is a tormented America suffering extreme economic stress.

I hope that the American public will do everything possible to bring the corrupt economic saboteurs to the bar of justice for their yellow collar crimes. And I hope that whatever God they serve will touch them and make them aware of the vastness of their inhumanity to their fellow citizens. Besides the economic damage that they have inflicted, they are responsible for unnecessary deaths, suicides, child beatings, mental illness, broken families, and the misery of a despondent nation. This much I know—their earthly reward cannot compensate them for the toll they have exacted from the American people by exploiting the public's trust. We hoped for a better way of life, but they had a deceitful, double-dealing plan to profit from the misery of the American people.

Now is the time for the American public to proclaim their commitment to economic democracy and to demand fair and equal opportunity under the laws of the land. We will not tolerate the Board's favoritism and parasitic interest rates any longer. The message must be strong and to the point: throw the nefarious money changers out.

Our pride, our individual welfare, and the preservation of our democracy dictate that we declare our independence and serve notice on the financial junta: Whatever our economic status—poor, middle-class, or wealthy—we will no longer be their economic serfs.

# PART II

# *Introduction*

The Federal Reserve Board occupies a unique position in our society. It is held in greater esteem than the Supreme Court. Perhaps the American public holds it in awe because it conducts its business one level higher than the Papacy with the attitude that they must answer only to God. (Ex-Chairman Arthur Burns said that he looked to God for his rewards, not the people.)

Does the Fed deserve our respect? As the chapter on the Fed's *Track Record* will demonstrate, the answer is a definite *NO.* The Federal Reserve has an infamous record of public service.

Since 1951 the Fed attacked inflation as though it were the plague. Our entire economy has suffered wave after wave of high interest rates and a succession of devastating recessions, justified as necessary to fight inflation—millions of jobs, homes, farms and businesses were sacrificed to save us from inflation. But what about inflation? Is it an economic boogey man that ravages the economy and the public? The chapter on *Inflation* puts the issue in perspective with some interesting conclusions.

The Fed's war on inflation has created havoc in our economy. Uncertainty dominates the market place. The Board's repeated use of high interest rates has created an economic cycle with periods of inflation preceding periods of recession: The Federal Reserve Cycle. The cycle is out of control. The magnitudes of the cycles are increasing and the Board does not have a solution. The cycle has forced the economy into a long-term structural maladjustment called stagflation. Stagflation is the most serious economic problem in the United States today. It is a cancer that smothers the vitality of the American economy. The chapter *The Federal Reserve Cycle* explains the cycle and its threat to the world economy.

What are high interest rates? What are low interest rates? After reading the chapter *History of Interest Rates,* you will be able to decide for yourself. This chapter will educate you to the abuse of interest rates by the Federal Reserve Board.

Some of the material covered in the following chapters were cited in Part I. For the sake of clarity, continuity and the readers convenience they are repeated when helpful.

# CHAPTER 13

# *Inflation*

> ***The unexpected upsurge of inflation during the past decade, and particularly during the last two years, has led many educated laymen to be skeptical of anything economists say about inflation.***
>
> *Sommers, Albert T. Ed.*
> **Answers to the Inflation and Recession:**
> *The Conference Board, NY 1976,*
> *Robert J. Gordon, p. 127*

"Inflation is simply a condition of generally rising prices. Like sin, everybody is against it." (Maisel, Sherman, p. 11) There are many definitions of inflation: the devaluation of the currency (dollar), erosion of purchasing power, increasing price level, too many dollars chasing too few goods, devaluation of the dollar in relation to gold, reckless increase in the money supply. Each definition describes a facet of inflation and may be useful in understanding the process of how our money buys less today than it did yesterday. The major cause of our long-term inflation is the Federal Reserve Board's monetary policies.

The word inflation conjures up images of economic horrors—disaster from fixed income, the shrinking dollar, wheel barrels full of money, eroding faith in the dollar.

The truth of the matter is that inflation per se is neither good nor bad. It is the magnitude of the inflation and how it is distributed through the economy that is good or bad. The majority of America's wealth—our land's value—was created by inflation. Without inflation, Chase Manhattan Bank would express the value of its Manhattan holdings as a "handful of beads." Downtown Los Angeles sold for a dollar an acre when the American settlers first arrived, and much of America's farmland was simply given to farmers. But today, thanks to inflation, Chase Manhattan's real estate holdings are an impressive part of its net worth; millions can be borrowed against Los Angeles real estate; and the farmer can sell that free land for a lot of money. The balance sheets of America are bulging with wealth created by inflation. Inflation has been such an integral part of America's economic success that an appropos metaphor for its achievement is that America has pulled itself up by its own inflationary boot straps.

Deflation destroys wealth. A deflation in the value of real estate causes the net worth of the nation to decline. Value of investments decline, home equity evaporates, and economic chaos can result. Deflation is dangerous. It occurred in the United States when the Federal Reserve Board caused the Agricultural Depression of 1921-1922, which diminished the value of the land so drastically that it did not recover for twenty years. The Great Depression of the 1930s was responsible for a damaging devaluation of the wealth of the nation and chaos did occur.

Most American homeowners can relate to the appreciation of real estate since the net worth of most families is the result of the appreciation of their home. If a family lives in their home for twenty years, they benefit from inflation in two ways. First, their monthly payments are based on the purchase price. In relative terms, their economic rent diminishes as the price level of homes inflates. Secondly, when a family sells the house, they realize a profit due to inflation. Simply stated, net worth is enhanced by inflation if we own stocks, real estate, real goods, and certain types of collectibles.

Inflation benefits most forms of investments and encourages risk taking. Since World War II, many investors made investments because they believed that their probability of success was increased because of the added value accrued from inflation.

The distribution of the effects of inflation among the public is a critical measure of its acceptability. For example, if the effects of inflation were distributed evenly throughout the population, there would be a minimum of economic inequity. Unfortunately, inflation tends to hurt the poor and lower-middle class the most because they own few real goods.

The poor and those on fixed incomes suffer the severest because they own few permanent possessions and spend a greater portion of their meager income for consumables. This burden is ameliorated if wages keep pace with inflation. As a general rule, inflation is benign if it is distributed throughout the economy and is relatively steady at a reasonable rate.

The magnitude of inflation is the most critical determinant of the acceptability of inflation. Obviously, double-digit inflation is unacceptable. Some economists have suggested that a predictable percentage per year of inflation is acceptable and desirable, while others have tried to create national income models that cranked in various inflation rates to determine the optimum rate of inflation for our economy. There is no realistic method to determine an optimum rate of inflation, because of the uncontrollable and unpredictable extraneous factors that affect price levels.

Inflation is inevitable since the many forces that accelerate inflation are the result of the course of events: war, international cartels, monopolies, environmental laws, depleting natural resources.

The "real" economic cost of extracting our raw material is increasing and will continue to increase. We have to drill deeper and search harder for petroleum. We must mine and process marginal ores at increasing "real" costs. Because deposits of resources are distant from the point of use, we must pay more to transport them further under more difficult conditions. (Example: Alaskan oil and pipeline.)

Government regulations are sometimes inflationary. An example is the inflationary impact that the environmentalist movement had on the price level in America. Milton Friedman has estimated that it cost the American economy billions of dollars. Inflation is inescapable in a maturing economy as more people vie for food, land, and other natural resources. While this looks like a simple deduction from an obvious set of conditions, it is not that pat. Technology modifies our resource patterns so that population growth is not always inflationary. Each resource pattern must be analyzed in terms of many complex factors to deduce the relationship between population growth and inflation. For example, our present population could not possibly survive on our present farmland using the technology of the 1800s. With the impact of farm technology in the 1920s and 1930s, the real cost of food declined, and food became a deflator of the price level, while in the early 1970s the increasing cost of food became an inflationary force.

Generally, as economies mature inflation becomes a fact of life. The economists have their own pet categories for inflation. We will look at three: (1) push-pull; (2) hyper; and (3) monetary.

(1) "Cost-push, demand-pull" inflation is the result of the interplay of factors within the economy. An example of "cost-push" is the economists' favorite whipping boy: wages. The rationale is that when the price of labor is forced up by labor unions, the additional cost is passed on to the consumer in higher prices. From 1950 to 1964, the inflation rate averaged 1.3% per year. Labor was typically singled out as the inflationary culprit. Generally, this was not true since wage increases during this period were related to increases in labor productivity. Since workers produced more goods per unit of labor, their wage demands were generally based on the added increment of production per hour. If the relation between increases in productivity and increase in wage is proportional, the wage increase does not elicit an inflationary response.

"Demand-pull" results where there is a strong demand for a commodity or commodities with a limited supply with the result that the excess demands bids up the price.

(2) The inflation that frightens all of us is called hyper-inflation. This is a true monetary inflation, caused and nurtured by monetary policy. This is the image of inflation that causes panic. It is a condition where inflation depreciates the value of money so rapidly that it is difficult, if not impossible, for an economy to function. The classic example of such economic chaos is the inflation that swept Germany after World War I.

The circumstances of the German inflation from the end of World War I to 1923 differed in almost all significant parameters from the inflation recently experienced in the United States. Gunter Schmolders commented on the German experience in the Academy of Political Science. "Many of the characteristic factors and institutions associated with inflation today appear quite different from those in Germany after World War I."

Two distinctive characteristics of the German Inflation were: (1) It was fed by printing too much money, and (2) it occurred in a country that distrusted the government and the quality of its money. It should be noted that hyper-inflation is caused by *printing money* and not by expanding credit.

There is a significant difference. To expand credit to the extent that Germany printed money would be impossible in the American economy. Banks would refuse to continue to make loans.

Though some people and perhaps some economists fear that America could experience this type of inflation, it is remote. Even the Fed, which has been maligned in this book, could not be so irresponsible. Besides, inflation is profitable to banks only if credit is restricted. There is no profit to banks in printing money.

(3) Many economists contend that excess money, per se, is the root-cause of inflation. Milton Friedman calls inflation a "monetary phenomenon." This concept is the basis of the Federal Reserve Board's anti-inflation policy. It is based on the theory that too many dollars are chasing too few goods. The cure looks simple: decrease the number of dollars.

But the policy works in reverse. Too few dollars cause inflation.

> First, interest plays a large part in the cost of living. All business firms borrow to conduct their operations – some more than others. These include firms at every stage of production. So, interest is a charge which is added on at each link of the production chain. This is a cost which must eventually be paid by the consumer. (Subcommittee on Domestic Finance, House Banking and Currency Committee. 88th Congress, 2d Session, 1964)

Every businessman knows that increase in interest rates are incorporated in the price of products, just like an increase in labor cost. Interest rates have additional inflationary impact. First, they inflame the inflationary spiral. The upward pressure of interest rates adds to the inflationary expectations of everyone. Merchants become speculators when pricing their inventory and add on an increment of "tomorrow's price." Their inflation expectations are triggered by the increase in interest rates.

Second, increases in interest rates have an amplified impact on the consumer price level. This is because commodities are financed many times during their manufacture. Take an automobile, for example. When the rubber for a tire is financed, higher interest rates increases its price. When the tire is manufactured, it, too, is financed, and its price reflects the increase in interest. When the automobile is manufactured, floored and sold, it is financed again and again. The net result is that the piece of rubber, like all components of the automobile, has been financed six or seven times and each time there is an additional increment added to its price reflecting the increase in interest rates. In addition, there is the inflationary impact of finance fees. During tight-money, financial institutions charge loan fees; these fees are compounded and add to the consumer price level. As a result, a 5% increase in interest may have a 7 or 8% impact on the price of the car.

An objective analysis of the inflation problem of the American economy indicates that inflation is not the economic bug-a-boo that we have been led to believe. It is the *Federal Reserve Board's purported cure that is the monster.* It's high-interest policy was the inflation. George Brockway commented, "In their choice of tactics the political bankers [the Federal Reserve Board] have choosen to fight fire with fuel." (*Washington Monthly,* June 1980, p. 50)

If the Board was honestly interested in controlling inflation by restricting the money supply, it would have curtailed credit by lowering interest rates to discourage banks from making loans. But stopping inflation was not the Board's goal, it was a publicly acceptable cover to justify its real objective: increasing interest rates in compliance with the profit strategy of the syndicate.

The tragedy of our present inflation is that it was totally unnecessary. There was an inflationary pressure because of the Vietnam War, petroleum prices, and other reasons. The prudent economic response was to let the inevitable inflation run its course and allow the marketplace to make adjustments.

The Board's anti-inflation propaganda was effective because it dramatized the inequities of inflation, especially its unfair impact upon the fixed income group. While there is no denying this was serious, it is equally true that today the fixed income group is worse off because of Federal Reserve Board policy.

The Fed's tight-money policy causes serious inequities in society. Tight-money hurts everyone that needs credit to conduct a business or maintain a standard of living. Tight-money causes unemployment and millions of people suffer.

Although the American public was propagandized to believe that inflation is an absolute social and economic evil, this is not the case. Moderate, steady, and widely-disbursed inflation is not only manageable and tolerable; it is preferrable to the economic havoc wrought by the policies of the Federal Reserve Board. The social and economic cost is staggering. The Board's policies benefits the idle wealthy at the expense of the working wealthy, the middle-class, and the poor.

# CHAPTER 14

# *The Federal Reserve Cycle*

***This Act gives the Federal Reserve Bank the power to create business cycles scientifically.***

***Congressman Charles Lindbergh***

In 1951, when the Accord was signed releasing the Federal Reserve Board from its agreement with the Treasury, a new era of American èconomics began. The Federal Reserve Board embarked upon a systematic monetary policy calculated to create "planned recessions." The Federal Reserve Board has intentionally created six "Federal Reserve Cycles" that have introduced new dimensions of uncertainty in our economy. The "Federal Reserve Cycle" is the legacy of the Federal Reserve Board's monetary policy of "tight-money, high-interest" rates. Economist Milton Friedman describes the Federal Reserve policy this way: ". . . it has continued, by swinging from one extreme to another, to produce not only booms, but also recessions, some mild, some sharp. It continues to promote the myth that private economy is unstable . . . its behavior documents the reality that government is today the major course of economic instability." (*Free to Choose,* p. 81)

When the Fed tightened credit in 1951, they programmed the 1953-1954 recession. In 1955, they again forced interest rates up and precipitated the recession of 1957-1958. The same process created the recessions of 1961, 1970, 1975, and 1980.

This chart depicts the Federal Reserve Cycle. Alternate periods of Board-created inflation followed by programmed recessions. The single line shows the changes in the interest rate. The shaded areas show period of recessions. Note how the interest rates increase until there is a recession. After a short period of decline, the Fed starts forcing the rate upward. Notice that for every cycle, the interest rate has gone successively higher.

When the Federal Reserve Board concludes that inflation is a threat or that the money supply is increasing too rapidly or that the economy is "too hot," it restricts the money supply. As a result, the banks increase the interest rate they charge to borrowers.

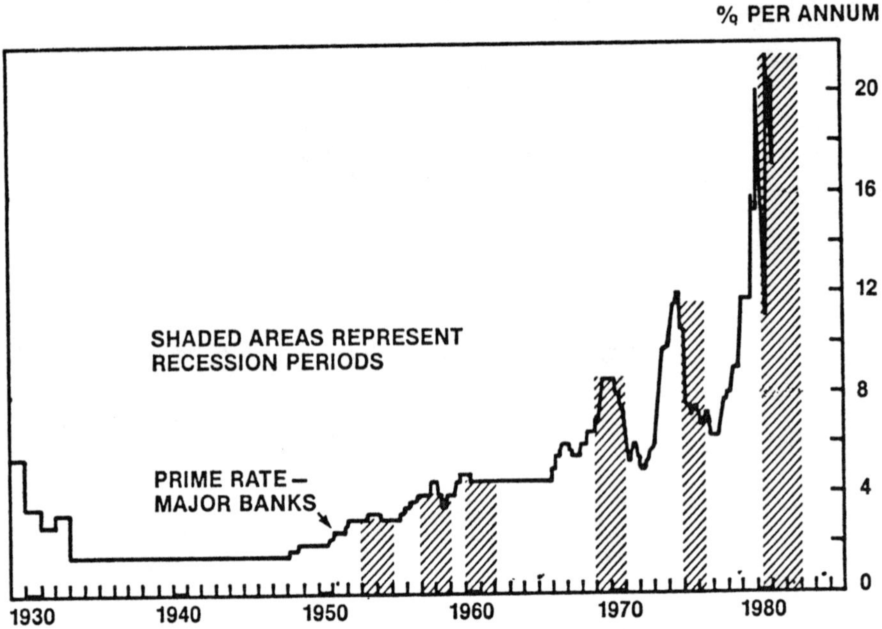


**THE FEDERAL RESERVE CYCLE**
This chart shows the six Federal Reserve Cycles since 1951. Each recession (shaded areas) was intentionally programmed by the Board increasing interest rates to restrict economic activity until there was a recession.

The interest rates are increased until the burden of the interest rates discourages investment and consumer purchases that require financing. As investment and consumer purchases decline, plants close; inventories accumulate; and unemployment increases because of the cutback in production. Industrial expansion or retooling is abandoned or modified downward. Bankruptcies and foreclosures increase, and profits decline. The stock market becomes timid as the interest rates increase and the nation's industrial output declines. We have idle plants, idle people and unsold inventories, in short, the beginning of a recession.

But even while these economic indicators of recession are flashing red, inflation continues because the Federal Reserve Board fuels inflation with its high interest rates. The scenario continues until interest rates become so high and restrictive that the recession stage is reached, causing the inflation to decline, temporarily. In response to public clamor about the depressed economy, the Federal Reserve Board then reluctantly starts to ease interest rates. When the interest rate is decreased to a level that is conducive to investment and consumer credit purchases, consumers and investors re-enter the market.

There is a strong pent-up demand ready to exert itself as soon as carrying charges are tolerable. If mortgage rates decline sufficiently, many potential purchasers who have been waiting to buy a house would enter the market actively. The supply of houses will be short because the home building industry's capacity to build homes and the number of homes under construction are at a minimum. The result is an inflationary impact on the price of homes.

The anti-inflation segment of the Federal Reserve Cycle lays the groundwork for the next inflation because it dams up consumer and investment demand and diminishes the capacity of the economy to meet the accelerated demand of the recovery. Inventory flow has been disrupted by the recession, and production capacity has atrophied or is idle.

It may be easier to understand the Federal Reserve Cycle if we examine the effects on a middle-class family as it experiences the cycle. The time is 1977; Mr. Carter has just been inaugurated. John and Mary are a forty-five-year-old, middle-class American couple with three children, two of whom are in college. They live in a modest home and have worked diligently most of their lives to provide security for their old age and to educate their children. John is an engineer who recently started his own company, Hi-Tech, to produce and market an electronic-control device that he had patented. The market potential was strong and John optimistically anticipated the future. John had to borrow money to start Hi-Tech. In order to help, his wife works as a real estate salesperson. Hi-Tech is doing a brisk business; the demand for the product has grown, and John plans for a major expansion of the business. He borrows $500,000 at 7% as interim financing to build a plant. He will need another $500,000 at a later date to equip the plan since it takes approximately a year and a half to design and build the plant.

In the meantime, Mary has been successful as a real estate agent. Because of the pent-up demand for housing, the relatively low interest rate has attracted many buyers to the market. Her major problem is that the demand has been pent-up so long and is so strong that it bids up the price of real estate every day, and sellers are setting higher and higher prices as they enter the market. In the meantime, John's plant is finished, and he must pay off the interim loan. He finds that the money market is significantly tighter and that no funds are available for him to borrow and pay off the $500,000 interim loan.

After much effort, he finds a bank willing to offer him a $400,000 loan. With his $100,000 cash reserves, he pays off the $500,000 loan. But the bank now charges 3% over prime, which is 15%, and in addition, the bank requires an originator's fee of 5% (which amounts to $20,000). Because Mary's income has been reasonably good and expectations in the business are good, John agrees to the loan. In the meantime, he must make arrangements to finance the plant equipment, which will cost $500,000. In his initial calculations, he had anticipated an interest rate of 7 to 8% for this financing and had calculated his profit margin on this rate.

In the six months necessary to obtain the equipment, the prime interest rate has soared to an astronomical 20% and money is very, very scarce. In the meantime, Mary's real estate business has soured because interest rates have driven monthly payments so high that no one can afford to buy a home, and it is extremely difficult to obtain real estate loans for her clients. Her income has diminished to almost zero. Once again, John has the problem of obtaining financing that is almost nonexistent. However, because of the high quality of his technology, he finds a bank willing to make a loan to him at 23% interest and a 15% originator fee ($75,000). He has no choice but to accept the terms or lose his building and business.

As he begins manufacturing his product, he realizes that he must raise the projected price by 20% to meet the added costs of financing. By the end of the following year, demand diminishes because Hi-Tech's product was used in manufacturing automobiles and due to high interest rates, automobile sales have declined dramatically.

The price of his product was forced so high on the consumer market by increased cost of money that it is no longer attractive. In six months, John can no longer make the very high mortgage payments nor the equipment payments. He regretfully adds to the unemployment rolls by dismissing his staff. Despite his attempts to find a refinancing package for his business to ride out the difficult times, he discovers that money is even scarcer and that interest rates are higher (21.5% prime). He is unsuccessful. In three months, he declares bankruptcy and finds himself personally broke and heavily in debt. The economy is in a recession, and he is unable to find a job that can use his particular skills. His wife, Mary, is working as a receptionist in a bank, and they are in danger of losing their home through foreclosure.

Although the recession has continued for two years, John is no quitter, and every day he hopes for the time that the interest rates will come down so that he can start his business anew. He has a new invention to manufacture. John has now become a part of the massive pent-up demand that waits for the Federal Reserve Board to lower interest rates. When this happens, he will be among the investors and consumers who will bid for a recession-diminished supply of goods, and the Federal Reserve Cycle will start over again.

The Federal Reserve Cycle is self-generative. Each cycle sets the stage and supplies the motivation for the next stage of inflation.

The economy develops an insensitivity to interest rates as an economic deterrent to control credit formation. Although 4% interest peaks discouraged investment and consumer credit purchases in 1960, 4% was low in 1970, and it required 8% to discourage credit formation; in 1974, it required 12%, and in 1980, it required 22%.

By increasing interest rates so drastically, the Federal Reserve Board is acting out of desperation. The Federal Reserve Cycle is out of control and unmanageable. Look at the chart: each peak of interest rate is successively higher. What will the next peak be? 30 to 35%? To break the cycle, the board must be restrained from using interest rates to control the economy.

The most damaging result of the Federal Reserve Cycle is that by periodically strangling the economy, the Board's self-defeating monetary policy has caused it to stagnate. If the Board's control of our economy continues, the Federal Reserve Cycle may cause irreparable damage to the fabric of American capitalism because of the continued stagflation. Stagflation is a paradoxical condition wherein the economy, even though experiencing high inflation, suffers economic stagnation such as under-utilization of plant capacity, relatively high unemployment, and low or negative economic growth rate. It is a signal that capitalism is in trouble. Stagflation epitomizes the perverse effect of the Federal Reserve's policies on our economy.

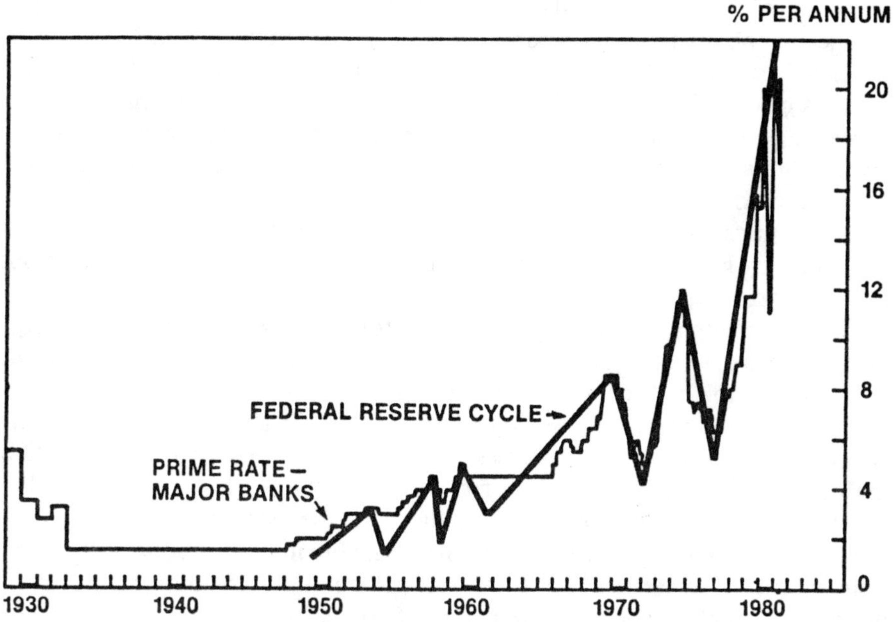


**AMPLITUDE OF FEDERAL RESERVE CYCLE**

This chart demonstrates four facts: (1) the amplitude of the Federal Reserve Cycle is increasing; (2) Interest rates lost their effectiveness as an economic tool. Higher and higher interest rates are necessary to precipitate a recession; (3) The Federal Reserve Cycle is forcing the trend of interest rates upward. Notice, they never return to their previous low; (4) The Federal Reserve Cycle is out of control.

Inflation has an undesirable and inequitable effect on the economy. But severe recession or depression, which the Fed prescribed, has disasterous economic and social consequences. Recession is not an acceptable remedy for inflation. It would be a tragedy if the misguided policies of the Federal Reserve Board were to result in a serious depression that could not be alleviated. It happened in 1920, and again in 1929 because of the monetary policies of the Fed were unresponsive to the economy's problems. It can happen again for the same reason.

Until now, this recession could be cured relatively quickly by decreasing interest rates. In the past, we have been able to count on pent-up demand to revive the economy. But if the Fed keeps interest rates too high for too long, it might extinguish the pent-up demand. If our current recession is allowed to continue too long or get too deep, the economy may suffer serious structural maladjustments. If these economic maladjustments become too extreme, it may be so difficult for the economy to right itself, a depression may be in our future.

There is a surprising parallel between present conditions and those of 1929:

In both instances there was a President who did not understand the imminent danger of the situation, a hollow stock market boom, historically high increases in interest rates, and a Federal Reserve Bank which has demonstrated an uncanny ability to do the wrong thing at the wrong time. In the 1930s, it was dedicated to saving the gold standard while the economy collapsed with horrendous results. Today, it is fighting inflation when a recession that threatens to become a depression is the problem. A stagnant economy threatens the survival of our standard of living. If the Federal Reserve Board does not face economic and social reality, it may well force us beyond the point of economic self-adjustment and plunge us into a severe economic depression. Although our economy has great resilience, it cannot withstand the abuse of continuous high interest rates.

Another potential for economic catastrophe is the manner in which high interest rates are causing a worldwide depression syndrome. Depression feeds on itself, and the bad economic condition of one country accentuates the problems of other countries. All Western Europe is suffering from a recession and the potential for worldwide depression is increased by the dollar shortage. Our high interest rates attract dollars from all over the world, creating a dollar shortage in other countries. For instance, the Belgians must conduct their international commerce with dollars, including buying oil. If dollars are short, Belgium must increase interest rates to attract dollars. The high interest rates discourage economic activity, deepening its recession.

Worldwide depression is a clear and imminent danger. The Europeans recognize this, and have pleaded with our government to decrease interest rates. We must avoid the drastic consequences of a worldwide recession, for continued economic declines will become fodder for anti-freedom forces throughout the world. While economic downturns and recessions cannot always be controlled with pragmatic policies, the effects can at least be ameliorated. But our problem is that the Federal Reserve Board intentionally created the recession and will not decrease interest rates sufficiently to encourage a recovery.

Business cycles have been a persistent problem for the capitalistic system. Socialists and Communists use the periodic depressions as "proof" that capitalism does not work and should be replaced by a planned economy that could avoid unmanageable economic collapses.

Twentieth century free market economics has been dedicated to the goal of eliminating or dampening business cycles. Many economists, including Mitchell, Hyack, Hansen, and ever ex-chairman of the Federal Reserve Board Burns, have written books dealing with the business cycle. Economists worldwide are trying to prevent or alleviate the economic ravages of cyclical business uncertainty and the resulting human trauma.

Since 1929, the downside or depression phase of the business cycle has received monumental attention because of the horrendous economic tragedy and human suffering of the Great Depression. For ten years, the economy refused to right itself, and even government intervention was not as effective as expected. Alleviating the devastation of the business cycle was a major reason for organizing the Federal Reserve Bank. With great optimism, the secretary of the Treasury announced the formal establishment on October 25, 1914, of the Federal Reserve Bank and promised the people, "Under the operation of this law such financial and commercial crises, or 'panics,' as their country experienced in 1873, in 1893, and again in 1907, with their attendant misfortunes and prostrations, seem to be mathematically impossible."

# CHAPTER 15

# *History Of Interest Rates*

> ***While we are tracing the history of interest rates and looking into the financial behavior of earlier generations, we should not forget the loan shark, who is alive and well in the United States masquerading as a banker.***
>
> ***– Comment of a foreclosed farmer.***

The average person does not understand how interest rates affect our economy. To most of us, interest rates are simply the finance cost we pay for an automobile, a refrigerator, or a home. The rate of interest is important to each and every one of us as is a major factor in the performance of the economy. It affects us financially, and influences the quality of our lives.* (The quotes are from the Congressional Record, Sub-committee on Domestic Finance, House Banking and Currency Committee, September 21, 1964.)

1. Interest rates influence the level of economic activity. Generally high interest rates retard economic activity and low interest rates may encourage economic activity. National indexes as the Gross National Product, National Income, and Unemployment, reflect the impact of interest rates. For example, as the Fed increased interest rates recently 1%, unemployment increased by 1,000,000 job losses.

2. The price level is influenced by interest rates; increasing interest rates are inflationary.

> Interest plays a large part in the cost of living. All business firms borrow to conduct their operations—some more than others. These include firms at every stage of production. So interest is a charge which is added on at each link of the production chain. This is a cost which must eventually be paid by the consumer.

3. Interest rates have an effect on the level of capital investment and production:

> Interest rates influence production, because interest rates influence the amount business spends for investment in plants and equipment.

4. Interest rates affect the productivity of our industrial complex. Low interest rates tend to encourage investments in new and sophisticated factories

and equipment, while high interest rates tend to discourage investment in new advanced production facilities. A lack of investment capital adversely affects productivity:

> When investment is cut by high interest, two things happen. (1) When business does not take as much advantage of the new, more efficient tools to produce goods as it might (2) industry slows down the rate of expansion of the total output capacity of the country's factories. The result of these twin effects is that tomorrow's workers work with less efficient machinery and fewer machines than they might. Having fewer and less efficient tools, tomorrow's workers, of course, produce less than they could. In other words, the rate of growth of output slackens when high interest prevails.

5. High interest rates encourage the concentration of economic power:

> Small business is especially hard hit because the larger firms tend to have their credit needs catered to first.

6. High interest contributes to the size of the government's budget deficits:

> It can be shown that if the interest rates of the early 1940s had prevailed throughout the postwar period, the total National Debt would be $40 billion less than it is now. This is just one of the terrific costs of tight money, and also proves that raising interest rates is not a simple solution to more serious economic problems.

7. Low interest rates tend to encourage economic activity. High interest rates cause recessions:

> Interest rates in the United States increased in steps between 1952 and 1964, and each major step upward was followed by a recession. . . . The economy pays for high interest in incomes not earned and in outcome not produced.

The rate of interest is a function of the supply of money. If money is tight, interest rates are high; if there is an adequate supply of money, interest rates tend to be low. Until recently, the national demand for low interest rates was always a hot political issue that generated intense public response and Congressional action. High interest rates were considered parasitic and a windfall profit to the banks. And they are. The nation's total interest payment is the amount of money the public pays to have credit manufactured and serviced. Historically, it was a relatively small portion of national income, around 3%, but in 1981 it skyrocketed to 13%! This means that the people of the U.S. paid 13% of their income for a routine service of their government — a currency system. Another way of saying it is that one out of every eight dollars of the public's income was a compulsory contribution to the moneylenders.

History shows that interest rates were relatively low for qualified borrowers in normal times. Records of interest rates go back to Sumerian documents circa 3000 B.C., which indicate a systematic credit structure on loans secured by grain and silver. In about 1800 B.C., the Sumerians' credit customs and rates were codified in the Babylonian Code of Hammurabi, which was sophisticated and socially oriented. For example, it set maximum rates of interest that were altered only once in 2,000 years. The lender had to wait until after the harvest before he could demand his money in repayment. If the crop failed by acts of God, the interest was cancelled. Loan contracts had to be signed in the presence of an official and a witness, and pledges of property, such as land, were noted in detail and signed by wives. Interest rates could be and often were negotiated below the maximum. In many ways, the Code was more humane than our current laws.

Interest rates were surprisingly low, considering the relatively high risk factor. For about 1,300 years, the legal maximum on silver loans was 20%, while the normal rate on silver was a low as 10%.

Hammurabi's Code limiting interest rates remained in effect for over 1,300 years. Greek interest rates went as low as 6% at the time of Christ, and Roman rates went as low as 4%. In antiquity, 300 B.C. to 200 A.D., interest rates rarely went above 6%.

In Greece, from the fifth century B.C. to the first century A.D., normal loans were made at interest rates that varied between 6 and 12%. Real estate loans were predominantly in the 8 to 12% range, a rate at which many young American families today would like to finance a home.

SUMMARY OF GREEK INTEREST RATES*

| Century | Normal Loans, % | Real Estate Loans, % | Loans to Cities, % | Earnings of Endowments, % |
|---|---|---|---|---|
| B.C. | | | | |
| Sixth century | 16-18 | – | – | – |
| Fifth century | 10-12 | 8-12 | – | – |
| Fourth century | 10-12 | 8-12 | 8½-12 | – |
| Third century (early) | 7½-12 | 10 | 8½-12 | – |
| Third century (late) | 6-10 | 7 | 10 | 6-10 |
| Second century (early) | 6-9 | 6⅔-10 | 10 | 6⅔-10 |
| Second century (late) | 6-9 | – | 7 | 10 |
| First century | 6-12 | – | 8-12 | 10 |
| A.D. | | | | |
| First century | 8-9 | – | – | – |

Source: Homer, *History of Interest Rates*

Greek loans to governments (cities) in good standing ranged from 7 to 12%. In 1981 the American government paid double the rate that the ancient Greek city-states paid in the late second century B.C.

Roman Empire interest rates followed the general pattern of those of Greece, except that the rates varied a little more between times of crises, such as wars and peacetime. When conditions were stable, rates were as low as 4%.

Sidney Homer, in his excellent book, *A History of Interest Rates,* summarized his findings:

> . . . we have excellent evidence of great stability in these "normal" interest rates over known long periods of time. This stability was due no doubt in part to tradition . . . These ancient "normal" loans, if they are to be compared at all with modern loans, were probably most like modern personal loans made by small banks or by individuals either on good collateral or to a substantial citizen.

Homer explains that it was not the risk of borrowing that set interest rates as high as they were, but the lack of large organized credit markets. Furthermore, the cost of doing business was high. (The implication here is that as credit markets grew and technology facilitated the lending processes, interest rates should reflect the lower cost of lending money.) These interest rates were for loans made with hard currency since creating money by credit had not yet been invented. During the Dark Ages trading was a disarray as were the money markets. There were no organized money markets of any consequence and fewer records of interest rates.

In the twelfth century, the papacy became very strong under Innocent III, and the power of kings expanded. As trade revived, money and how it flowed became a critical problem. This is the period of the Thomas Aquinas debate in the church over usury and "interesse." The doctrinal definition of usury is "where more is asked than is given." (Homer, p. 73) As used here, usury is "interest" in our terminology. In 325, the Council of Nicea passed a canon prohibiting usury by clerics, and St. Jerome argued that permission for layment to take usury from strangers should be withdrawn. Pope Leo the Great (440-461) "forebade clerics to take usury and declared laymen who take it to be guilty of 'shameful sin.'" During the time of Charlemagne, the Hadriana canons forbade usury to anyone. Usury was considered to be an invasion of property rights and a sin against man, and the userer could be treated as a thief and excommunicated. Interest as we know it was forbidden; the compensation for loans was paid in psychic income to the lender from the knowledge that he had been generous or had helped his neighbors and friends. St. Raymond stated, "One ought to lend to one's needy neighbor only for God and principally from Charity." (Homer, p. 71) St. Thomas Aquinas (1225-1274) referred to usury as breeding money from money and said that to accept usury as evil. Sidney Homer commented that, "It is probable that in essence the early attack on usury was aimed not very differently than it is today: against exorbitant rates." (Homer, p. 81)

As commercial activity in the secular sector increased, commercial demand for credit soon outweighed clerical edict. Interest became differentiated from usury by the introduction of the concept that the lender was not gaining anything if he was merely being reimbursed for the gain he gave up to lend the money. "Interesse," a form of the Latin verb "intereo," meaning to be lost, developed into the word "interest." The use of the word "interesse" to refer to a legal payment for the use of money became common around 1200-1220. It is interesting to note that risk was not considered as a just cause for establishing the rate of "interesse." Interest was differentiated from usury by the secular authorities and the protestant church. Interest was compensation for loss and not gain. The term "usury" was used if the lender charged more than his loss of the use of the funds.

Deposit banking, which is the method of extending credit beyond the total amount of deposits in a bank and thereby creating money, was developing rapidly in the thirteenth century by Italians, especially in Venice, Genoa, and Florence. Despite some initial church opposition, deposit banking developed into a respectable and lucrative endeavor for the moneyed class of Italy and medieval Europe. (Homer, p. 76)

Martin Luther denounced the church's ban on charging a fee (interest) for loaning money and contended that the common man must obey the secular laws. It was for princes to enact reform, not the church. While Luther condoned payment of 5 to 6% interest and tolerated 8%, he rather perceptively denounced those who charged higher interest as being responsible for the inflation in Germany.

John Calvin was the Protestant intellectual leader who condoned interest as being acceptable – even desirable – in a prudent society. He disagreed with the arguments of Aristotle and St. Thomas Aquinas that money should not beget money. In 1547, in Switzerland, he set the maximum legal rate of interest at 5%.

(By 1836, the Catholic church finally accepted that Catholics could legitimately earn interest in the eyes of God. In 1950, Pope Pius XII sanctified the banking business by noting that bankers earned an honest living.)

During the thirteenth century, some stable money markets were established, particularly in Italy. Interest rates were relatively high, particularly in unsettled areas, but commercial loans and loans to stable states had reasonable rates of interest.

By the fifteenth century, commercial loans ranged from 5 to 15%, and the "usual rate" in Venice as low as 5%. Long-term mortgages ranged from 5 to 10% and averaged around 5% in cities.

INTEREST RATES PAID BY GENOA
BANK OF ST. GEORGE

| Year | % | Year | % | Year | % | Year | % |
|---|---|---|---|---|---|---|---|
| 1600 | 2 7/8 | 1606 | 4 3/8 | 1613 | 1 3/8 | 1619 | 1 1/8 |
| 1601 | 3 | 1607 | 2 3/8 | 1614 | 1 3/4 | 1620 | 1 1/4 |
| 1602 | 2 7/8 | 1608 | 2 5/8 | 1615 | 1 5/8 | 1621 | 1 5/8 |
| 1603 | 3 5/8 | 1609 | 2 5/8 | 1616 | 1 5/8 | 1622 | 4 1/4 |
| 1604 | 2 3/8 | 1610 | 2 3/8 | 1617 | 1 3/8 | 1623 | 3 3/4 |
| 1605 | 2 1/8 | 1611 | 1 7/8 | 1618 | 1 3/8 | 1624 | 5 1/2 |
| | | 1612 | 2 | | | 1625 | 5 1/2 |

Source: Homer, *History of Interest Rates*

From 1600 to 1625, the interest rates charged on loans to states (principally Genoa) by the Bank of St. George ranged between 1.5 to 5.5%. It is interesting to note that Genoa was financing its government, on the average, at 2.5% in a primitive money market, whereas the United States recently paid 14% in the most sophisticated money market in the history of the world!

The fourteenth, fifteenth, sixteenth, and seventeenth century money markets were better organized and extended throughout most of Europe. From the fourteenth through the seventeenth century, commercial loans averaged 5%. During the seventeenth century, they declined below 2%.

By the eighteenth century, England had become a world power and possessed a well-organized money market. The chart below traces the history of English government bonds from 1796 to 1900. The British government financed the American Revolutionary War at a lesser interest rate than the Federal Reserve financed the Vietnam War. With all the unsettled conditions of the eighteenth century, the average interest rate that the government paid for financing was about 4% – rarely exceeding 6%. Mortgages (variable rate because they could be renegotiated yearly) ranged from 4 to 4⅛%. Public utility financing for building turnpikes and canals ranged from 3.5 to 5%, while on the Continent, many of the Dutch rates during the eighteenth century were lower, ranging from 2 to 6%.

English government bond yields from 1800 to 1900 were characterized by a downward trend that lasted the entire century. The yield on English government bonds decreased from 5% in 1800 to 2.5% in 1900, dipping to an all-time low of 2.20% in 1897. During a hundred years of tremendous expansion of industry and empire, England was able to maintain a very low, constant interest rate. No doubt England's expansion of industry and commerce was promoted by the low interest rates.

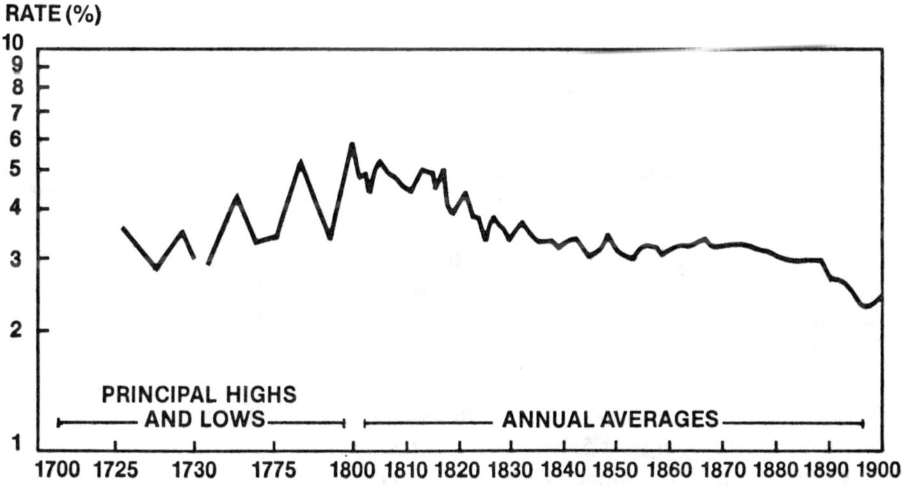


Source: Homer, *History of Interest Rates*

**ENGLISH GOVERNMENT BONDS 1700-1900**

For a century English Government Bonds averaged less than 3%. The trend of rates was downward for the 100 years.

During this period, short-term interest rates were more volatile, ranging from 2 to 7% average annual rate. Still, the highest average annual interest in England during the nineteenth century was only about one-third of the 22% prime rate established in 1980 by our Federal Reserve Board.

From 1900 to 1960, during which time the English fought two devastating world wars, the yield of long-term government bonds did not exceed 6% and ranged from 2.66 to 6%.

Long-term English government rates from 1730 to 1960 on the average have remained low through a turbulent epoch of economic growth and terrible wars: between 2.25 and 6%, averaging less than 4%.

The long-term American experience with interest rates has not been much different from the English experience. Part of America's problem was that it was slow to develop adequate money markets. Nonetheless, on the average, long-term interest rates averaged around 4% and stayed below the 6% level in that New York-dominated market.

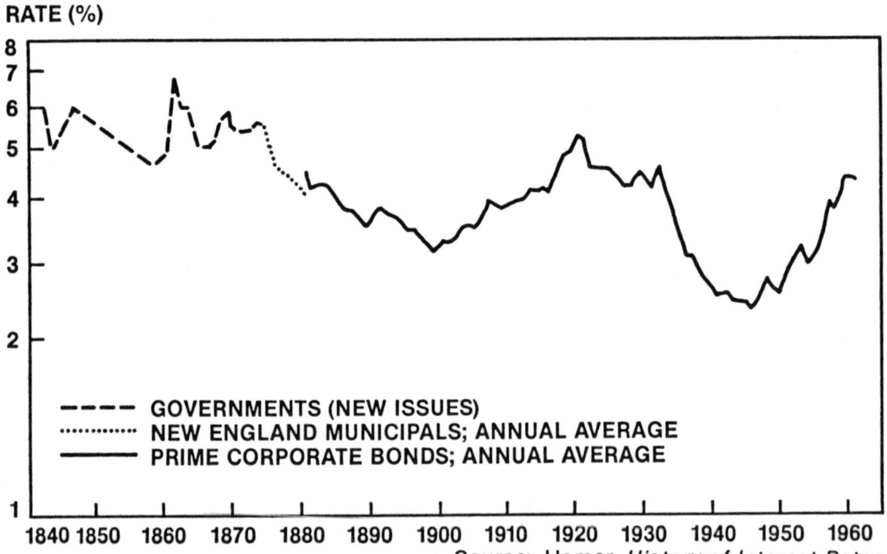


Source: Homer, *History of Interest Rates*

**HIGH GRADE AMERICAN BONDS 1840-1960**

For 110 years prime bonds interest rates averaged less than 4%. The trend was toward lower interest rates until the Fed was released from Roosevelt's Treasury Agreement in 1951.

The interest of prime American bonds from 1920 to 1961 ranged from 5.5% in 1920 down to 2.5% in 1946, and back up to 3.5% in 1961. Compare this with what has happened between 1965 and 1980, when Corporate AAA bonds (Standard and Poo's) went from 4.75% to 11.5%.

The following chart shows a long-range composite of the lowest interest rates of long-term loans in Western Europe and the United States.

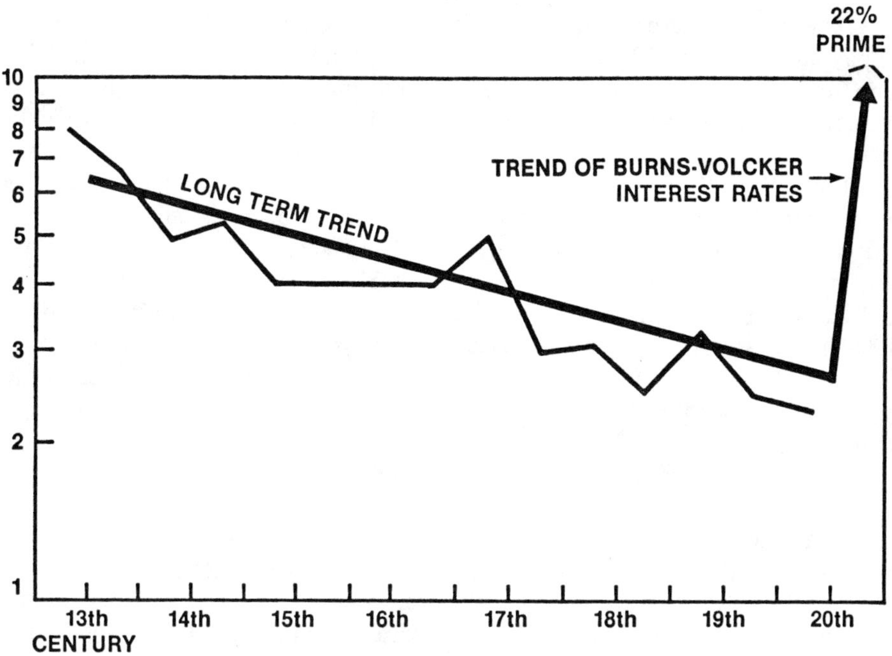


**700 YEAR TREND OF INTEREST RATES**

Since the 13th century the trend of the interest rates was downward. Notice how the Burns-Volcker interest rates reverse a 700 year trend and forced them off the chart to historic heights.

The important conclusion to draw from these figures and dates is that *the trend of interest rates has been downward since the thirteenth century and that historically, they have been relatively low.*

From 1805 to 1960, the yield of long-term high-grade American bonds varied between 2.5 and 6%, averaging somewhere around 4%. Interest rates on Moody's Corporate AAA bonds increased from 4% in 1965 to 14% in 1980, a 250% increase.

By any measure, money should be cheaper today. Before the thirteenth century until the early nineteenth century, most of the money was loan in coin, not credit. This meant that the lender had to forego the use of his money while it was out on loan. This is not the practice today. The vast majority of current loans consist of bank credit. Banks are franchised by the government as agents empowered to create money by extending credit. In essence, the bank creates the money that it lends. Today we have a stable, relatively risk-free, highly organized credit market with qualified borrowers in abundance, as opposed to the dearth of such customers in the early days of "country banking." Interest rates should be the lowest in history. Because the creation of money is mechanized by numerous sophisticated labor-saving devices, the cost of processing and servicing loans is decreasing. The productivity of banks has increased; interest rates should reflect the decreased cost. But that is not the case.

The Federal Reserve Board has forced blue-chip American corporations to pay more interest (22%) for a loan than a second century merchant (8-9%). The Board has forced American citizens to pay mortgage rates as high as 18%. A second century B.C. farmer paid 6%, and a 1670 British mortgagor paid 4%.

Since 1951, the Fed has increased interest rates at a phenomenal rate. The outrageous increase in interest rates in America were so extreme that it tests our credulity. Read these figures carefully. The Federal Reserve Discount Rate (NY) rose from 1% in 1946 to 14% in 1981, a 1300% increase. Prime Commercial Paper (four to six months) soared from ½% in 1945 to 15% in 1980, a 3000% increase. Three-month Treasury bills skyrocketed from .5% in 1946 to 14% in 1981, a 2700% increase. Can you believe that over the last 33 years, the government's short-term cost of money has increased at an incredible average yearly rate of nearly 50%?

Thanks to the Federal Reserve Board, in 1981 the American government, the strongest and wealthiest in history, was forced to pay 14% for short-term financing, almost ten times the rate that Genoa paid in 1614!

Interest rates during the last twelve years have been abnormally high, contrary to the long-term trend. Furthermore, interest rates should be at an all-time low, considering market stability, risk factor, and cost of servicing loans.

At the beginning of this century, Congress recognized that a "neutral" currency system was critical to our free enterprise system and the problem was how to guarantee that it would be managed fairly and impartially to provide the nation with a flexible money supply to meet the needs of an expanding economy.

Congress made it clear that the Federal Reserve Board was mandated to supply the economy with a low, constant rate of interest. The Senate majority report noted the wild interest rate fluctuations in the United States:

> The stabilizing of the rate of interest in the United States will be one of the very important functions of the proposed Federal Reserve System . . . and will enable the banks of the country to extend accommodation at a comparatively stable rate of interest upon a lower basis than heretofore, because the element of hazard, of panic, and of financial stringency will be removed by the proposed system.

The Congress that passed the Federal Reserve Act understood that low, stable interest rates were prerequisite for American industry to grow and prosper. Today they are still the prerequisite for a stable, dynamic, growing economy if the American dream of a good life and a high quality standard of living for everyone is to be realized. Low, stable interest rates are particularly important today because in the next decade our industries will need massive amounts of capital and credit to retool for an age of complex automation. To avoid the consequences of industrial obsolescence, we are today faced with the same objectives of the 1913 Congress—to create an elastic money supply with low, stable interest rates.

A strong, pervasive effort is under way in America to convince us that high interest rates are necessary and should be continued. This is dangerous propaganda. It serves only one purpose: to enhance the power and wealth of the money lenders while everything else in the economy suffers. If high interest rates continue, America will decay into technological antiquity and become a second-rate economic power. High, volatile interest rates are an economic straight jacket that saps the strength of a nation.

As the medium of exchange, the money supply is the life blood of an economy. A neutral money supply is the economic lubricant that facilitates economic activity. Providing a neutral money supply is the obligation of our government. It is our duty to require the government to fulfill its obligation.

*The tables and charts in this chapter reproduced by permission from Rutgers University Press from the book by Sidney Homer, *A History of Interest Rates, 1963*.

# CHAPTER 16

# *Track Record*

***The Federal Reserve System with its enormous power, with its large bureau of research, with every opportunity to know the facts and take action to help us, has not given this country any relief, and has done all it could to worsen the situation.***

***Senator Robert L. Owens, 1939***

## FEDERAL RESERVE BOARD POLICY

The Federal Reserve Bank, sometimes referred to as our "National Bank," is the central bank for the American economy. It is called a "reserve bank" because it was established as a credit reservoir for the banking industry in times of unusual heavy demand for credit and to increase the mobility of reserves, enabling them to be moved readily from one geographical area to another. Thus the Fed was to serve as a national bank to facilitate the expansion of credit when the economy needed it.

The Federal Reserve Bank is a private bank, owned by the member banks and operated as an independent organization with two important ties to the federal government. First, the board of governors is appointed by the president and ratified by the Senate for fourteen-year terms. Secondly, Congress delegated to the Fed the right to coin money.

Even though the Fed is incorporated as a private organization, the Congress of the United States has authorized it to issue currency in the form of Federal Reserve notes, on government credit, making the Fed our central bank of issue. More importantly, Congress delegated to the Fed's Board the authority to control the nation's credit system, the major portion of our money supply.

Congress recognized that fair and impartial management of our nation's money supply is the most crucial safeguard of every American's individual economic rights. Money – its supply, its availability and to whom, its cost, its distribution – determines survival in our economic system.

Senator Robert Owens of Oklahoma, a sponsor, co-author, and chief advocate of the Federal Reserve Act of 1913, stated in a speech to the Senate on behalf of his Banking Committee:

Mr. President, the purposes of this great measure should be kept steadily in mind in considering the bill.

PURPOSES OF THE MEASURE

The purposes of this measure are:

First. To ensure the *stability* of our commerce, of our manufacturing enterprises, of our industries, and the safety of our merchants and manufacturers and businessmen generally.

Second. To make *available* effective *commercial credit* for individuals engaged in manufacture, in commerce, in finance, and in business to the extent of their just desserts.

Third. To put an end to the pyramiding of the bank reserves of the country and the use of such reserves for gambling purposes on the stock exchange.

Fourth. *To keep constantly employed the productive energies of the nation.* And this consideration is of vital importance to the laboring men of the country who are dependent for their daily bread upon constant, regular employment. Our crimes, our vices, our chief social evils come from lack of regular remunerative employment.

Keep Senator Owens' purposes in mind while reading the track record of the Federal Reserve Bank.

When the sponsors and promoters of the Federal Reserve Act spoke to the people and Congress, they painted enticing pictures of a stable economy and promised that banking crises would be a thing of the past. With the built-in flexibility of the monetary system, they claimed that bank failures would be a rare event. The major banking benefit of the Bill, is that it was supposed to help small banks weather crises with the assurance that if they needed help, it was only as far away as the nearest friendly Reserve branch.

But it did not work out that way. From 1884 to 1912, out of approximately 30,000 banks nationwide, an average of 67 banks closed yearly. From 1902 to 1912, the decade before the Federal Reserve Bank was organized, bank failures averaged 83 per year. From 1920 to 1930, after the Fed was in charge, almost 6,000 banks failed, an average of 588 per year. This deplorable sevenfold increase in bank failures occurred under the supervision of the Federal Reserve Board.

The worst was yet to come. From 1930 to 1933, the failures averaged 2,276 per year! In three years, 9,106 banks failed.

Many people were convinced that the attack on smaller banks was directed by large bankers in a move to consolidate their control of banking in the United States, aided by the "mismanagement" of the Fed. The co-author of the Federal Reserve Act, Senator Robert L. Owen, said at a Senate Finance Committee hearing in 1939, " . . . Under the influence and direction of the Federal Reserve system, 16,000 banks have failed in sixteen years through mismanagement of the system."

Since its formation in 1914, the Federal Reserve Board has contributed to sixteen thousand bank closures, two depressions, the severest and longest inflation in our history, and six recessions.

Between 1915 and 1918 (the end of World War I) the wholesale price index increased by approximately 75%, a strong inflationary force that continued after the war was concluded. Although it would be unfair to blame this inflation on anything except America's preparation for and participation in World War I, it should be noted that during these years, the Federal Reserve Board followed an inflationary money policy, supporting President Wilson's inflationary fiscal policy. At that point in history, the Federal Reserve was considered as part of the administration team and was expected to implement the goals of the administration. Besides, Wilson had appointed the Board. As economic historian W. Elliot Brownlee has observed, the policy of the Board during the war years was clearly inflationary: "The impact of this rapidly expanding money supply has sharply increased competition for a limited supply of goods." (Brownlee, *Dynamics of Accent,* p. 258) "The inflation was created by an infusion of too much money into an economy with shortages and a great deal of uncertainty. As a result of the war effort and the inappropriate policy of the Fed, prices increased almost three fold from 1914 to 1920" (Brownlee, p. 260).

In an attempt to correct its errant monetary policy, on June 20, 1920, the Board increased the discount rate to 6%, the largest increment of increase in the history of the Fed until that time. As a result, the money supply declined 9% from September 1920 until July 1921, a drastic decline.

With a post-war depression already under way, prices began to decline in May 1920. The Fed's monetary policy coincided with and accentuated the downward pressure on prices. Within a year, prices nose-dived by 50%, the most precipitous price decline in American economic history. By July 1921, the bottom of this depression, industrial production was down significantly and unemployment reached 10%. Williams Jennings Bryan wrote in *Hearst's* magazine in November 1923, "The Federal Reserve Bank that should have been the farmer's greatest protection has become his greatest foe. The deflation of the farmer was a crime deliberately committed."

The Depression of 1920-21 is known as the Agricultural Depression because it had a devastating impact on the American farmer and because a great number of rural or western banks were ruined. Singling out the farmer, the Fed raised the discount rate to 7% on agricultural and livestock paper. This was higher than the rate on other paper and had the effect of depreciating this type of security and increasing the cost of those banks that had to use it as collateral in borrowing from the Fed. There was speculation that the Federal Reserve Board directed its policy against the agricultural community because many of our rural banks would not join the Federal Reserve system. Eugene Meyer, Jr., Chairman of the Fed from 1930-1933, testified at a Senate hearing in 1923, "I believe that a great deal of trouble would have been avoided if a larger number of the eligible non-member banks had been members of the Federal Reserve System." Furthermore, in the Senate Hearings of 1923 that investigated the causes of the Agricultural Depression, Frank Vanderlip, President of National City Bank of New York, testified that the rural banks had not joined the Federal Reserve System as had been expected and that many of those banks which did join dropped out during the War. There was an undercurrent of suspicion that the Federal Reserve had made its policy move to convince the rural banks of the danger of their wayward ways.

The co-author of the Federal Reserve Act, Robert L. Owens, testified at a Senate Silver Hearing in 1939:

> In the early part of 1920, the farmers were exceedingly prosperous . . . and then they were bankrupted by a sudden contraction of credit and currency which took place in 1920. The Federal Reserve Board met on the 18th day of May, 1920, and it was a secret meeting. . . . Only the big bankers were there, and their work of that day resulted in a contraction of credit . . . reducing the national income fifteen billion dollars, throwing millions of people out of employment, and reducing the value of lands and ranches by twenty billion dollars.

Because of the violent manipulation of credit and the severe loss of agriculture, farmers did not share in the prosperity of the twenties. Economic historian W. Elliot Brownlee referrs to the Depression of 1920-1921 as a "Tarnished Age." For over twenty years, agriculture was a poor cousin, a second-class economic partner that did not completely recover until World War II. During the twenties, net farm income fell to about 40% of the 1919 level and never returned to 75% of the 1919 price level during the thirties. Needless to say, agriculture's share of national income receded significantly during this period. Credit one depression to the Federal Reserve Board; soon there would be a second.

Though we are all acquainted with the Great Depression, we may not be aware that its severity and duration were an unnecessary result of the policies of the Federal Reserve, as historian W. Elliot Brownlee has observed:

> To be sure the economy had flaws, but they were not serious enough to account for the scale of the Great Depression. Rather, that severity resulted from the failure of public officials to use effectively the stabilization instruments at their disposal, particularly those of the Federal Reserve System.

The most dramatic aspect of the Depression was the "crash" of the stock market. But the stock market was merely a barometer that reflected what was taking place in the economy in general. As an economic institution, the stock market of 1929 had problems that were self-generated. Since 1927, stocks were oversold on great expectations, margin requirements were set low by the Federal Reserve Board, and money was easy to obtain for speculation. From the end of 1927 to September, 1929, prices of stocks escalated as much as 60%. At the Senate investigation of the Federal Reserve Board in 1931, Board Member Adolph C. Miller stated, "If we had had no Federal Reserve System, I do not think we would have had as bad a speculative situation as we had."

Many economic historians attribute the depth and length of the Great Depression to the Federal Reserve Bank's failure to alleviate the negative cyclical impact on the economy.

John R. Bunting, the chief executive officer of Philadelphia's First Pennsylvania Bank and Trust Company and an economist with the Federal Reserve, criticized the Federal Reserve:

> I think if you ask a hundred economists—any hundred, as long as they have the degrees and a reasonable amount of objectivity—they'll say that what happened in 1929 was absolutely stupid Federal Reserve policy. It caused the depression in 1929—that along with a President of the United States who really didn't understand what was going on in 1929. There's no question that the monetary policy of that time was absolutely stupid.

During the House Hearings on Stabilization of the Purchasing Power of the Dollar in 1928, there was an indication that the Depression of 1929 had been planned by the Federal Reserve Board in cooperation with the heads of European central banks at a luncheon in 1927. In an article in the *North American Review*, May 1929, Dr. Henry Parker Willis, a legislative consultant and the author of the Federal Reserve Act and later secretary to the Federal Reserve Board, related how a group of bankers planned the stock market boom and subsequent deflation. He contended that they realized enormous profits from the ploy. It is reasonable to suspect that bankers were planning all sorts of schemes to exploit the money market, and we should not rule out the possibility that the greed of the moneymen contributed to the start of the Great Depression. John Bunting said, "The banks were responsible for the Great Depression of 1929, 1930 and 1931." However, none of them, in their right mind, would have caused a depression of such depth and extent. That was left to the Federal Reserve Board to achieve.

Many competent economic historians have recognized the fact that the Fed's policies not only precipitated the Great Depression, but were actually responsible for its duration and severity.*

During the Depression, the Fed's policies were committed to protecting the international gold standard while callously ignoring the dire plight of the domestic economy.

Concerned about the heavy flow of gold into the United States during 1930-1931, the Board took action to stem the flow of gold. When England went off the gold standard in September 1931, worldwide demand for gold soared as many nations, fearing that the United States might follow England, demanded to trade dollars for gold. The resulting heavy outflow of gold from the United States further increased the fear that the United States would abandon the gold standard. The Federal Reserve responded with an abrupt policy change by sharply raising the discount rate to increase short-term interest rates to stabilize the international gold market. Even though the increase in interest rates made the dollar more attractive than gold, it put a damper on the domestic recovery and deepened the depression by contracting the money supply drastically.

Herbert Hoover, the President of the United States during this period, is generally blamed for the failure of government to come to the aid of the economy. Because he was quite conservative, it is questionable how much government intervention he would have tolerated to avoid economic chaos. Whatever Hoover's domestic recovery efforts may have been, they were sabotaged by the Board's policy commitment to maintaining the international gold standard. In his *Memoirs, Vol. III, The Great Depression*, Hoover lamented that the Federal Reserve was a "weak reed on which to lean in time of trouble." Hoover's ex-officio representative on the Federal Reserve Board was Secretary of the Treasury Andrew W. Mellon, a Pittsburgh financier, whom Hoover depicts as a self-righteous man who felt that the hardships of the depression were punishing those who deserved it. According to Mellon, the "less competent" should be penalized, and the depression should be allowed to do its work without governmental interference. Hoover described Mellon as the leader of the "leave-it-alone liquidationalists" who advocated leaving the depression free to run its course as per his formula: Liquidate labor, liquidate stocks, liquidate the farmers, liquidate real estate. Mellon moralistically rationalized that "panic will purge the rottenness out of the system. High living will come down. People will work harder, live a more moral life. Values will be adjusted, and enterprising people will pick up the wrecks from the less competent people." (Hoover, pp. 51-52) Mellon influenced Board policy and the economy was devastated.

The national economic recovery from the Great Depression was protracted, slow, and uneven. By 1937, real income had increased by only 3% since 1929, and per capita income did not reach the 1929 levels until 1939. In 1937, six million people, 14% of the workforce, were still unemployed.

In 1933, the United States had a new President who was committed to action and did not defer to the sacred cow—the Federal Reserve Board. Roosevelt went after the Fed with his own aggressive economic policies. Roosevelt let the Board know that he held the cards and that on important economic issues, he would play them his way. He further indicated to the Fed that the control of the banking industry was not the exclusive right of the Federal Reserve Board. He exerted his power through the emergency Banking Act and the declaration of a bank holiday that closed all banks for a week. In the 1933 Banking Act, he built confidence in banks by creating the Federal Deposit Insurance Corporation. One of Roosevelt's strongest moves against the Fed was the Banking Act of 1935, which centralized control of the system and moved decision making from New York to Washington. (Unfortunately, this proved to be a long-run enhancement of the Board's powers.) Demonstrating his disdain for the Reserve Board's concern over the gold standard, Roosevelt, with the help of Congress, reduced the gold content of the dollar up to 50% by the Gold Reserve Act of 1934, and changed the price of gold from $21 to $35 per ounce.

Predictably, the Federal Reserve Board began to fear the radical innovations of "that man in the White House," fearing that he would go overboard and take the United States completely off the gold standard. The Fed even feared that if Roosevelt did not get cooperation from the Reserve Board, he would nationalize the banks.

When threatened, early in the Roosevelt Administration, the Federal

Reserve Board cooperated by avoiding any action that would restrict monetary expansion. It refrained from raising the discount rate or engaging in open market sales or following its previous policy of protecting the gold standard when enormous amounts of gold flowed into the country as a result of the Gold Reserve Act of 1934. From 1934 to 1940, the amount of gold in Fort Knox tripled. Roosevelt's manipulation of the gold prices had a very fortunate impact on the recovery of the economy. He did just the opposite of what the Federal Reserve Board had done between 1931 and 1933, when the Board discouraged the large influx of gold.

Despite an improvement in the unemployment statistics, from 24.9% of the labor force out of work in 1933 to 14.3% in 1936, the Depression was not over. As a matter of economic history, there was a sharp depression in 1937-1938. The British economist Douglas Fisher (*Money and Banking*, 1971, Richard D. Irwin, Inc., Homewood, Ill. p. 175) describes this debacle: "The second sub-period is that of the short, but sharp, recession of 1937-1938, which might have been precipitated by the doubling of reserve requirements which occurred immediately prior to it." He explained further:

> As is visible in the figure, the required reserve ratio was doubled over a very short period . . . the timing for these changes was most unfortunate, for the peak of the business cycle expansion was also reached in May 1937. This coincidence is probably not an accident, and thus it is that the Federal Reserve is accused by many of killing the boom in its attempt to solve a problem which probably did not exist. (Douglas Fisher, *Money and Banking*, p. 182)

Once more the Federal Reserve Board failed the American public, for the weight of the evidence suggests that the serious downturn and the recession of 1937-1938 were caused by the Federal Reserve Board's action.

Senator Robert L. Owen described the terrible cost of the Great Depression through the mismanagement of the Federal Reserve:

> The loss in production in the last ten years reached $220 billion in products and services which might have been enjoyed by the people under a management which had their interests at heart, and the country would be free of debt and heavy interest charges. These facts are proven by the record of the Federal Reserve Board of Governors.

Considering the inept policies of the Federal Reserve Board, the Depression would probably have continued into the 1940s. However, the preparations for World War II provided a stimulus to the American economy. Roosevelt was determined that the Board's policies would not interfere with the war effort. To restrict the Federal Reserve's interference in the financing of World War II, in April 1942, Roosevelt forced the Federal Reserve Board to peg the market for government securities.

According to monetary theory, Roosevelt's policy of pegging the interest rate low should have resulted in a runaway money supply and hyper-inflation. But it did not. This fact is important because it casts serious doubts on the very foundation of current Federal Reserve policy. After war-time inflation subsided in 1948 without monetary interference by the Fed, the money supply declined of its own volition, and prices fell sharply.

Because of the power and foresight of a President who practiced pragmatic economics and did not blindly follow theory, post-war inflation was kept under control. Even with unusually high deficit spending, the American government financed the most expensive war in history at low interest rates. Business financed the retooling to a peace-time economy at low interest rates (prime commercial paper was about 2%). In 1948, prices fell even though there was an *abundant money supply*. The important point to note is that during the war and post-war period, the availability of sufficient money at low interest rates allowed the economy to make the necessary adjustments and we had twenty years of low inflation. Under the Roosevelt plan, the Fed was not allowed to interfere with the market mechanism with a "tight-money" policy.

EXCESS RESERVES
AND BORROWINGS
($ Billions)

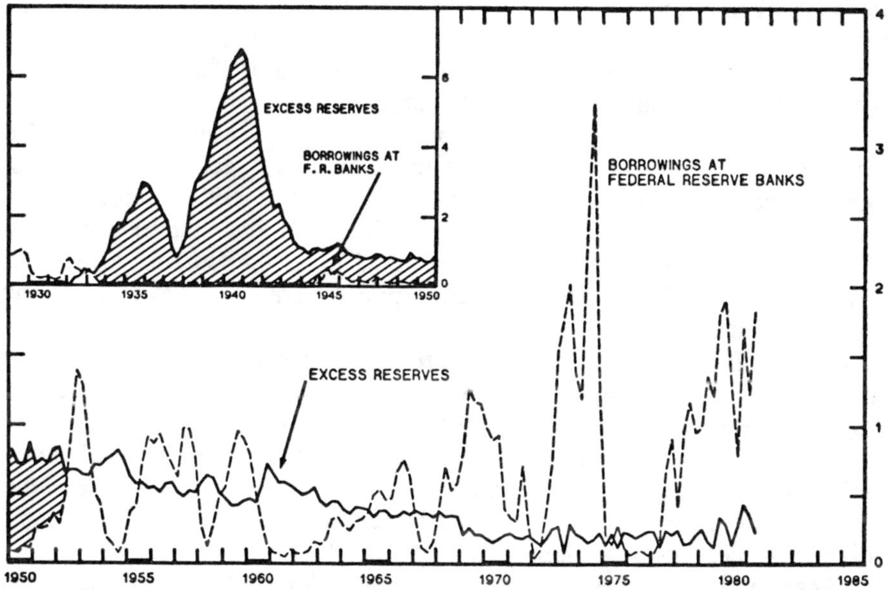


This chart disproves another Federal Reserve myth. The Fed argues that high interest rates are necessary to discourage credit growth. This chart demonstrates that low interest rates are more effective. During twenty years of low interest rates, banks were cautious and did not loan to the limit of their reserves. (The shaded area shows excess bank reserves to 1951.) As soon as the Accord was signed in 1951, the Fed increased interest rates and banks accelerated lending and exceeded their reserves.

The Truman era, 1945-1953, was characterized by a short but significant post-war inflation, the Korean adventure, and a restrained Federal Reserve, which was obligated to assist the Treasury in supporting the market for United

States Treasury bonds. Because of the restricted role of the Federal Reserve, an adequate money supply was available for the conversion to peace.

During the period that the Fed was under Treasury control, it made many attempts to extricate itself from these controls, for without the authority to manipulate interest rates, the Board was powerless. The Fed resented the restraints on its ability to invoke monetary controls and began a propaganda campaign to regain its independence. Threatening that inflation was going to ruin the nation, the Fed made inflation its battle cry.

As soon as the war was over, the Board began an intensive assault against the Roosevelt controls, with the chairman of the Federal Reserve Board, Marriner Eccles, leading the way: "In making a cheap money policy for the Treasury, we cannot avoid making it for everybody. All monetary and credit restraints are gone. Under such conditions the Federal Reserve becomes simply an engine of inflation." (Kross, p. 297) As usual, the Fed was wrong, for events have proven that keeping the Federal Reserve under wraps and maintaining low and steady interest rates was the best anti-inflation program in our history. The powerful banking elite resented their inability to force interest rates higher and applied pressure to release the Fed from its commitment to low interest rates. During the Truman administration, the Fed regained its freedom to control the money supply by the Accord of 1951, which released them from their obligation to the Treasury.

In retrospect, inflation was not a major economic problem from 1952 to 1965. But the Fed was obsessed with inflation and it dominated monetary policy since 1951. During Eisenhower's administration (1953-1960), the Federal Reserve Board was so paranoid about inflation that its over-reaction to relatively low inflation is sometimes referred to as the Board's "overkill of inflation." From 1948 to 1963, consumer prices increased an average of only 1.6% per annum.

Despite this low level of inflation, the American economy suffered three recessions during the Eisenhower administration. In the 1954 recession, unemployment rose to 5%, and in the 1957-1958 recession, unemployment was approximately 7%. The third recession was in 1960-1961 and unemployment again reached 7%. In all three recessions, the sequence of events was the same: the Fed tightened the money supply and forced interest rates up until the economy was forced into recession.

Sherman Maisel questioned the Fed's policy during the Eisenhower recessions: "There had been three recessions between 1953 and 1960. The last downturn had come well before output had approached capacity or full employment of the labor force. Why had the Fed tightened them? Did it believe the economy should always run with excess labor and plant capacity to avoid any price increases? (Maisel, *Managing the Dollar*)

These Eisenhower recessions signaled the start of the Federal Reserve Cycle and set the pattern for the Federal Reserve Board's control of our economy. The Federal Reserve Board learned that its monetary policies were a powerful tool to control the American economy and that high interest rates were the cutting edge.

From the Eisenhower era recessions, the Federal Reserve Board learned that the home building industry and certain other industries that required long-term financing could be used as an economy flywheel. When money became tight, mortgage money and other long-term funds dried up first, and as a result of high interest rates, the demand for homes and other goods diminished dramatically. But as soon as money loosened and funds became available at reasonable rates, the "pent-up demand" for homes exerted itself as a powerful force that turned the economy upward.

After the Gulf of Tonkin Resolution in 1964, President Johnson significantly escalated the Vietnam War commitment. Despite the added burden of increased military production, the Board followed a restrictive monetary policy designed to force a cutback in economic activity even though inflation was not yet a threat. From late 1963 until early 1969, the Federal Reserve Board doubled the discount rate, from 3% to 6%.

The Board's record of its conduct of economic policy since the Vietnam War was chronicled in earlier chapters. The Fed has never been an effective institution to control economic instability. The reverse has been true. A great deal of the economic instability experienced in the United States since the Fed was organized was caused or aggravated by Fed policy. It has a consistent record of damaging the economy and failing the American public.

* (See Friedman, Milton & Anna, *A Monetary History of the U.S. 1867-1960,* and Brownlee, Elliot W., *Dynamics of Accent.*)

# BIBLIOGRAPHY


ALLEN, Gary, *The Rockefeller File,* '76 Press, 1976, Seal Beach, CA

ALLEN, Gary, *None Dare Call it Conspiracy,* 1971, Concord Press, Rosmoor, CA

BALOGH, Thomas, *The Irrelevance of Conventional Economics,* Liveright Publishing (Norton) N.Y. 1982

BROWNLEE, W. Elliot, *Dynamics of Accent,* Alfred A. Knoff, Inc., 1978

BRZEZINSKI, Zbigniew, *Between Two Ages,* Viking Press

CARTER PRESIDENTIAL PUBLICATION, N.Y. 1970

ELIAS, Christopher, *The Dollar Barons,* 1973, MacMillian

FISHER, Douglas, *Money and Banking,* Richard D. Irwin, Inc., 1971

FRIEDMAN, Milton, SCHWARTZ, Anna, *A Monetary History of the United States,* National Bureau of Economic Research, Princeton University Press, Princeton, 1963

FRIEDMAN, Milton & Rose, *Free to Choose,* Avon, N.Y., 1979

GARRISON, *Roosevelt, Wilson & the Federal Reserve Law*

GOLDWATER, Barry M., *With No Apologies,* William Morrow & Co., Inc., Copyright 1979, N.Y., N.Y.

GROSECLOSE, Elgin, *Fifty Years of Managed Money,* 1913-1963, MacMillian Co., Ltd., London, 1965

HOMAN, Paul T., MACHLUD, Fritz, *Financing American Prosperity,* 1945 Twentieth Century Fund, N.Y.

HOMER, Sidney, *A History of Interest Rates,* Rutgers University Press, 1963, N.J.

JOSEPHSON, Matthew, *The Money Lord,* Weybright & Talley, N.Y. 1972

KEYNES, John Maynard, *General Theory,* Harcourt Brace & Co., N.Y. 1936

KOLKO, Gabriel, *The Triumph of Conservatism,* Copyright 1963, The Free Press, MacMillan Publishing Co., Inc., N.Y.

KROSS, Herman E., *Documentary History of Banking and Currency in the U.S.,* Chelsea House Publishers, McGraw-Hill, 1969, Vol. 3

LARSON, Martin A., *The Federal Reserve and Our Manipulated Dollar,* The Devin-Adair Co., Old Greenwich, Conn., 1975

LASKY, Victor, *Jimmy Carter: The Man & the Myth,* 1979 R. Marek, N.Y.

LEVINSON, Charles, *Capiital, Inflation, and the Multi-Nationals,* The MacMillan Co., N.Y., N.Y. 1971

LUNDBERG, Ferdinand, *Rockefeller Syndrome,* Lyle Stuart, Inc., Seracuse, N.J., 1975

MAISEL, Sherman, *Managing the Dollar,* 1973, Norton, N.Y.

MAYER, Martin, *The Fate of the Dollar,* Times Books, N.Y. 1980

MULLENS, Eustice, *The Federal Reserve Conspiracy,* Christian Educational Assn. 1954

RITTER, Lawrence S., SILBER, Wm. L., *Money,* Basic Books, Inc., N.Y., 1973

PATMAN, Wright, *A Primer on Money,* 88th Congress: House Committee on Currency & Banking 1964

SIMPSON, Anthony, *The Money Lenders,* Viking Press, N.Y.

SKLAR, Holly, Editor, *Trilateralism,* South End Press, Boston, MA., 1980

STOESSINGER, *Henry Kissinger, the Anguish of Power,* 1977 Norton, N.Y.

SOMMERS, Albert T. Ed., *Answers to the Inflation & Recession, The Conference Board, N.Y. 1976*

SUTTON, Anthony C., WOOD, Patrick M., *Trilaterals Over Washington,* The August Corp., Scottsdale, AZ., 1981 Vol. I & II

TRILATERAL COMMISSION: TASK FORCE REPORTS, 1977, 1978, New York University Press

WILLIS, Henry P., *The Federal Reserve System,* 1923, Arno Reprint 1975

*There are a number of books which every concerned American should read:* Trilaterals of Washington, *by Anthony C. Hutton and Patrick M. Wood. These two volumes bring us up-to-date on Who's Who in the Trilateral power structure.*

*A delightfully candid book by Barry Goldwater entitled* With No Apologies. *Senator Goldwater has an uncanny ability to cut through the "B.S." of politics and determine what is really happening. In that book, he has a chapter about the Trilateral Commission called "The Non-Elected Rulers."*

*A comprehensive, well-researched book entitled* Trilaterism, *edited by Holly Sklar.*

# AUTHOR'S NOTE

I have done what I can to bring your attention to the sordid political and economic affairs of our country. We have been the victims of serious crimes by men who were chosen to serve the public in the highest offices of national trust. Every American must become involved and demand redress from the economic saboteurs who perpetrated this infamy on our nation. I have indicted the Federal Reserve Board, but you hold the power to regain control of our government and national bank.

You can do your part by signing petitions, participating in public expressions, and demanding reform from your Congressmen and Senators. This is non-partisan; make it clear that you will vote and work against anyone who fails to actively promote reforms. If you have any ideas that would be beneficial, please write to me in care of the publisher.

The Author.

# NOTES

# NOTES